In the Shadow of the Mountain

THE KADE FAMILY SAGA

VOLUME 5

In the Shadow of the Mountain

LAUREL MOURITSEN

STRATFORD
BOOKS

ISBN: 0-929753-29-1
The Kade Family Saga, Volume 5: In the Shadow of the Mountain

Stratford Books
Eastern States Office
4808 37th Road North
Arlington, VA 22207

Stratford Books
Western States Office
P.O. Box 1371
Provo, UT 84603-1371

In the Shadow of the Mountain
First printing: November 2008

The acid-free paper used in this book meets the guidelines for
permanence and durability of the committee on Production Guidelines
for Book Longevity of the Council on Library Resources.

Dust jacket painting: *Celebration*
by Al Rounds
© 1996 Al Rounds
Used by permission.

Printed in the United States of America

"Come unto me,
all ye that labour and are heavy laden,
and I will give you rest.
Take my yoke upon you, and learn of me;
for I am meek and lowly in heart:
and ye shall find rest unto your souls.
For my yoke is easy,
and my burden is light."

MATTHEW 11:28–30

CHAPTER ONE

The wind rustled the tall grass and moaned through the trees. Rebecca turned her face into the hot breeze, hoping it would dry her tears before they began sliding down her cheeks. The bishop from Draper was standing at the rim of the open grave reciting the Twenty-Third Psalm, but Rebecca's ears were tuned to the sighing wind rather than the text in the Bible. At this moment, it seemed to offer more comfort than the words written in the book of Psalms. She gazed up through the branches of a tree crisscrossing her view of the sky; high, thin clouds gave it the appearance of blue marble. To the east, the jagged mountains hemmed in the landscape, and a hawk soaring across the foothills cried out in its plaintive voice. All around her the wind wailed. The sights and sounds of the land intermingled with her grief.

Realizing that the bishop had finished his remarks, she turned to stare into the grave. The pine casket holding her father's remains rested at the bottom of the deep hole. A sob tore from her throat, and her shoulders shook. Rebecca's sister, Rachel, slipped an arm around her and drew her close; she wanted to bury her face in Rachel's neck and unloose her grief in a torrent of tears over the loss of their father.

Having completed the graveside service, the bishop stood with his hands folded. Rebecca glanced at his face; she found kindness and compassion there, and sorrow, too. Although her family had not regularly attended the Draper Ward because of their responsibilities on the ranch, she felt the love of this good bishop. He'd come to the ranch to comfort her as soon as news of her father's passing had reached him, and he'd handled the funeral arrangements according to her wishes, bolstering her both spiritually and temporally.

Rebecca appreciated the friends from several miles around who had come to attend the service, although she and Rachel were the only kin. Her father's younger brother and sister, Samuel and Birgithe, both lived a long distance away, and a cousin and her husband who had been especially close to Rebecca's family resided in Arizona Territory. Rebecca had sent each of the relatives a telegram informing them of her father's passing and knew they would be grieved at the news. She shuddered, remembering her own shock and pain upon realizing that Ethan was dead.

Clearing his throat, the bishop invited the mourners circled around the grave to drop a handful of dirt onto the coffin as an expression of their love and respect. Rachel stepped forward first. Pale and trembling, she took some earth from the mound carved out for the grave and slowly emptied it into the hole. Rebecca watched the dirt sift through her sister's fingers and saw the wind catch the dust and scatter it away.

Rebecca watched the others, one by one, add their sorrowful offering—neighboring ranchers, friends from town, cowpunchers, and business associates. Micah Grant, her father's trusted friend and foreman of the Double K Ranch, scooped up a fistful of dirt from the pile heaped beside the grave and tossed it onto the casket. The sound was like pebbles flying against glass.

Feeling dazed and nearly numb with grief, the scene passed before Rebecca's eyes as if she were viewing it from the haze of a cruel nightmare. But this image was real, and bearing silent witness to it was the rough stone slab lying on the ground that would mark her father's resting place. Chiseled across its face were the words *Ethan Kade, Age 42, Died 11 July 1895.* The granite stone marker matched in color and size, as well as surname, another that lay embedded in the ground a few feet away. The only comfort Rebecca felt was in knowing that now her father rested beside her mother.

The bishop's eyes gently prodded Rebecca. She forced her feet to move forward until she stood at the edge of the open grave. With tears blurring her vision, she withdrew a clean, white handkerchief from her skirt pocket filled with a scoop of earth she'd taken from the ground near the ranch house. Carefully unfolding it, she turned its contents into the grave.

"Goodbye, Papa," she whispered.

The wind snatched her words as soon as they left her lips and carried them across the wide, silent hills.

After the service at the Draper cemetery had ended and the mourners had drifted away, Rebecca and her sister joined Micah in the buckboard for the short drive to the train depot. Rachel was leaving for Salt Lake City on the afternoon train.

"Can't you stay with me at the ranch for a few more days before going home?" Rebecca asked her sister as the team of horses lurched forward.

Rachel shook her head. The broad-brimmed hat she was wearing, embellished with a wide, black sash and large bow, wobbled as the wagon bounced over the rough road. "But I'll come out to the ranch soon. I promise."

"All right," Rebecca said in resignation. She hoped Rachel would keep her word. She knew that her sister, too, was grief-stricken over their father's passing; but Rachel had been away from the ranch for nearly two years, living in the city, and the ties that had bound her to Rebecca and their father had grown frayed.

Rachel gave her an encouraging smile. "You won't be alone. You have Micah to help you."

Rebecca glanced at the lanky ranch foreman. She could count on Micah for almost anything she needed, but it wasn't the same as having her sister near. Even though her relationship with Rachel had become strained over the past few years, and the tension between them often erupted into angry outbursts of temper, still Rebecca relied on her sister for emotional support. "I won't make any decisions concerning the ranch until you get there," she said.

Rachel nodded. "We'll talk about the ranch and go through Papa's belongings together."

"Just don't wait too long before you come," Rebecca reminded her.

When they reached the station, Micah stayed with the team and wagon while Rebecca accompanied her sister inside the adobe station house to wait for the train. She dreaded the moment when she would have to return to the ranch, yet at the same time she yearned for it. The familiar surroundings of the ranch had always been a source of happiness and comfort to her, but she wondered if she would ever feel the same about it now that her father would not be there. She tried to make conversation with Rachel while they waited for the train to arrive, but all her words felt hollow and the pain in her heart throbbed with each breath.

When the locomotive steamed into the station, Rebecca stood to give her sister a hug. "Have a safe trip back to the city," she said with tears welling in her eyes.

"Join me in Salt Lake City," Rachel urged. "Micah and the cowhands can take care of things at the ranch. It will do you good to get away."

For an instant, Rebecca reconsidered the idea. Her sister had been suggesting this same thing for the last three days while she'd been at the ranch in preparation for their father's funeral.

"You can stay with me at the rooming house," Rachel added.

Rebecca shook her head regretfully. "Maybe later. I'll think about it."

"I hope you will."

The locomotive sounded a long, shrill blast of the whistle that reminded Rebecca of the wind shrieking across the grasslands, signaling the passengers to board. Rebecca's eyes darted to the train, and she felt a sudden panic knowing her sister was about to leave.

"I wish you'd change your mind about living on the ranch," Rachel said, straightening her hat as she prepared to step aboard the train.

"I can't leave the Double K—I have responsibilities there. Especially now, so soon after Papa's death."

Rachel heaved a sigh of frustration.

Rebecca watched her sister hand the conductor her ticket, then disappear inside the passenger car. Through the window of the car she saw Rachel take a seat, turn toward her, and briefly wave.

With a loud burst of steam, the train began to pull away from the depot. Rebecca watched until it was out of sight, then she returned to the wagon and climbed into the seat beside Micah. The wooden seat was rough and splintery and snagged her skirt when she sat down. Slapping the reins against the horses' broad backs, Micah urged the animals forward for the long ride back to the ranch house. He tugged his hat over his brow and squinted straight ahead as he handled the team, keeping his customary silence.

Rebecca closed her eyes and let the jolting of the wagon dull her thoughts. The dust churned up by the horses' hooves and the creaking wheels soon deposited a layer of dirt on her best, black dress. The hot wind loosened wisps of hair from beneath her hat and lashed them against her cheeks. She sat in the seat as still as stone, trying to block out every thought—trying to rest her mind from the worries, fears, and concerns that would meet her when she got back to the cattle ranch.

It was late afternoon by the time they reached the gate leading to the ranch property. The tall, wooden archway marking the entrance to Kade ranch lands stood out starkly in the waning sunlight. Rebecca read the lettering sprawled across the wooden beam—*DOUBLE K RANCH*. The name stirred poignant emotions, bringing a lump to her throat. Micah snapped the reins and the pair of horses pulling the wagon moved forward at a trot.

"You've had a long day, Miss Rebby. When we get to the house, you relax for a spell. I'll tend to chores outdoors."

Rebecca gazed at the older man. "I noticed the other day that the door to the feed stall in the barn is loose," she said wearily.

"I'll take care of it."

She studied Micah's lined face, brown and weathered from years of working outdoors. His eyes were a faded blue, but razor sharp—quick to spot a steer tangled in the brush or a calf that had become separated from its mother. The old cowboy hat he always wore covered a head of sparse, graying hair, and gray whiskers hid his chin. Micah was the only ranch hand to accompany her to Draper for the funeral and graveside service; the other hands were needed at the ranch to attend to the daily chores.

Rebecca sighed, focusing her attention on the foothills to the east. The Kade ranch covered more than 2,000 acres of grassy range land, streams, and rocky canyons. At one time, the ranch had run about 1,500 head of cattle, but that number had declined in recent years to about 1,000. Rebecca would get an accurate count when they conducted the fall roundup.

Rebecca wiped away the perspiration collecting along her brow. Although this summer was one of the hottest she could remember, the winter before had been a harsh one. The Double K had lost a dozen head of cattle in one particularly fierce snowstorm and the ensuing freezing weather. Her father had been forced to supplement the sparse grass with winter feed, which left them short of cash. A countrywide depression was further depleting resources. Rebecca gave another worried sigh. The problems facing her at the ranch were difficult ones, and she would not have the guidance from her father to solve them.

When the wagon pulled into the yard, Rebecca climbed down and went inside the ranch house while Micah unhitched the horses. The house was silent and gloomy, and afternoon shadows were already clinging to the walls. Rebecca removed her hat and brushed the dust off her skirt, then walked down the short hallway and past the kitchen. She avoided looking at the closed door leading into her father's bedroom. Entering her own room, she sat down on her bed. Muted sunlight splayed on the quilt, giving the patches of color a somber hue. Restless, she got up again and paced the room. The adobe house her father had built was small, but it was sturdy and cozy. She and Rachel had shared the bedroom, and a second room off the kitchen had served as a bedroom for her parents. Her mother had chosen the color for the walls, painting them a bright blue. The plank floors were covered with rugs, and an oak rocking chair sat in the small parlor in front of the hearth.

When her mother was alive, the house had rung with the sound of laughter and conversation; it seemed someone was always paying a visit. Susannah Kade had liked people and enjoyed their company. Her husband had been less socially minded, but he'd indulged his wife in her every whim. Pleasing her was his greatest joy. When she died, Ethan nearly lost his mind. It was months before he was able to function again. Rebecca believed that he never really got over Susannah's death.

Rebecca went to the kitchen to prepare herself some supper. Her mother had cooked all the meals for both the family and the ranch hands, but after her death, Ethan built a cookshack beside the bunkhouse for the cowhands so that he and the girls could eat together privately. Rachel had taken over the duty of cooking for the three of them. She preferred cooking and keeping the house, rather than working outdoors with the cattle. The ache in Rebecca's heart grew sharper as she thought about the hours she and Ethan had spent together in the saddle overseeing the ranch. Since her mother's passing, Rebecca had become her father's companion and confidant. He'd shared his joys and concerns with her, taught her enough to fill a volume about cattle ranching, and taken her with him on the semi-yearly roundups where they spent several days together working with the cattle. Just about the only time he shut her out of his life was on long winter evenings when he sat before the fire, staring into its flames, keeping his thoughts to himself. It was at such times Rebecca knew that he was thinking of her mother.

When she'd finished eating, Rebecca stepped out of the back kitchen door. Standing on the porch step, she shaded her eyes with her hand against the glare of the lowering sun. A pair of tall trees shading the house stood out in silhouette against the orange sky. She could hear the murmuring of the brook as it flowed past the house. She sat down on the step to watch the sun sink out of sight and nurse her wounded heart.

Later, when Rebecca climbed into bed, she lay awake listening to the wind wailing through the grass. The wind had grown stronger; she could hear it rattling the gate to the horse corral as if trying to force it open. She finally nodded off, drifting into a fitful sleep.

The wind was whistling across the hillside and the creaking branches overhead swayed in the stiff breeze. Shifting in the saddle, Rebecca pulled the brim of her hat over her brow to shade her eyes from the gusting wind and the hot July sun.

"The creek is running low," her father said, riding beside her on his chestnut gelding. "We'll have to move the cattle further up the canyon to water them. I'll have Micah and the hands herd them upstream this afternoon."

Rebecca stared out across the green hills and gullies, taking a mental count of the cattle foraging along the slopes. "I'd say nearly half of the herd is grazing here on the mountainside. It shouldn't take too long to round them up and move them to higher ground."

Ethan grunted in agreement.

"It sure is a pretty sight, isn't it, Papa?" she asked, looking out over the rippling grass. The wind sang through the brush growing on the slope, creating its own distinctive melody. Rebecca sighed in contentment. The sounds, sights, and smells of the land were familiar friends. She heard her father give a low chuckle. "What?" she asked, smiling at him.

"You. You're too much like your father. It doesn't take much more than a horse between our knees and a few bellowing steers on the hillside to make us happy."

Rebecca laughed. "I can think of a few other things I enjoy."

Ethan reached into his vest pocket and drew out his pocketwatch. He snapped open the cover, glancing at the time. "Let's go back to the house for lunch and then I can speak to Micah about the herd and you can get started on the account books."

Rebecca reined her black gelding down the slope. The horse tossed his head and whinnied as if in protest; Onyx enjoyed being out on the range as much as Rebecca did. "I went over the ledgers last night, Papa. No matter how you juggle the figures, it comes out the same. We're short of cash."

Ethan spurred his gelding to keep pace with Rebecca's black. The handsome quarter horse he rode was a rich shade of reddish-brown with a star-shaped patch of white on the forehead. Her father hadn't given the animal a name, but Rebecca called him Star. "We're going to need some money before November rolls around and we can get the cattle to market. How much do we have in savings?"

"About fifty dollars," Rebecca responded.

"We'll have to take some of that to buy winter feed for the cattle."

Rebecca frowned as she subtracted the figures in her head.

"We'll be all right," her father said with a confident smile.

"I'm amazed at the end of every year how you've managed to make ends meet," Rebecca remarked.

"It's luck and a little bit of horse sense," Ethan replied, grinning.

Rebecca awoke with a start. It was still dark outside, and the wind was still howling. Fresh tears started in her eyes as she recalled the dream she'd been having. She wanted to go back to sleep and continue on with it. She wanted to be with her father again, hear his voice, and feel his kiss on her forehead. She turned over onto her side, listening to the wind blowing outside her window, and was glad the sound of it muffled her sobbing.

Rebecca opened one eye and squinted at the shade shutting out the morning sun. A sliver of light escaped from beneath the bottom of the shade where it didn't quite meet the window sill. She narrowed her eyes against the blaze of horizontal light, envisioning the scene outside the window as clearly as if there had been no curtain concealing it from her sight. The sunlit, grassy slopes. The jutting hills. The hundreds of roving brown specks that were cattle grazing on the mountainsides. She threw off the covers, realizing that it was much later than she normally arose. Hurriedly dressing, she pulled a comb through her hair and then started for the kitchen. She'd always eaten breakfast with her father, and now she was painfully aware of his absence at the table. Pausing only long enough to gulp a glass of milk, she strode outside.

She spotted Micah at the corral saddling his horse and hastened over to him. "Morning, Micah. Which direction are you riding today?"

Micah tipped back his hat and passed a hand across his brow. "Day before yesterday I noticed a sick cow up by the creek. I thought I'd check on her."

She nodded.

"I'll be back in a couple of hours. Then I'll be working at the cattle pens if you need me."

Rebecca stood with her hands tucked inside the pockets of her skirt and watched Micah tighten the cinch around his horse's belly and then step up into the stirrup. He settled into the saddle as if it were the most comfortable of rocking chairs.

"Mr. Kade was a good man," he said, squinting off into the distance. "His death is a real loss."

Rebecca knew her voice would break if she tried to reply. She silently gazed off in the same direction as Micah, blinking back tears.

"You let me know if there's something else that needs doing," he said, glancing back at her. He pulled his hat over his forehead and touched his spurs to the horse's flanks.

Rebecca's eyes followed the cowboy until he was out of sight. She knew he shared the same urgent questions as she about the future of the ranch, but he wouldn't voice them until she'd had a chance to sort things out in the aftermath of her father's death. She could depend on Micah to go about his work as usual without any direction from her. Her father had counted on Micah's dependability and experience; she, too, would take advantage of those virtues. Micah had been the ranch foreman for the past six years, and under his supervision the ranch had operated smoothly and efficiently.

Dashing the tears from her eyes, Rebecca unlatched the gate to the corral and let herself inside. Three horses roamed the enclosure—a strawberry roan that belonged to the ranch's string of horses, Ethan's chestnut gelding, and Rebecca's black. The roan raised its head when she entered the corral, then lazily shuffled toward her, nosing her pockets for an apple or some other treat. She rubbed his chin, then walked over to her father's gelding. "How are you doing, Star?" she said. No one had ridden the horse since Ethan's passing; the gelding had remained confined in the corral for nearly a week now.

Rebecca moved on to her own horse, a tall gelding and black as midnight. The animal had distinctive markings—a white blaze down his face and a narrow band of white above each of his front hooves. "How's my boy?" Rebecca murmured to the horse, stroking his sleek neck. The animal snorted and restlessly pawed the ground. "Oh, Onyx, you know something is wrong, don't you?" she whispered. She threaded her fingers through the animal's coarse, inky mane, pondering the enormity of the problems facing her. With her father gone, what would happen to the ranch? Would Micah stay on as foreman? Who would make the myriad of decisions necessary to keep the ranch operating?

The questions tumbled through her mind in a kaleidoscope of colliding dark colors. "What am I going to do, Onyx?" she sighed, resting her cheek against the horse's neck.

Getting back into the routine of work was the best way to clear her mind and take the edge off her grief, Rebecca decided. She'd neglected her normal chores for the past four days since her father's death, leaving the work of running the ranch and tending the crops to the cowhands. Four hands were working at the Double K at present; Micah, two younger cowboys whose names were Andrus and Hernandez, and Jake Baxter, who looked after the horses. All of the men had offered their condolences, then given her a wide berth to allow her the privacy she needed to grieve.

Rebecca gave her horse a final pat on the rump, then went to the barn to get her saddle and bridle. When she stepped inside, it took a moment for her eyes to adjust to the dimmer light within the frame building. The familiar smell of horseflesh, mingled with the scent of fresh hay was soothing. She scooped a pail full of oats from the grain bin in the storage stall and noticed that Micah had already repaired the loose hinge on the door. Carrying her gear outside, she fed each of the horses some grain and then saddled and bridled Onyx.

As she climbed into the saddle, she saw Jake at the trough watering his horse. He tipped his hat when she glanced at him. Apparently, he'd been watching her saddle up—that thought made her skin twitch. Her father had only recently hired the cowboy, and of all the ranch hands, she liked him the least. She gave him a slight nod of acknowledgement, then nudged the gelding with her heels and Onyx started forward at a trot.

She hadn't been out riding for over a week; the last time she'd tended the cattle was with her father. They had looked over the herd together and made plans for the fall roundup; discussed the health of the cattle and the price per head they hoped to get for the steers and heifers at market. Typically, the cattle were kept on the range for four or five years in order to fatten them for market. Twice a year, in the spring and in the fall, the herd was collected and counted, then the animals to be sold were separated from the rest of the herd. Income from the sale had to last six months, until the cattle were ready to be sold at the next market. Rebecca had kept the accounts for her father and managed the financial records.

As Rebecca reined her horse toward the foothills, she gazed across the Kade ranch lands that straddled the boundary between Salt Lake and Utah counties. The ranch house was located in the northeast corner of the property. Her father had built the single-story, adobe house there because it was the closest point on the ranch to Salt Lake City where her mother had grown up. Susannah Hamilton had tended the counter at her father's book shop on Main Street, and it was there that Ethan Kade had first set eyes on her. Rebecca had heard a dozen times from her mother how Ethan had come into the shop on the pretense of buying a book just so that he could meet her. She'd been a beautiful woman with dark hair, green eyes, and dimples in her smile. She'd liked pretty things and enjoyed going into the city to see the latest dress fashions. Ethan had once purchased for her a lovely coral necklace and matching set of earrings, which she'd treasured. After she died, Ethan had given the coral necklace to Rebecca and the earrings to Rachel.

Of the two girls, Rachel had inherited their mother's attractive looks—she had the same lustrous dark hair and emerald eyes. Rebecca favored her father. Her hair was as yellow as his, and her blue eyes too easily revealed her thoughts and emotions, as his had. Both girls had been the center of their parents' affections and had enjoyed their constant care and attention.

Urging Onyx into a canter, Rebecca experienced a moment of relief from the sorrow cloaking her like a shroud. The air was calm this morning and the sky a brilliant blue. It felt good to be on the range again, to feel the sun on her face and to hear the bellowing of the cattle on the hillsides. Her shoulders relaxed and the tension drained from her body with the steady rhythm of the horse's gait. She rode southeast, cutting across the foothills of the vast, raw land.

After a time, she reined in her horse and slipped down from the saddle. The spot where she paused provided a spectacular view of the valley floor. Standing on the top of a large, slanting rock, she surveyed the varied landscape spreading around her like a calico skirt. She could see the adobe ranch house her father had built, the cattle pens, barn, and corral. She sat down on the sunlit rock and let her thoughts wander. Near her feet grew a clump of wild sunflowers. She pinched one off from its bristly stalk and tucked it in her hair. Among all the wildflowers that grew on the benches and valley floor, sunflowers were her favorite because they looked like splashes of sunlight she could hold in her hand. Twenty miles to the north lay Salt Lake City, where her sister had taken up residence. To the south stretched a number of smaller towns. But here, on this rocky point, it seemed as if she were perched on an island separated from the rest of the world. As she gazed idly around, her eyes lighted on a broad meadow filled with wildflowers and fronted by a rocky draw. With a sudden start, she recognized the spot. She hadn't gone near that narrow gully in the past five years—deliberately avoiding it whenever she went riding. A band of sweat broke out along her brow. The sight of that place filled her with such anxiety and torment that she could hardly draw a breath.

Clamoring to her feet, she scrambled off the rock and in her haste the yellow sunflower tumbled from her hair. Heedlessly, she trampled it underfoot as she hurried to mount her horse. Her only thought was to get away from this spot as quickly as possible, before the specters of the past arose to haunt her mind. Lashing Onyx with her heels, she reined the gelding down the hillside, ignoring the beauty of the shimmering streams and the high rocky ridges. She didn't slow or turn aside until she had the corral in sight. It was only then that she stopped shaking.

CHAPTER TWO

Rebecca sat down at her father's desk to write a long letter to Ethan's cousin in Arizona Territory, explaining the details about Ethan's death and the ensuing funeral. Jessica, her father's cousin, was married to Rory McKellar, who had been Ethan's best friend from the time both of them were young cowhands working on a ranch called the Willows in the southern end of the valley. Together they'd purchased the land for their own spread and bought 500 Durham cattle with which to stock it. They'd christened the ranch the Double K—K for Kade and K for the letter in McKellar— and worked it together for seventeen years. Jessica and Rory had built a house on the flats near the Jordan River on the southwest section of the ranch, a lush, green parcel of land bordered by willows, and Rebecca and Rachel had spent nearly as many hours in the McKellar home as they had in their own. The girls had grown up alongside the McKellars' five sons, and Jessica and Rory were like second parents to them. Rebecca had been heart-broken when the McKellars had sold their interest in the ranch to Ethan and moved with their family to Arizona at the request of Church president Wilford Woodruff to manage a cattle ranch owned by the Mormon Church.

She tapped her pen to the paper, sorting through the myriad of details whirling in her head. The sheet of paper rustled in the hot breeze coming from the open window next to her. As she was writing, she heard the sound of a horse's hooves echoing on the hard-packed dirt road leading to the house. She set down her pen and went outside onto the porch. Coming up the road was a buggy pulled by a single horse. The black roof of the carriage glimmered in the glare of the afternoon sun like sunlight reflecting off a raven's wing. She let out her breath in a long sigh of relief. Finally, Rachel had come. She waited impatiently for the covered buggy to pull into the yard. "Rachel!" she shouted, waving a hand.

The buggy came to a halt, and Rebecca hurried toward it. But she stopped abruptly when she saw a tall man step out first and then offer a hand to the woman still inside. Rebecca stared at the man, quickly determining she'd never seen him before. Rachel, stylishly dressed, climbed down from the buggy. "Thank you, Judson," Rebecca heard her say.

A swell of indignation rolled through Rebecca. Her sister had brought a guest with her to the ranch, and his presence at this sorrowful time would be an unwelcome intrusion. Rebecca felt her face flush with resentment.

"Hello, Rebby," her sister called, smiling. She walked to Rebecca's side and gave her a hug. "How are you?"

"All right," Rebecca answered, striving to curb her displeasure. She glanced past Rachel at the stranger who had just finished tying the reins of the buggy to the hitching post and was reaching for a pair of traveling bags. He was dressed as fashionably as Rachel, wearing a smartly tailored suit, fancy shirt, and square-toed boots. His dark hair was combed smoothly into place and glistened with hair tonic.

"This is Judson Carter, a friend of mine," Rachel told her. "Judson, meet my twin sister, Rebecca."

Judson took a step forward, focusing his gaze on Rebecca. "It's nice to make your acquaintance," he said, extending a hand.

Rebecca noted that his eyes were a rich shade of brown with flecks of green gleaming in them, and his voice was deep and resonant. She nodded and accepted his firm handshake, then she turned to Rachel. "I was expecting you before now."

Rachel took her companion's arm and shrugged off Rebecca's testy remark. "I came as soon as I could get away. We've been busier than usual at the millinery shop."

Rebecca struggled to put a smile on her face. Leading the way to the house, she opened the door.

"After you," Judson said, bowing slightly. He held the door while she and Rachel passed through. Their eyes met again briefly as she stepped inside the house, and Rebecca noticed a twinkle of good humor shining in them. Rachel settled on the couch while Judson set down their bags beside the door, then joined her on the sofa. Rebecca took the chair opposite them.

"How have you been getting along?" Rachel asked, taking off her gloves and frilly hat and placing them beside her. "You've been on my mind constantly. I could hardly bear the thought of you out here alone on the ranch without Papa."

Although her tone was sincere, the words sounded rehearsed, as if intended more to impress her guest than to comfort Rebecca. "It has been hard. I miss Papa every day," Rebecca answered.

"May I offer my condolences on your father's passing," Judson said, leaning forward. "I'm sorry for your loss." Sympathy echoed in his voice, and his eyes seemed to express genuine concern.

"Thank you," she said, reddening under his steady gaze.

"I know this is an inopportune time for you to be receiving guests—"

"Nonsense, Judson," Rachel interrupted. "Rebecca doesn't mind a houseguest. We're used to guests staying at the ranch."

Rebecca tried to overlook her sister's insensitive remark; turning to Judson, she said, "You're welcome here, Mr. Carter." As she spoke, she took the opportunity to study his face. His wide, brown eyes were expressive, and his mouth seemed quick with a smile. His hair, curling slightly at the ends where it fell onto the collar of his shirt, was dark and thick. He looked older than Rachel, perhaps twenty-six or twenty-seven years of age, and reminded Rebecca of a handsome prince she'd once read about in a storybook. Rebecca glanced away, feeling suddenly embarrassed by her scrutiny of him.

"I've been telling Judson about Papa and Mama and the wonderful times we had together here on the ranch," Rachel said, absently stroking the blue silk bow on her hat.

Rebecca nodded.

"And I explained about Papa's death." Rachel lowered her voice. "I wasn't here when Papa passed away, but you were with him. Tell Judson what happened."

Rebecca hesitated for she disliked talking about such an intensely personal matter with a stranger; but Rachel was leaning forward in her seat, waiting expectantly. Rebecca couldn't keep her voice from quivering as she began the story, describing how Ethan had been working with the cattle in the foothills that morning. She'd taken him some lunch and he'd seemed fine, although he'd complained about a pain in his chest. She should have known then that he needed a doctor, but she'd believed him when he'd shrugged off the symptom as nothing serious.

About two hours later, she explained, Micah had come riding in, shouting for her. When she hurried out of the house in response to his call, she saw Ethan propped up against him in the saddle. He was unconscious but still breathing when Micah carried him into the house. She cringed, remembering the gray pallor of his skin and the paleness of his lips as he lay unmoving on the bed. Micah had sent Andrus for the doctor in Draper, but by the time the doctor arrived, it was too late. Ethan had died without ever regaining consciousness.

"The doctor said he suffered a heart attack, but he didn't think Papa experienced much pain," Rebecca finished in a whisper.

When Rebecca looked up, tears were standing in Rachel's eyes. She saw Judson fish in his pocket for a handkerchief and offer it to her. They sat in the parlor talking for a while longer, then Rebecca went to prepare supper and the three of them ate outdoors in the cool of the shaded porch. It was awkward for Rebecca to have a stranger staying at the house at this time of sorrow, but she tried to put her emotions aside and make Rachel's guest feel comfortable. She found a spare pillow and blanket and made a bed for Judson in the bunkhouse with the hands. After he retired for the night, she and Rachel stayed up late talking together.

The next afternoon, Rebecca and Rachel started on the difficult task of sorting through their father's personal belongings. "What should we do with these?" Rachel asked, holding a well-worn pair of Ethan's riding boots.

Rebecca looked up from the bureau drawer she was sifting through. The sight of the boots brought a fresh pang of sorrow to her heart. "I don't know. I suppose we should give them to someone."

"One of the ranch hands?"

Rebecca disliked the idea of passing them along to just anyone. "What about saving them for Uncle Samuel? He might be able to use them."

"That's a good idea." Rachel set the boots beside a growing pile of items collecting in the middle of Ethan's bedroom floor.

The room belonging to Rebecca's parents was painted a bright blue with white trim around the windows and door. Susannah had sewn the patchwork quilt covering the bed as well as the white curtains fluttering at the open windows. The room contained the bed, a maple chest of drawers and matching nightstand, and a washstand and mirror. On the walls were framed pastoral scenes done in pastel watercolors.

Rebecca closed the bureau drawer. "It's hard to see Papa's things getting scattered. It's like losing him all over again with each item we dispose of." She eyed the pile sorrowfully. "Don't you want something of Papa's for yourself?"

Rachel glanced about the room. "I don't know what it would be."

"Would you mind if I kept a few things?"

"Of course not. Keep whatever you like," Rachel answered. She removed the rest of Ethan's shoes and clothing from his closet, then turned her attention to the nightstand.

Rebecca stood with her hands on her hips and sighed. She was glad that she didn't have to tackle this task alone.

"What about this?" asked Rachel, lifting an object from the nightstand.

"Papa's pocketwatch," Rebecca said with a lump coming to her throat. She took the silver-plated watch from Rachel's hand and stared at it. "I can see Papa as plain as if he were standing here, taking this watch out of his vest pocket to check the time. He always wore it."

"Mama gave it to him, didn't she?"

"Yes. He valued it because of that."

Rachel inspected the watch. "It's a beautiful piece. It was probably expensive."

Rebecca nodded absently as she gazed at the pocketwatch, recalling images from the past.

"Let me look at it again, may I?" asked Rachel. She took the watch back into her hand and studied it. The silver case was discolored and slightly scratched from years of use, but the delicately etched design on the front of it still retained its original beauty. "Yes, it's a fine timepiece. I'd like to have this."

"All right," Rebecca said slowly. "If the watch is special to you."

"Oh, it's not for me," Rachel replied, looking suddenly embarrassed. "I'd like to give it to Judson."

"Judson?" echoed Rebecca in surprise. "He didn't even know Papa. You want to give our father's watch to a stranger?" She felt her face flushing in consternation.

"He's not a stranger. He's very special to me." Rachel closed her fingers around the timepiece. "You said I should have something of Papa's. This is what I want. Are you telling me I may not have it?" Rachel challenged.

"Rachel, please. If you must give Judson something of Papa's, choose an item less personal. Less . . . important."

"Less important?" Rachel repeated with a lift of her dark brows. "That's always the way it is with us, isn't it? You're the one who gets more, and I wind up with less."

"What are you talking about?"

Rachel's face darkened, like a black cloud at midday. "You've always been Father's favorite. He gave you everything you wanted."

"That's not true. Papa loved you the same as he did me. Only you didn't want to stay close or have much to do with him."

"That's a lie," Rachel retorted. She gripped the timepiece tighter. "Papa meant the world to me."

"Then why were you so anxious to leave the ranch? To leave Papa and me?" Rebecca's pulse was racing. Feelings of hurt and anger that she'd buried inside since Rachel's departure burst to the surface.

"After Mama died, I didn't see much point in staying," Rachel answered with a catch in her voice. "And besides," she added, moving away from the nightstand, "there's more to life than what's here on this barren plot of dirt and weeds and smelly cattle."

Rebecca swallowed the sharp reply that was on the tip of her tongue. She didn't want to argue with her sister. Not now; not a mere two weeks after their father's death.

"If you wouldn't seclude yourself on this isolated ranch, you could experience more of the world," Rachel said, "and enjoy the company of friends."

"I like it here," Rebecca countered. "I'm happy at the ranch."

Rachel rolled her eyes, and a sour expression settled on her face.

From the doorway of the bedroom, Rebecca heard someone clearing his throat. Darting a glance toward the door, she found Judson standing there looking uncomfortable, as if his shirt collar was too tight for his neck. "How long have you been there eavesdropping?" she demanded.

"Pardon me for interrupting," he responded. "I wondered if you ladies might like to take a break from your task and go for a buggy ride into the canyon." His eyes swept to the pile of Ethan's belongings resting on the bedroom floor.

"No, thank you," Rebecca said stiffly. She regretted snapping at him the way she had, but she was too proud and too agitated to make amends.

"Just ignore her, Judson," said Rachel, walking to his side and taking his arm. "She's being difficult, as usual."

Glancing from one sister to the other, Judson looked as though he were facing a panel of judges.

"I'd love to go for a buggy ride. This house is becoming too cramped," Rachel added with a look at Rebecca, her inference painfully clear.

"Perhaps later you might like to join us," Judson suggested to Rebecca. His eyes were apologetic.

Rachel tugged at his arm. "Let's go, Judson."

After they left, Rebecca sank down onto her father's bed. She was still smarting from her sister's harsh words and frustrated by her inability to get along with Rachel. Their interests and ambitions seemed always at odds. Rachel disliked ranch life and made no pretense about her feelings, staying away from the Double K for long periods of time. Rebecca knew their father had missed her, but he'd resigned himself to her physical and emotional distance—something Rebecca had not been able to achieve for herself.

She reached for the pillow resting at the head of the bed and buried her face in it. Her father's scent still lingered on the pillow slip. She breathed in the faint odor, the smell of it triggering memories of him. Before long, the pillow was damp with her tears.

The rest of the afternoon passed slowly. Rebecca continued to sort through her father's things, stacking them in piles to be dispersed later to various persons. The chore was heart-wrenching, but she kept at it, knowing it had to be accomplished. She searched briefly for her father's pocketwatch, and not finding it concluded that Rachel must still have it in her possession. Dispirited, she guessed that Rachel had already given the timepiece to her beau.

When she had done all that she could, she left her father's room and went to prepare supper for her sister and their guest. The heat of the afternoon had faded, and the breeze coming in through the open kitchen window beckoned invitingly. Rebecca decided to go outside while supper cooked on the wood-burning stove. She slipped out the back door. Rachel and Judson had been gone for a couple of hours on their buggy ride, and Rebecca didn't know when they'd be returning. Standing on the back porch for a moment, she gazed across the yard to the cattle pens, then started down the porch steps. She was nearly to the stream flowing past the house when Judson rounded the corner from the direction of the barn. He was alone, probably stabling the horse while Rachel went inside the house. He looked startled to see her, but then his eyes brightened with a smile.

"Evening," he greeted her.

"Good evening." She paused in her stride, determined not to be impolite again with him. If her mother had emphasized anything while Rebecca and Rachel were growing up, it was the virtues of a pleasant demeanor and a polite manner. Rebecca tried to put on her best face. "How was your ride?"

"Scenic. I'm sorry you didn't come with us."

"Perhaps next time."

"I'll look forward to it." He gave her another quick smile. "Taking a stroll?"

She nodded.

"Nice time of evening for a walk. Mind if I join you?"

His unexpected request flustered her. "I suppose so. If you want to." She felt her cheeks burn.

"Thank you. I would enjoy it." He locked his hands behind his back and fell in step with her. He was taller than she'd first thought and broad-shouldered. As they walked side by side, Rebecca could not think of a single word of conversation. They strolled in silence for a few paces.

"I wasn't eavesdropping," Judson said abruptly, turning to face her.

"What?"

"Earlier this afternoon. I wasn't eavesdropping on your conversation with Rachel. I had just entered the house when I made my presence known."

"Oh."

They continued on without speaking for several steps more. As he walked beside her, Rebecca could hear his quiet breathing and feel his gaze lingering on her. A soft breeze came up, rustling the leaves on the trees and carrying with it the scent of wild sagebrush. She heard Judson clear his throat. "You don't like me, do you?"

"Well, I . . . I don't dislike you, if that's what you mean. I hardly know you." She gave him a furtive, sideways glance.

He chuckled. It was a low, deep sound laced with self-deprecation.

"Is there something about that you find humorous?"

"Only my own stupidity. I should have known better than to come here at a time like this."

Rebecca glanced up at him again. The sunlight heightened the color of his eyes and made his dark hair gleam. "What do you mean?"

His expression sobered. "I came because Rachel wanted me to meet you and see the ranch. I wasn't prepared for what had transpired here."

"You're talking about my father's death?"

"Yes. I'm afraid my visit has been untimely. I'm sorry I've been hindrance to you."

"You're not exactly a hindrance," Rebecca replied slowly.

A smile drifted across his face. "Well, I want you to know that I am sincerely sorry about your father's passing. Even though I had never met him, I gather from what Rachel told me that he was a remarkable man."

"Yes, he was. A wonderful father and a successful rancher."

Judson paused and leaned against the trunk of one of the tall trees shading the yard. "The ranch is important to you, isn't it?"

Rebecca was surprised by the question. "Yes, it is. My father worked hard to establish this ranch." Her gaze strayed to the wood frame barn and corral, the fenced cattle pens and outbuildings.

"How long did he have the Double K?"

"Before Rachel and I were born," Rebecca answered, moving to stand in the shade of the tree a few paces from him.

Judson rubbed a thumb across his chin, apparently thinking about her answer. "He must have acquired it as a young man."

She nodded. She told him how Ethan and Rory had purchased the ranch lands together when they were both young, unmarried men and built up the herd.

"Does Mr. McKellar still own an interest in the ranch?" asked Judson.

Rebecca shook her head, then explained how the McKellars had sold their share in the Double K and moved to Arizona Territory six years ago. As she related the story, she thought longingly about Jessica, Rory, and their sons, wishing they were here to extend their sympathy and solace and to advise her on the hard questions she faced in running the ranch.

Judson straightened and moved away from the tree. Rebecca fell in step beside him as they continued walking. "You and Rachel were born here on the Double K?" Judson asked, putting his hands in his pockets as they walked.

"That's right. I've spent my whole life here."

"I can see why you like it. It's beautiful country." Judson's gaze moved to the rugged hills in the distance. "Do you plan on keeping the ranch now that your father is gone?"

"Of course. I'd never consider letting it go." She abruptly remembered the pocketwatch and Rachel's desire to give it to Judson. Was he as preoccupied with material possessions as her sister? "Why do you ask? Are you interested in buying it?"

Her question obviously surprised him. "Me? No, not at all. I have my hands full with my own business. I was only curious if you intended to hold on to it. It must take a concentrated effort to run a spread like this one."

"We have a competent foreman in Micah Grant and reliable ranch hands who know their business." Her thoughts lingered on Jake Baxter, and she frowned.

Judson paused in his step to give her a close look. "Does that scowl mean you've a worry or two about tackling your father's responsibilities all on your own?"

She looked up at him, feeling a flare of annoyance. She had no intention of revealing her concerns to him. "I'm perfectly able to manage the ranch by myself, Mr. Carter. I don't need any outside help."

"That's exactly what Rachel said."

Rebecca sent him a sharp look. "I'm sure my sister has told you a great many things," she said coldly. She thought again about the timepiece. It chilled her heart to think that this stranger would be the owner of one of her father's most prized possessions. "If you'll excuse me, I'll finish my walk."

"Certainly. Enjoy your evening."

"Thank you." She strode away into the gathering dusk without a backward glance.

"What do you think we ought to do about the ranch?"

"What do you mean?" Rebecca replied in answer to her sister's question.

"Just what I said. You can't stay here and run the Double K by yourself. What do you intend to do with it?"

Rebecca was taken aback by Rachel's remark. The two of them were making sandwiches for lunch and talking as they worked. Their disagreement from the day before was still sore and festering, like a thorn working itself out of the flesh. Rebecca paused before answering. "I intend to see that the ranch continues operating just as before."

"You can't do that, Rebby. It takes a man to run a big outfit like the Double K. And besides, you can't stay out here alone."

"I hoped that you'd come back home, and we'd work the ranch together."

Rachel snorted. "That isn't going to happen, and you know it."

Rebecca cut a slab of yellow cheese and placed it onto the bread. "Then I'll do it alone. I have Micah to help me and all the ranch hands. We'll be fine."

"You'll be the only woman for miles around and without Papa here to protect you," Rachel pointed out.

"I've been the only woman out here for quite some time now. And I can take care of myself."

"It's not practical, Rebby. There's too much work that needs to be done," Rachel insisted as she put a slice of bread on top of the cheese to complete the sandwich.

Rebecca stared at her sister. "What are you suggesting? That we sell the ranch?"

"It seems a sensible solution to me. We could sell the ranch and split the money between us." Rachel reached for the kitchen knife to cut the sandwich in two.

Rebecca shook her head. "You know Papa wouldn't want us to sell the Double K. It was his life. He worked day and night to make it a success."

"Exactly my point," Rachel said emphatically. The knife she was using flashed in the sunlight coming through the window. "It takes enormous effort to keep the ranch afloat."

Rebecca frowned. Her sister's words rang with the same discouraging tones she'd heard from Judson the evening before. "I don't mind that," Rebecca said. "I'm used to hard work. And I know cattle ranching."

"You won't listen to a thing I say, will you?"

"I am listening to you, Rachel, but you're wrong about this. Papa would be incensed if he heard you talk about selling the Double K. And Mama, too."

"Mama was never fond of ranch life," Rachel replied, arching her brows.

"She may not have liked it as well as Papa, but she did everything she could to help make the ranch successful. I plan to do the same."

Rachel arranged the sandwich onto the plate. "You can be more stubborn than a mule when you get your mind set on something. It's useless to discuss this with you."

As Rachel put together another sandwich, Rebecca worked sullenly alongside her. The square-shaped kitchen was roomy and comfortable with a large window to let in the sunlight. On one side was the counter, sink, and pump; across from that sat the old wood-burning stove. On the opposite walls were cupboards, and in the center squatted the worn oak table, scratched and marred from countless meals served and eaten there. When they had three sandwiches ready, Rachel left the kitchen to find Judson and invite him inside for lunch.

Rebecca sat down at the table while she waited, her chin in her hands. There was some truth to what Rachel had said, she knew that. But she also knew that she couldn't bear to lose the ranch. She loved the Double K too much to ever allow it to slip out of her hands. Rachel didn't have the same emotional ties to the ranch as she did.

Rebecca chewed on a thumbnail, thinking back. The two sisters had shared a close bond throughout their childhoods; and after their mother died, they had clung to one another for support. But as Rebecca's relationship with her father deepened as the two of them worked side by side on the ranch, Rachel grew more distant. Rachel seemed to increasingly resent her sister as the months passed, perhaps jealous of the attention she felt Rebecca was receiving from their father. Rachel and her mother had always enjoyed a special closeness; and with Susannah's death, it was as if Rachel lost her moorings and began to feel adrift.

Rebecca stood up when she heard her sister and Judson come into the house. Judson was talking as they entered the kitchen. When he saw Rebecca, he turned to give her a broad smile, revealing a dimple in his cheek that Rebecca had not noticed before. His smile made her heart unexpectedly skip a beat. She nodded in return as Judson pulled out chairs for both sisters to be seated. He had impeccable manners, Rebecca thought. And he was nice looking and well dressed.

Her mother would have liked him, she decided, as she took her place at the table.

Rachel passed around the plate of sandwiches, and they started on their meal. As they ate, Rachel prattled about inconsequential things, occasionally giving her beau a beguiling smile or brushing her hand up against his. He leaned his head close to hers in response, talking in low tones. Rachel had on a flattering striped dress with white cuffs and collar, and her dark hair was arranged on the crown of her head in an attractive style. As she and Judson conversed, Rebecca eyed her own rumpled cotton skirt and plain blouse. Her blonde hair, plaited loosely down her back in a single braid, rebelled against confinement. Wisps of it fell in disarray against her neck. The toes of her dust-stained shoes poked from beneath her wrinkled skirt. The contrast between her dark-haired, pretty sister and herself was striking. It was no wonder Judson Carter sat hovering at Rachel's side like a honey bee drawn to a flower. Rebecca looked away, feeling a pang of envy. She wondered how sincere Rachel's feelings were for him and if the two of them might be considering marriage.

After they'd eaten, Rebecca sat at her father's desk to finish the letter she'd started writing to Jessica the day before. She hoped Rachel would carry it into Salt Lake City with her when she left the ranch and mail it. That would save Rebecca a long trip into Draper to post it herself. She spent a few minutes scribbling out the note while Rachel and Judson went for a walk. The afternoon was hot, but the thick adobe walls of the house kept out much of the heat. Outside the windows, the July sun beat down on the grasslands, turning the wild grasses yellow and brittle.

When she finished with the letter she slipped it inside an envelope, addressed it, and set it aside. Then she went outside to replenish the water in the troughs for the animals and set out more rock salt for the cattle and horses to lick. She tended to chores for the rest of the afternoon, leaving Judson and Rachel to entertain themselves while she worked.

CHAPTER THREE

Rachel and Judson left the ranch the next day after spending the weekend with Rebecca. At first Rebecca was relieved to see them go for she was weary of the constant tension between Rachel and herself; but as the days wore on, Rebecca missed her sister's companionship, thorny as it was. She tried to put aside her grief over her father's passing and concentrate on her work at the ranch.

One hot, windy afternoon she sought out Micah Grant as he sat outside the bunkhouse refastening the metal handle to a coal oil lantern with a piece of baling wire. "Can you give me a report on where we stand on things, Micah?" she asked him.

Micah scratched at his bearded chin. "The land's as dry as the rattles on a snake's tail, Miss Rebby. The streams are runnin' low and some of the smaller creeks have dried up altogether. This drought is going to hurt cattle prices come fall."

Rebecca nodded. "With the grass as poor as it is, the cattle aren't going to put on much weight. We won't be getting much of a price per head."

"That's a fact," Micah said, squinting into the distance as if he could read the future written there.

Rebecca shaded her eyes against the wind-driven dust. It had been an unusually dry summer; almost no rain had fallen since the beginning of July. The range grasses were sparse and stunted, and the cattle had grown thin; with market prices already low, Rebecca worried that she might not be able to sell her cattle for enough money to get them through the winter. "I've kept my father's account books long enough to recognize the fluctuation in cattle prices from year to year. But I think this year is going to be the worst I've seen when it comes to losses." Rebecca sighed and brushed away a fly buzzing around her head.

Micah gave the baling wire fastened around the handle of the lantern a sharp twist. "Gonna need some new gear before winter sets in. This lamp is comin' apart at the seams." He held up the battered and rusted lantern for Rebecca to see.

"We'll have to buy what we need. We can't skimp on equipment."

Micah put the lantern aside and stood up. Tall and lean, he had bushy eyebrows and a gruff-looking face. The many seasons spent outdoors had weathered him, making him look older than his fifty-four years. Rebecca's father and Rory McKellar had run the Double K jointly; but when the McKellars left for Arizona, Ethan had hired Micah to oversee the operation of the ranch. Micah had directed the labors of the cowhands and reported directly to Ethan.

Micah swept off his sweat-stained hat and wiped the perspiration from his forehead with the sleeve of his shirt. "This is one of the hottest summers I can remember," he said. "The boys have had to haul water to the cornfield. Looks like the hay is fairing all right, though."

Rebecca nodded, pushing out her bottom lip in thought. "I'll have the cowhands make sure the crops are getting plenty of water."

"Might ask one of them to cut another trench through the field. I reckon the corn could use a little more water."

"All right, I'll do that."

"Andrus and Hernandez are out on the range. You might ask Baxter to tend to the irrigation ditch."

Rebecca winced at the thought of having to initiate a conversation with Jake Baxter. His surly disposition tried her patience. She left Micah to his chores and walked to the hen house across the yard to gather a few eggs for supper. The feisty, red rooster perched atop the pen crowed at her and flapped his wings. "Don't get yourself all riled," Rebecca said to him. As if to challenge her remark, the rooster flew at her feet, squawking loudly. Rebecca stepped easily out of his way. "Shoo!" she said, waving her arms as she ducked into the hen house to get the eggs.

After taking the eggs to the house, she went out to the garden to dig some potatoes for supper and pick an apron full of pod peas. She pried open one and saw that the peas were small and shriveled. She frowned, hoping the rest of the peas in the garden were in better condition. After gathering all her apron could hold, she moved to the corn patch to get a look at the crop. Micah was right; the broad leaves cradling the ears looked yellow and withered.

She started supper for herself, shelling the peas for cooking and setting the potatoes to boil. Then she went in search of Jake Baxter. She found him inside the barn, cleaning the stalls. "How is everything here?" she asked.

He looked up from his work. "All right, I guess, Miss Kade." He leaned on the handle of his shovel. "Can I help you with something?"

He waited, his round face glistening with sweat and his dark eyes like two chips of coal. The smell of perspiration and manure clung to him. Only a couple of inches taller than Rebecca, he was stocky in build. His head was bare and stringy brown hair hung down to his collar.

"Yes. We need another ditch dug to water the cornfield. The crop isn't getting enough water. Would you do that when you finish here in the barn?"

Jake's eyes hardened and he frowned. "I was hired on as a wrangler, not a field hand, Miss Kade."

Rebecca was surprised by his objection to her request. "My father employed you as a ranch hand, Mr. Baxter, and I believe that includes doing whatever chores are necessary to keep the ranch running smoothly."

"Your father would have wanted me to tend to the horses, like always," he countered, his scowl deepening.

Rebecca swallowed a sharp retort and said instead, "Since my father is no longer alive, I'll be making the decisions now."

Jake scuffed the toe of his boot through the straw scattered on the floor of the stall. "I ain't used to taking orders from a woman," he muttered.

"And I'm not used to managing the ranch without my father's direction. So we'll both have to get used to a new way of doing things."

He glared at her from beneath a mop of shaggy, unkempt hair.

"Are we agreed on that point?" she asked when he made no further comment.

"We're agreed," he mumbled. He set the shovel in the corner of the stall, shot her a disgruntled look, and strode out of the barn.

Rebecca chewed on her lip in dismay. She'd gotten off on the wrong foot with the cowhand, and she knew it wouldn't be easy now to win Jake's confidence or his cooperation. She wished her father were here to take matters in hand. She remembered Ethan's seemingly effortless skill in managing the ranch hands and despaired of ever acquiring that ability for herself.

She wondered how Rachel was coping with their father's death. At least she had Judson Carter to comfort her. An image of Judson's wide, brown eyes and dimpled smile sprang to her mind. She was curious about how he occupied his time when he wasn't courting her sister.

Although he'd spoken of attending to his business, she had no idea what sort of work he did.

Erasing Judson from her thoughts, she picked up the shovel Jake had discarded and began shoveling out the soiled straw. Jake was responsible for taking care of the horses used on the ranch. Each of the cowhands had his own string of horses; most were quarter horses, a breed well suited to working cattle because of their agility. Quarter horses were adept at starting, stopping, and turning quickly—traits imperative in herding cattle. Out on the range, a horse had to respond promptly to commands from the rider in order to keep the cattle together and moving in one direction and to cut out individual steers, heifers, calves, and cows. The horses had to be able to negotiate steep mountain trails and cross swift streams without balking. The Double K kept a string of good cutting horses for its ranch hands to ride.

When she'd finished with the stall, Rebecca tended to her other chores while her supper cooked. The meal that evening consisted of boiled potatoes, a slice of bacon, and scrambled eggs. Rebecca ate by herself, staring out the window above the table. Afterward, she cleared the dishes from the table, pulled out the ranch account books, and settled down to review them.

The past couple of years had seen a sharp decline in cattle prices. The country was in the grip of one of the worst economic downturns it had ever experienced, and this had a direct bearing on the marketing of cattle. The sale of cattle last spring had yielded the lowest returns Rebecca could remember since she'd begun keeping the accounts for her father. She and Ethan had discussed the situation often.

United States president Grover Cleveland, who was completing a second term in office, was providing little effective leadership to a country reeling under economic chaos. After being elected in 1884, Cleveland lost the presidential seat in 1888 to Republican Benjamin Harrison and then returned victorious in the election of 1892. Although President Cleveland was respected for his integrity, honesty, and courage, he had failed to resolve the issues dividing the country—the persistence of an unpopular tariff on foreign goods, a controversy over the coinage of silver versus gold, and a debate on civil service reform within the federal bureaucracy.

Rebecca didn't fully understand the political and economic ramifications of these problems, but she felt their effects—cattle cost more to buy and sold for less at market. Her father had often complained that politicians, both Republican and Democrat, skirted controversial issues in order to appeal to the largest number of voters. Neither party would clarify its position on any given question for fear of driving away more voters than it attracted. Political indecisiveness was a chronic problem plaguing the country, Ethan had often said. He felt that politicians avoided the real issues; and, therefore, effective solutions to problems were not addressed. With these matters weighing on her mind, Rebecca sat at the kitchen table hunched over the account books for most of the evening, familiarizing herself with all aspects of the ranch's financial picture.

By the time dusk settled, Rebecca was tired in mind and body and decided a quick dip in the cool pond near the house would refresh her before going to bed. She put the books away in the desk drawer and slipped outside. The pond lay a few yards from the house, ringed by a thick stand of willows. Rebecca had been coming here to bathe ever since she was a child. She had her own special name for the pool of shimmering water: Willow Pond. She had been baptized in its waters as a young girl and well remembered the occasion—her father's strong, secure arms holding her tightly as he lowered her beneath the water and brought her safely up again, her mother's tears of joy, and the warm, sweet sensation that filled her own heart.

As blue clouds drifted across the moon, Rebecca shed her clothing and slipped into the cool water. She moved quietly through the pool, barely causing a ripple. Closing her eyes, she slipped beneath the surface, then rose again with water streaming down her hair. She stirred the surface with the palms of her hands, watching the moonlight reflected on the glittering water. Gliding beneath the ripples, she swam to the far end of the shallow pond.

When her head broke the surface, she was facing the direction of the house. Within the patch of willows cloaking the edge of the pond, she caught a glimpse of sudden movement. She froze, staring at the spot. In the dim light from the moon, she recognized the silhouette of a man. The figure disappeared almost as quickly as she'd seen it, and she wondered if her eyes had played a trick on her. Yet the chilling feeling that remained, of being watched, shook her to the core. She quickly swam to the edge of the pond, crawled out of the water, and crouched close to the ground as she dressed.

The next morning after breakfast, Rebecca went out to the vegetable garden to pull weeds before the sun became too hot. Squash and pumpkin clung under thin, withering leaves. Carrots, turnips, and potatoes struggled for nourishment in the poor soil. Scraggly vines were dotted with a few knobby tomatoes. When she was through weeding, she moved to the cornfield to inspect the ditch Jake Baxter had dug the day before. She walked its length, a scowl growing on her face. Jake had done a sloppy job of digging out a trench for the water to flow into the field. It was neither deep enough nor wide enough to accomplish its purpose. Her annoyance with the cowhand flared. She resolved to speak to him about the ditch at the first opportunity.

She suspected that it had been Jake staring at her from the willows the evening before while she was bathing. She'd be more wary of the cowhand from now on. Jake had been at the ranch for only about eight months before her father's death. She had never heard Ethan complain about him, but she'd never heard any words of praise from him either concerning his new wrangler.

That afternoon she took the buckboard into Draper, more than an hour's drive from the ranch, to purchase some supplies. The day was hot, and a strong wind blew from the canyon. Dust swirled around the wagon wheels as they rolled through brush and over stones along the dirt road. When she arrived in town, she went first to the post office located on Fort Street, where homes and businesses sat intermixed along the busy road like pieces of a puzzle. Tying her horse to the hitching post outside the post office, she shook the dust from her skirt and went inside.

The postal clerk had three letters waiting for her. One was a notice of sale for beef cattle to be auctioned off in September, but the other two were from members of her family. She hurried outside with the letters and sat down in the buckboard to read them. The first was from her Uncle Samuel, thanking her for her telegram informing him of Ethan's death and expressing his sorrow over his brother's passing. Samuel was a teacher at a small, rural school about 100 miles north of Salt Lake City. He asked how she was getting along at the ranch and what he could do to help her. He promised to make a visit to the Double K to see her before school started again in the fall.

The second letter was from Ethan's younger sister, Birgithe. She, too, had been grieved to learn of Ethan's death. Her letter was comforting, containing affectionate sentiments regarding her brother. Rebecca appreciated the consoling words and the expressions of love and concern; she invited Rebecca to visit her home in St. George, Utah, where she lived with her husband and children. Rebecca's feelings were tender as she refolded the letters and tucked them inside their envelopes. Her uncle and aunt's kind words warmed her heart and soothed the raw wound of grief she carried inside. She put the letters in her handbag for safekeeping, then gathered the reins for the short drive to the mercantile.

The Rideout general store was a convenient place to shop for the items she needed. As she stepped inside the brick building, she hoped to see her friend, Lettie Miller, at work stocking the shelves. The store shelves were laden with groceries, dry goods, shoes, ready-made clothing, dishes, hardware, lumber, feed for livestock, and other merchandise. Rebecca passed by a table with magazines for sale on it. She thumbed through them, pausing to study the cover of the latest *Ladies Home Journal*. She would have liked to buy the magazine to read on the long, lonely summer evenings, but the money she had for goods and supplies was strictly budgeted; there was none to spare for frivolous purchases such as magazines.

Lettie wasn't anywhere in sight. Perhaps she'd gone on an errand for Mr. Rideout or was out making a delivery, Rebecca thought. She made her selections and took them to the front of the store where Mr. Rideout usually tended the counter, but today a middle-aged man Rebecca didn't know stood behind the long counter helping customers. He rang up her groceries at the cash register and with each press of a key, the register clicked in the amount. Rebecca's breath tightened as the total mounted. When he had finished, he looked up expectantly at her.

"Will you please put that on my father's account?" Rebecca asked him. "His name is Ethan Kade. He passed away three weeks ago. I'll be making the payments from now on."

The clerk brought out a large ledger book from beneath the counter and made a notation in it. Rebecca watched his finger move across the column of figures. "It appears your father's account hasn't been paid for some months, Miss Kade. Will you be bringing the balance up to date soon?"

Rebecca felt her face flush, although she knew she shouldn't be embarrassed by the clerk's words. Most of the ranchers and farmers who lived in outlying communities purchased their groceries on credit. That was nothing to be ashamed of. Buying the goods on time had been a standing arrangement between Mr. Rideout and her father. He knew that Ethan always paid his debt promptly after marketing the cattle. But, still, she felt uncomfortable knowing she was short of money. "Yes. I'll be paying the balance of the account after we get our cattle sold at market."

"All right," the clerk said, but Rebecca thought he looked dubious about the arrangement. Rebecca signed the store credit ledger for the amount of the purchase, then the clerk loaded her groceries into boxes—flour, sugar, molasses, dried beans, nails, and a gallon of coal oil for the lamps—and then motioned to a lad who was waiting nearby. The boy whisked up Rebecca's boxed groceries and carried them out to the buckboard for her.

Before leaving town Rebecca walked to the cemetery, which was adjacent to the Rideout store, and placed on each of her parents' grave a bouquet of wildflowers she'd picked on the ranch property and brought in a vase of water with her. The bright flowers created a contrast against the drab, gray brush and weeds dotting the cemetery grounds—a splash of color like an oasis in the desert. Standing silently beside the graves, she thought about her parents and how much she missed them. She yearned for her mother's companionship and her father's wise words of counsel. Her gaze drifted to the mountains sculpting the eastern sky with their high, sharp peaks, shadowed valleys, and rocky outcrops. She remembered how much her father had loved the mountains and how he had instilled that feeling into her. Sighing, she turned away and retraced her steps to the buckboard for the ride back to the ranch.

After supper that evening, she summoned Jake Baxter to the house to talk with him about the ditch running through the cornfield; but he was defensive and uncooperative. When the interview ended, Rebecca felt she had bungled the whole conversation and began to question her ability to manage the ranch by herself. Perhaps Rachel was right— perhaps the best thing would be to sell the Double K. Her heart recoiled at that thought; the ranch was her whole life and her link to the past she had lost.

That night, before crawling into bed, she considered getting down on her knees to pray for guidance and comfort. But she hadn't prayed—really prayed—for a long time. The Lord could comfort her in her loss, she knew, if she would only ask for His help, but she couldn't bring herself to do it in spite of the pain she was suffering over her parents' deaths. She'd been taught to pray as a young child, and when her parents were alive prayer was a daily habit. But after her mother's death, Rebecca found it impossible to approach her Father in Heaven in prayer. This night, like many others since her mother's passing, Rebecca climbed into bed without kneeling, feeling a deep sense of loneliness and despair.

The next morning Rebecca was up before sunrise, her horse saddled and bridled, and ready at dawn to ride out with the cowhands Andrus and Hernandez. The three of them planned to herd the cattle to higher pastures where the grass grew thicker and water was more plentiful. Together they rode southeast, gathering the herd. Even at the higher elevations, the grass was short and dry. Along the creeks grew cottonwoods and willows. Rebecca often spied beaver in the streams, foxes and bobcats slipping through the grass, and eagles, hawks, and ravens soaring through the clear skies. Once, she had spotted a black bear loping through the brush.

But today, her mind was concentrated on the cattle. Many of them were thin and weak. Some of the cows were so sickly that they weren't able to produce milk to feed their young. The calves milled around their mothers, bawling plaintively for nourishment. She called to Juan Hernandez, who was riding a big, broad-chested sorrel, pointing out to him some of the sickest calves. Juan would herd the calves, along with their mothers, back to the ranch and pen them in the corral where he would feed them grain and hay and nurse them back to health. The weakest one of the calves Juan would carry back to the ranch across the front of his saddle.

Most of the cattle, however, were faring well, despite the drought. They had ranged long distances in order to find grass and water and they were tired; but at least, for the most part, they were healthy. Andrus cut out a few of the steers who needed attention. One seemed to be limping on a sore hoof, another suffered from a wound in its hide. Rebecca liked Charles Andrus, who had been with the ranch nearly as long as Micah. A middle-aged bachelor who enjoyed his whiskey and his chewing tobacco, he could be depended on to put in a full day's work and do whatever was asked. He usually rode the same blood bay quarter horse each day. The gelding was his favorite because of its smooth gait and physical strength. Andrus whistled and waved his lariat at a cow that was veering off in the opposite direction from where he wanted it to go. An instant later, he had the cow trotting back to the group.

Both Andrus and Hernandez were dressed in typical cowboy gear—sturdy Levi denim jeans, chaps, long-sleeved cotton shirts, and broad-brimmed hats to protect their faces from the sun and wind. They wore spurs on their boots and carried saddle ropes. Rebecca wore a more feminine version of the same outfit. She had on a split skirt for riding, cotton blouse, hat, and spurs. While growing up, her mother had insisted that Rebecca and Rachel wear skirts on the ranch, even when riding. Susannah would never allow her daughters to dress roughly or slovenly, although they often worked alongside the ranch hands tending cattle out on the range or in the fenced pastures. The habit had stuck, and Rebecca seldom put on a pair of trousers, except perhaps during the roundup when she spent long hours in the saddle. Each cowhand owned his own saddle and bridle. Rebecca's saddle had been given to her by her father. It was a comfortable, well-made saddle with handsome leatherwork, and it fit snugly on Onyx' broad back.

Spying a cow on the far side of a narrow ridge, Rebecca spurred Onyx into a canter. Just as the horse cleared the ridge, Rebecca spotted the cow's calf lying on the ground near its mother. She reined in her horse beside the white-faced, roan calf and dismounted to check on it. What she saw caused her breath to stick in her throat. The calf's hindquarters were raked with deep, bloody gashes from the claws of a wild animal—most likely a cougar. It was still alive, but struggling to breathe. The mother cow was bawling to her calf, and the calf was feebly trying to get to its feet. Rebecca knew the calf wouldn't survive unless it was taken off the mountain and cared for at the ranch. Kneeling beside the injured animal, she glanced around, searching for the cougar that had attacked it. The cat was probably still close by. The wounds on the calf's haunches were fresh, and the calf's eyes were still wild and white with fear.

Rebecca checked the ground for paw prints. She found one set of tracks leading off in the direction of a narrow slot canyon. Grabbing her rifle from the saddle, she mounted her horse and began following the tracks. She kept a sharp eye out, knowing the big cat could be crouching behind a boulder along the trail or hiding in the branches of a tree overhead. Onyx could smell the cat. He pranced nervously, tossing his head and snorting. She had to urge him forward with her spurs.

Just when she thought she'd lost the cougar's tracks, she spotted a faint set of prints leading into the narrow canyon. She gripped her rifle, thinking twice about entering into the steep-walled, rocky gorge. If the cougar surprised her in an attack, she could have trouble getting out of the canyon. She tightened her grip on the reins, slowing the horse's pace. The air was close and quiet except for the twittering of birds as she guided Onyx into the rocky mouth of the gorge. Scrubby trees grew on the ledges of boulders, and loose rocks skidded down the sides of the steep ravine as she rode along a narrow dirt path that wound through brush and rock. It was nearly impossible to track the cougar in this terrain, and she was feeling as jittery as Onyx knowing the cat was somewhere in the canyon. She had just decided to turn back when, from the corner of her eye, she spotted the cougar a few feet ahead, crouched in the branch of a tree. It was a full-grown adult, and its yellow eyes were fastened on her.

"Whoa," she said quietly, pulling on the horse's reins. Slowly, she raised her rifle and sighted along the barrel. As if sensing it was in the line of fire, the cougar bared its sharp teeth and let out a snarling scream. Then it sprang. Rebecca saw a blur of motion. Instinctively, she shielded her face with her arm as the powerful cat surged past her in a flurry of teeth, fur, and claws. Onyx reared up on his hind legs, whinnying shrilly, and Rebecca felt herself sliding sideways off the saddle. Desperately, she got off a shot in the cat's direction as it sped away before she lost her balance entirely and tumbled from the horse's back. The sound of the shot boomed in the still air and reverberated off the rock face of the canyon.

When she got to her feet, the cougar was gone. Rebecca was certain she'd missed hitting the cat and worried that it might still be hiding nearby. She muttered under her breath in frustration and brushed the dust from her skirt. Her hip hurt where she had fallen on it, and she'd skinned her elbow. Onyx was standing a few yards away, pawing the ground. If the cougar decided to return, she wouldn't be able to reach the gelding in time to escape on horseback. The close encounter with the cougar unnerved her. She whistled through dry lips, coaxing Onyx to come to her. The horse's black mane danced as he tossed his head and pawed the ground, but he wouldn't approach Rebecca. Instead, he backed up, sidestepping nervously.

Rebecca retrieved the rifle that had fallen out of her hand when she fell and started limping toward her horse. Her hip ached with each step. Before she reached the gelding, she spotted Hernandez and Andrus coming at a gallop toward her.

Hernandez reined his horse to a halt beside her. "I heard the rifle shot. Are you hurt?" he asked anxiously.

Rebecca flushed, embarrassed to have the two cowhands know she'd been thrown from her horse. "A cougar attacked one of the calves," she explained. "I went after it, but it spooked Onyx and got away."

Andrus had ridden over to the black horse and collected the reins. He led the gelding back to Rebecca. "Did you wound it with your shot?" he asked as he handed her the reins.

"I don't think so." She stepped into the stirrup, grimacing with the movement, and swung up into the saddle. "I'll take the calf back down to the ranch and clean its wounds. The two of you keep working here."

Both men nodded. Hernandez followed her back to the calf and lifted it up onto her saddle. The calf's breathing was more shallow than before, and blood from its wounds trickled onto Onyx's ebony coat, making a ribbon of scarlet. Rebecca worried that the young animal might die before she could get it off the mountain. Steadying the calf with one hand, she reined Onyx toward the ranch house.

Rebecca tended to the injured calf throughout the afternoon, but as she prepared for bed that night, she doubted the calf would still be alive when morning came. The gouges made by the cougar's claws were deep and already showed signs of becoming infected. The calf was too weak to suckle, and Rebecca had fed it a little milk in a bottle fitted with a nipple. But it had only been able to swallow a bit of it.

As she slipped into bed, her thoughts dwelled on the calf and the rest of the cattle that Hernandez and Andrus had herded to higher ground that afternoon. After she'd left, Andrus's horse had stumbled and gone down with him.

Although Andrus had managed to jump clear of the animal as it fell, he'd sprained his ankle and hurt his shoulder. He'd still be able to work, but he'd be stiff and sore for a few days. Rebecca slipped her arms underneath her head, pondering the day's events. Ranching was difficult work and often dangerous. Accidents happened while on horseback and working with the cattle; doctors were miles away and so most injuries had to be dealt with on the ranch. A year ago, a ranch hand had been killed when he was thrown from his horse and struck his head on a rock. She remembered her father telling her about his experiences as a young cowhand working on the Willow Ranch. The ranch's owner and a neighboring rancher had been feuding over water rights, and on one occasion Ethan and Samuel had been caught up in an exchange of gunfire with the cowhands from the adjacent ranch. Ethan had been struck in the chest by a bullet, and Samuel had ridden all night to get their father, who was a physician living in Salt Lake City. If it hadn't been for his father's prompt medical attention, Ethan would have died. Rebecca had seen the scar on Ethan's chest left by the bullet.

Rebecca shuddered and turned onto her side, blocking out the disturbing images. She thought again about the calf safely secured for the night inside the barn. Each animal was important; the cattle were her livelihood, and Jessica hated losing even one of them. She closed her eyes, yawning. Even though she thought she would be unable to fall asleep, before long she was dreaming. But her dreams were haunted by the piercing cries of a cougar.

CHAPTER FOUR

Judson Carter ran a soft cloth over the drop-front desk. The walnut desk was equipped with both drawers and racks, as the customer had specified, and was symmetrically shaped with tapered legs and a flat top. Its simple, traditional lines reflected a timeless style. Judson hoped Mr. Owens would be pleased with it. Owens was a repeat customer; Judson had built a four-drawer cabinet for his wife a few months earlier.

Judson stood back to scrutinize the desk with a critical eye. He had done all of the labor on this piece of furniture himself. The assistant he'd employed had recently moved away from the city, and Judson hadn't yet replaced him. It was difficult to find a skilled craftsman who worked in wood. Most furniture was commercially produced, and only a handful of cabinetmakers, such as Judson, continued to design and construct their own products. Judson gave the desk top one more swipe with the cloth and then put away the cloth and linseed oil he'd used to bring out the shine of the wood.

Owens was scheduled to pick up his desk that afternoon. While he waited for his customer to arrive, Judson resumed the work he'd been doing on a Victorian chair with an elaborately carved back. He'd spent hours shaping the curved wood slats that formed the back of the chair and carving the floral ornamentation on the armrests. The seat, when it was finished, would be upholstered in brocade.

Few clients could afford such a luxurious commodity because of the effects of the countrywide economic depression. Over the past two years, Judson had seen a steep drop in the number of orders placed for his custom, hand-made furniture. Luckily, a few high-priced specialty pieces, such as the Victorian-styled chair, kept him in business. He himself had cut corners to save money by limiting his private quarters to a couple of rooms behind the shop—a kitchen, small sitting area, a single bedroom. He didn't need a large amount of space for just himself. In the workshop he had room for his work bench, his tools, and an uncluttered spot where he conducted business with clients. The building with his shop and living quarters was situated on a busy corner of town and constructed of adobe brick painted a pale straw color. Behind it was a place to keep his horse and wagon.

He'd been at work on the chair for about an hour when Owens entered the shop. Judson set down his tools and greeted the man, then led him to the desk. Owens said nothing for a moment as he studied the piece of furniture, then he rubbed a thumb across his chin and nodded. "Excellent work, Mr. Carter. That's a fine piece of craftsmanship."

"I'm glad it meets your satisfaction," Judson replied.

The two men talked together as they examined the desk. Then pleased with his purchase, Owens paid Judson the agreed-upon price for the work, and Judson helped him carry the desk out to the waiting wagon.

After Owens had pulled away from the shop with his merchandise, Judson went back inside. He hung the "Closed" sign in the window, then walked through the cabinetmaking shop to the rear door that led into his private rooms. After letting himself inside, Judson considered whether to make supper for himself at home or to visit his favorite dining house. He felt restless and tonight preferred the companionship of friends. As he changed out of his work clothes into a fresh shirt and a pair of stylish, striped trousers, he toyed with the idea of inviting Rachel Kade to dine out with him, but decided he wasn't in the mood for Rachel's company this evening. As he straightened his high, stiff collar and pulled a comb through his dark hair, his thoughts wandered from Rachel to her twin sister. He pictured Rebecca Kade's slender form, candid blue yes, and light hair. He smiled ruefully as he recalled her prickly reception when he'd arrived at the Double K a week and a half before in the company of her sister. Later on during his visit she had mellowed, but he knew that she had been unhappy with Rachel for bringing him to the ranch so soon after their father's death.

He caught himself thinking about Rebecca again as he buttoned his vest and pulled on his top coat. Grabbing his hat from the peg beside the door, he pushed the image of Rebecca Kade from his mind and stepped out into the summer evening. The air was muggy and without a whisper of a breeze. He said hello to an acquaintance he passed on the board sidewalk as he headed for the dining house a few blocks from his home. After a solitary supper, he crossed the street to the saloon for an after-dinner drink. The Blue Fly saloon was owned by one of his friends, and Judson often retreated there for conversation and card playing to while away the evenings.

The saloon was filled to capacity when he entered. The smell of cigar smoke and sweat permeated the room. He walked over to the long wooden bar that was nicked and stained from frequent use and took a seat on a stool. Lorin Stotts glanced at him from behind the bar and nodded a greeting. When he'd finished serving a drink to the customer at the far end of the bar, he moved to Judson.

"Evening, Judson. How is work at the shop?" he asked as he reached for a glass, filled it with whiskey, and set it in front of Judson.

"Business is good," Judson replied, swirling the liquid in his glass. Judson drank the same brown, rye whiskey whenever he came to the saloon. Lorin had gotten used to his habit and didn't bother anymore asking Judson what he wanted to drink when he sat down at the bar. "You?"

Lorin nodded toward the gaming tables. "About the same crowd as usual."

"How's that pretty gal of yours?"

Lorin smiled, showing crooked front teeth. "Married life is good. You ought to find yourself a girl and settle down."

"How long have you been married now? Eight weeks?" Judson asked, sidestepping his suggestion.

"Ten. And I've put on the extra pounds to prove it." Lorin patted his stomach.

Judson had already noticed that his friend had grown rounder in the face and belly since his marriage. "The missus must be a good cook."

"She bakes the best apple pie I've ever tasted."

"Give your wife my regards."

"Come for supper a night this week. Then you can say hello to Catherine yourself."

"I'd like that." Judson lifted the glass of whiskey to his lips and took a swallow.

From the rear of the room came a sudden burst of raucous laughter. Judson glanced over his shoulder and saw three men seated at a table in the back playing cards. One of them had evidently just won a hand at poker and was raking a pile of cash and coins toward him with a gleeful grin. He laughed again. It was a harsh, grating sound.

Judson turned back to his drink.

"It's hot as blazes in here tonight," Lorin said, taking a swipe across his forehead with the sleeve of his shirt. "Any cooler out of doors?"

"Not much."

"We could use some rain."

Judson nodded. He looked again at the threesome at the card table. Two of them were arguing over the winnings, and the third was taking a long swig from his whiskey glass.

"What magnificent piece are you crafting at your shop this week?" Lorin asked, resting his elbows on the bar.

Judson focused his attention on his friend. "I just sold a walnut desk to a customer. I've been working on it for the past several weeks."

"Did you make a good profit on it?"

"Some."

"I believe you'd work for free, just for the sheer pleasure of shaping the wood."

Judson chuckled as he ran his finger around the rim of his drink, making the glass ring. "I like to turn a good piece of change as well as the next man."

"And you're apt to squander it all on clothes and the ladies," Lorin said with a wink.

Another loud outburst came from the table at the rear of the room. This time there was an unmistakable edge of anger to the voices raised in argument.

Lorin wiped his hands on a towel he kept beside the counter, then walked from behind the bar to the table where the threesome sat. "Can I get you boys anything else?" he asked, directing his question to the man who seemed the most agitated. Judson watched the exchange going on at the table.

"Nobody invited you over here, bartender," the whiskered, ruddy-faced man growled in reply. Judson thought the man's round, red face and whiskered chin resembled a radish.

"If you boys have a bone to pick between yourselves, I suggest you take it outside," Lorin said firmly.

"You tellin' us to leave?" the man at the table challenged, rising to his feet. He pushed his chair away from the table and glared at Lorin.

Lorin stood his ground. "I don't allow fighting in my place. If you men want to do more than drink whiskey and play cards, then you'll have to do it elsewhere."

Judson admired his friend's skill in defusing the tense situation at the table. His voice was firm, yet remained cordial. Judson knew he'd dealt with belligerent customers many times before and usually prevented drunken disagreements from escalating. Judson wondered if this time he'd be as successful.

The man glowered at Lorin, then swept up his hand of cards and flung them on the table. "Come on, boys. This place is beginning to stink. And I hate the smell of a pigsty."

Judson watched to see how the bartender would handle that insult. Lorin's expression didn't change, nor did he budge from his spot. The other two men got up from their chairs and started toward the door. One of them turned and spat a wad of chewing tobacco onto the floor.

Judson turned back to his drink. The dull, brown fluid languished in his glass. He wasn't much of a drinker.

It was primarily the companionship he sought at his friend's establishment, rather than the alcohol. He picked up his glass and carried it with him to a table where some acquaintances were in the midst of a game of poker. "Mind if I join you?" he asked the men gathered around the table. A couple of them moved their chairs to make room for him, the chair legs scraping shrilly against the wood floor. Judson set down his glass in front of him. "Deal me in," he said to the man on his left who was shuffling the cards.

The following evening Judson called on Rachel at the boarding house where she lived, a small, two-story brick building with individual rooms for boarders on the upper floor. On the lower floor was a common parlor and dining room, together with the private rooms occupied by the owner. The owner's wife responded to Judson's knock at the door and then went upstairs to summon Rachel.

After Rachel had seated herself on a parlor chair, Judson asked about her work at the millinery shop. "Mrs. Howells purchased some new fabric for embellishing the hats," she replied. "There's a lovely sky blue satin I have my eye on. It will make the prettiest bow for the straw hat I have in mind to make for myself."

"How many new hats do you already have?" asked Judson with a chuckle.

"Not nearly enough," she smiled.

Rachel smoothed the skirt of her dress and adjusted the lace cuff on her sleeve. Judson had already noticed the green and black striped dress she had on with its tight-fitting waist and black silk collar. Her dark hair was done up in a stylish knot with curls fringing her face, and her emerald eyes reflected the light from the electric street lamps filtering through the parlor window. As he sat opposite Rachel in a garish upholstered chair, he decided she was one of the most attractive girls he'd ever known.

"I'm thinking about making Rebby a fashionable hat with a big, pink bow on the brim as a gift for our 20th birthday." She frowned slightly. "But I don't know where she'd ever wear it. She seldom leaves the ranch."

Judson pictured Rebecca in a fancy, bow-festooned hat and could hardly refrain from smiling. Although he barely knew Rachel's sister, he guessed she would never wear such a concoction; she seemed much too practical and serious-minded.

"What do you think about that idea? You've met my sister," Rachel added.

"I can't quite imagine her in something as frivolous as you've described," he answered. "Why don't you make her something a little less festive?"

"Oh, Judson. She needs something lively to spice up that dreary existence she lives. A stylish hat with bows and feathers is just the thing."

"Whatever you say." He leaned forward and took her hand in his. It was soft and warm and made his heart leap. "And what about yourself? What birthday gift do you want?"

She glanced down at her left hand, clasped in his. "Perhaps a bit of jewelry?" she responded with a coy smile.

He easily determined the meaning behind her words. He and Rachel had been courting for the past five months, and he knew she expected him to ask for her hand in marriage. At one point in their relationship he had contemplated doing that very thing. She certainly appealed to him in a physical way, and he was charmed and amused by her coquettish manner. But if he were to propose marriage, he wasn't entirely sure that she'd accept. She might respond by flirting and teasing, instead of giving him a straightforward answer. She seemed to enjoy keeping him dangling just out of reach. Her words and actions encouraged his affections, yet he sensed that her feelings for him were superficial. Perhaps it was that very issue that both attracted and repelled him.

He let go of her hand and leaned back in his chair. "Your sister's and your birthday is still a few months away. Plenty of time for me to mull over the perfect birthday gift," he said.

A flicker of annoyance passed across her brow. Apparently, his response was not what she'd expected. "Rebecca wants me to come out to the ranch to help her. I'm going to ask Mrs. Howells for some time away from work so that I can do so. She was very sympathetic upon hearing about my father's death and told me to take all the time I needed to tend to family affairs." She lifted her gaze to stare at Judson, measuring his reaction to her words.

"Your sister would probably appreciate your support. When we were at the ranch she seemed nearly overwhelmed with sorrow and worried about shouldering the responsibilities there."

"I'm just as grief-stricken as she is, Judson. Even more so. I haven't had the opportunity of seeing much of Papa over the last year or two. At least she got to spend every day with him."

Judson didn't doubt the sincerity of her feelings—only the suggestion that she'd been prevented from visiting her father because the opportunity was denied her. He said nothing, however, and his silence seemed to aggravate her further.

"I haven't seen you carrying Papa's expensive pocketwatch yet," she said with a chill in her voice. "I gave it to you because I thought you'd appreciate the sentiment behind it. But apparently you don't."

He was surprised by her accusation. "Do you wish it back?"

"No, of course not. But Rebecca was upset with me when I told her I wanted to give it to you."

Judson wasn't aware of this fact. "Then why did you?"

"I just told you the reason. I wanted you to have something of Papa's that he valued."

"Perhaps you should have given it to a family member instead."

"I'm sorry I even brought up the subject." She turned her gaze to the window and stared out with a petulant expression on her face.

Outside the window the night sky was sprinkled with stars, and Judson thought their reflection seemed to wink and shine like jewels in Rachel's dark hair. "When are you planning to go to the ranch?" he asked, seeking to placate her.

"Soon."

"Do you want me to accompany you?"

She turned to stare at him, and her gaze was as cold as a winter's evening. "I wouldn't want you to trouble yourself."

"I can manage to take a weekend off from work at the shop, if you'd like."

"It makes no difference to me."

"If that's the case, then I'll remain here," he said, anger springing into his voice. "I have plenty of work to keep me busy."

She lifted her nose in the air and turned back to the window as if the scene outside was infinitely more interesting than was his company.

He stood up abruptly from his chair. "It's getting late. Perhaps I should be going."

"Yes, perhaps you should."

He jammed on his hat and started for the door. Jerking it open, he strode out into the night without another word. He was fuming as he stalked down the porch steps toward his horse, tethered at the hitching post in front of the boarding house. He wondered why he continued to put up with Rachel's ill humor. Her frequent outbursts of temper were getting on his nerves, and tonight her behavior galled him more than usual. As for the matter of her father's pocketwatch, he made a decision not to keep it. He doubted that the timepiece held much sentimental value for Rachel;

it likely meant more to her sister. Sometime in the near future, he resolved, he would return the watch to Rebecca.

He grabbed the reins from the hitching post and mounted his horse. Casting a glance over his shoulder, he saw a movement at the parlor window—a quick lowering of the corner of the curtain. Rachel's furtive spying brought a scowl to his face. Jabbing the horse with his heels, he reined it away from the boarding house, the scowl burrowing deeper into his brow. His thoughts were dark and his disposition sour as he rode down the dirt road.

Instead of returning to his house, Judson headed for the Blue Fly saloon. It was late, and when he entered the saloon he found few customers at the counter and the gaming tables. Judson strode directly to the bar and chose a stool.

Instead of his friend, Lorin Stotts, behind the bar, the assistant bartender was on duty. He sauntered over to Judson. "What can I get you?" he asked.

"Whiskey," Judson answered.

The bartender poured Judson a glass and set it in front of him. Judson immediately took a swig and grimaced as the whiskey slid down his throat. The bartender gave him a close look. "We close in twenty minutes," he said.

"That should be time enough," Judson muttered. He lifted the glass again, tipped back his head, and gulped another mouthful. This time the whiskey went down without burning.

CHAPTER FIVE

The next morning Judson's head was pounding when he awoke. He climbed out of bed and dashed cold water onto his face. Rubbing his eyes, he stared at his reflection in the mirror above the washstand. A somber-faced man with puffy eyes and rumpled hair stared back at him. A dark patch of bristly whiskers shadowed his chin. He passed a hand over his face and frowned. He'd drunk too much whiskey last night—something he didn't often do—and wondered why he'd allowed himself that indiscretion. As he shaved and dressed for the day, his thoughts dwelled on Rachel. He was still angry with her and frustrated by her behavior. Her petulance was beginning to weary him.

Thrusting the troublesome thoughts from his mind, he opened the door to his workshop. Yesterday he'd received two new orders for furniture—a chest with a hinged lid and a sideboard. He had other projects he was in the midst of constructing, including the Victorian chair which was requiring many hours of labor. Judson was used to working alone when it came to designing each piece of furniture, choosing the appropriate wood, and doing the finish work. But he often employed one or two others to help with the assembly. He needed an assistant, preferably someone skilled in joinery. As he worked in his shop that morning, he considered placing an ad in the Salt Lake City newspaper for an apprentice cabinetmaker.

Thinking about the new order he'd received for the sideboard, he began to plan out its shape on paper. He calculated how much time the piece would require to build and from which supplier he would purchase the cut wood. He frowned, thinking again about the need for an assistant. He spent the morning working on the design for the sideboard, and in the afternoon he ordered the wood for it. He worked in his shop until the sun set. When he finished for the day, he felt satisfied with what he'd accomplished. He took pleasure in seeing the raw wood transforming under his fingers into an article of beauty and utility and appreciated the artistic and aesthetic qualities of the finished product.

Judson saw Rachel only once, and that was briefly, during the following week. On Thursday evening, he finished the Victorian chair he'd been working on. To celebrate the completion of the chair, he dined out for dinner and then made a stop at the Blue Fly. The saloon was crowded. He walked to the bar and ordered a drink from the bartender filling in for Lorin.

As Judson drank his whiskey, he spotted the three men who had caused a disturbance at the saloon a few nights earlier. They were seated at a corner table sharing a bottle between them. The florid-faced man with the whiskers was lazily shuffling and reshuffling a deck of cards.

Judson went back to his drink. A stranger sitting next to him at the bar initiated a conversation, to which Judson contributed only slightly. He listened with one ear as the man told about an amorous encounter he'd had with a saloon girl in another town. While the man's voice droned on, Judson sipped his whiskey and let his thoughts ramble. The August heat made the room close and stuffy, and the bar was sticky from spilled drinks. Judson took another swallow from his glass. From the corner of his eye, he saw a young man enter the saloon; the fellow caught his attention because of his youth and his striking appearance. The young man had dark eyes and hair as black as a crow's wing, broad cheekbones, and a bronze complexion. Judson watched him stand in the doorway of the saloon, his eyes darting about like a wild bird's, before he came inside and moved to the far end of the bar.

Judson turned back to his neighbor. The man had finished his story about the saloon girl and started another colorful tale. Gulping the last of his drink, Judson shot a look down the length of the bar to where the young man stood, stiff as an arrow, waiting for the bartender. He had on a pair of brown cotton trousers, a white collarless shirt, and a striped vest. Judson noticed an ornamental piece hanging from a leather strand around the boy's neck. From his vantage point at the opposite end of the counter, he couldn't make out the shape of the carved wooden ornament.

He turned to his empty glass, considering a refill. The stranger next to him was still rambling, starting one tale before even finishing the last. Judson tuned him out. He was about to signal the bartender for another drink when he heard the raised voice of one of the men sitting at the corner table. "What are you doin' in here, Injun?"

Judson swung around to look at the puffy-faced, whiskered man who had spoken. The man's name was Murdock, Lorin had informed him previously, and he'd started more than one brawl at the saloon since he'd begun frequenting the Blue Fly. Murdock's face was flushed and his eyes belligerent.

"I'm talkin' to you, red man," Murdock said in a slurred voice.

Judson's gaze slid to the Indian youth standing at the end of the bar. He could see the young man's shoulders stiffen as he turned to face Murdock.

"That's right. Show some respect when your white brother is talkin' to you." Murdock let out a snort of laughter, as if his remark was somehow humorous. His two companions at the table snickered.

Judson watched the youth to see how he would respond. The young man stared at Murdock without speaking, then shifted his gaze to the bar. Judson was close enough to him to see the anger sparking in his eyes.

Murdock, finished with needling the young Indian, resumed his conversation with his friends at the table. Judson saw the bartender approach the youth and speak to him. "We don't serve Indians in here. You best be moving on," he heard the bartender say.

The youth said something in reply, and Judson saw the bartender shake his head, frown, and point toward the door. The men at the table apparently overheard the exchange. Murdock's head jerked up, and he nudged the shoulder of the man sitting next to him. All three of them watched the youth with scowling faces.

When the youth didn't move from his place at the bar, Murdock abruptly stood up, knocking over his chair in the process. The chair fell onto the floor with a loud clatter. Swaying on his feet, he swaggered over to the youth with his two cronies following. "Didn't I hear the bartender askin' you, nice and friendly-like to leave?" Murdock said in a drunken voice. "You best be gettin' back to the reservation, boy."

The picture of the three men glaring hatefully at the Indian youth stirred Judson's sense of indignation. He watched the scene a moment longer as Murdock continued to taunt and insult the boy. Then Judson saw Murdock shoot out a hand and yank the necklace from the young man's neck.

"What's this? Some sort of Injun charm?" Murdock snarled. He held up the carved piece attached to its leather thong like a trophy so his friends could see it. One of the other men made a grab for the necklace, but Murdock snatched it out of his reach.

Nearly everyone in the saloon was watching the exchange going on at the bar, including the bartender, who made no attempt to step in and defuse the situation. If Lorin had been tending the bar, Judson thought, the altercation would never had gotten this far. As Murdock and his companions continued to harass the youth, Judson could sit still no longer. He got up from his stool and strode over to the four men.

As he approached the group, Judson could see the fury in the young man's eyes. The youth looked no older than seventeen or eighteen, but he stood facing the men without cowering. Wordlessly, Judson stepped between the youth and the drunken man who held the necklace in his fist. "That doesn't belong to you," Judson said, motioning to the necklace. "Perhaps you'd like to return it to this young man with an apology." There was no mistaking the determination behind Judson's words.

Murdock turned to stare at him. "Who do you think you are, mister, interferin' with somethin' that ain't none of your business?" he growled.

"Return the necklace to the boy. Now," Judson ordered. "And tell him you're sorry for your comments."

"I ain't apologizin' to no Injun," Murdock spat out.

The youth hadn't backed down at all. From the look of defiance on his face, he looked as though he might attack Murdock. Judson hoped to put a stop to the quarrel before it worsened. "Hand me the necklace and go back to your whiskey before someone gets hurt," he said.

Murdock responded by taking a wild swing at Judson. Judson easily dodged the man's fist, then landed a solid blow of his own on the other man's jaw. Murdock sprawled backwards. His body glanced off the back of a chair, and the necklace he was holding skidded across the wooden floor of the saloon. He grunted and tried to sit up, but fell back, groaning.

Judson retrieved the necklace while Murdock's friends helped him to his feet, then handed the necklace to its owner. "I believe this is yours," Judson said to the young man.

The youth took it without speaking and quickly slipped the ornament around his neck. Judson had an instant to glimpse the handsome piece, carved into the shape of a wolf, before the young man stuffed it inside his shirt. He nodded at Judson without any change in expression, then turned and strode out of the saloon.

Judson sent Murdock a dark look as he slowly climbed to his feet with the help of his two companions. The whiskered man glared back at him. "You ain't seen the end of this, mister. I'll remember your face, that's for sure," Murdock bellowed.

"I hope so," Judson retorted. He turned his back on the three men and started for the door of the saloon. On his way out, he tossed a coin onto the counter to pay for his glass of whiskey.

When he was outside, he scanned both directions of the street for the Indian youth and caught sight of him just ahead rounding the corner. He quickened his step in order to catch up with him.

As he drew near, the young man paused and warily turned around. His posture was rigid, as if he expected to confront a foe. When he saw it was Judson approaching, the tenseness in his body eased.

Judson came to his side. "May I speak with you for a minute?"

The youth nodded slightly, his dark eyes alert and intense.

Judson smiled, trying to reassure the young man that he meant no harm. "I wanted to make sure you're all right," he said. "Those men in the saloon were way out of line."

"I am fine," the boy responded. His voice was low pitched and decisive, and Judson heard in it a note of acrimony.

Something about the youth appealed to Judson's sense of compassion. "Are you from around here?" he asked in a friendly tone.

"No."

"Have you a place to stay?"

The young man nodded briefly, keeping his eyes on Judson as if he didn't quite trust him.

Judson wondered if the boy was telling him the truth about his circumstances. He wanted to help him, if the youth would let him. His eyes flicked to the leather thong around the youth's neck. "From the quick look I got at the carving hanging from your necklace, I saw that the workmanship was excellent. Did you carve the piece yourself?"

The youth nodded again.

"Well, then you appear to have a knack for woodworking." Judson paused as a sudden thought occurred to him. "I own a cabinetmaking shop a few blocks from here. I make chests, cabinets, and the like."

The young man looked steadily at him, his eyes never wavering from Judson's face.

"And at the moment, I'm in need of an assistant." Judson felt the youth's dark eyes studying him, but he couldn't read their expression in the flickering light of the street lamps. "Would you be interested in the job?"

The boy's brown eyes narrowed in distrust. "Why would you offer me such a position? You know nothing about me."

Judson thrust his hands into his pockets. "I told you. I need some help at my workshop." Judson watched him carefully, gauging the youth's reaction to his words.

The young man glanced up the street and then back at Judson. "How do you know I would be able to do the work?"

"Well, I don't. But I'm willing to teach you. And if that carved wolf you're wearing is any indication, I believe you'd learn the trade quickly and be successful at it."

The Indian youth said nothing for several seconds, and Judson thought he would turn down the offer. It was probably better that way, Judson decided. He didn't know the first thing about this young man. He could be a troublemaker or a thief. He'd felt sorry for him after seeing the treatment he'd received in the saloon, and the glimpse he'd gotten of the carving intrigued him, but perhaps it was just as well if he didn't get involved with the boy.

The young man shifted on his feet. "All right."

"All right?" Judson repeated in surprise. He nodded, mulling over the consequences of his invitation. "All right, then," he said again. He put out his hand and the youth gripped it in a firm handshake.

Judson gave him directions to his shop and instructed him to come by around noon the next day. As they parted, heading off in opposite directions, Judson abruptly turned back around. "Wait a minute. I didn't give you my name. It's Judson Carter."

"Daniel Briggs," the young man said in return.

"Good to meet you, Daniel." Judson tipped his hat, then continued up the road. He had mixed feelings about the offer he'd just extended. If the youth didn't work out, he reasoned, he could easily dismiss him. But if he did possess a talent for cabinetmaking, then that would be advantageous for both the boy and for Judson. Judson shoved his hands into his pockets as he walked back toward the saloon to untether his horse, content to wait and see what the morrow would bring.

At precisely noon the next day, Daniel Briggs stepped into the woodworking shop. Judson set aside the plane he was using to smooth a section of board and met Daniel at the front of the shop. "Come in," Judson invited, feeling mildly surprised that the young man had kept his appointment.

"Good afternoon, Mr. Carter."

Judson noticed that the youth was wearing the same brown trousers, but with a different shirt and waistcoat. The wolf necklace hung around his neck, resting against his chest. The carved piece swayed on its leather strand as Daniel reached out to shake Judson's hand. "Good to see you. Are you ready to get started?" Judson asked.

"I am, sir."

Judson indicated a chair for him to sit on and pulled another close to it for himself. Folding his arms, he studied Daniel to determine his demeanor. He was a handsome young man, Judson thought, with high cheekbones, a slender nose, and broad mouth. But he was probably not a full-blooded Native American, even though his hair was as black as ink and his eyes nearly the same color. There was a Caucasian look about his features, too. His gaze was direct and alert, ready to assimilate whatever Judson had to say. That was a good start, Judson decided. "If you're willing to work hard and follow directions, I can teach you the art of cabinetmaking."

"Yes, sir."

Judson ran a hand across his chin, considering the best place to begin his explanation. "Unlike a carpenter who uses nails to secure the parts of a piece of furniture together, a cabinetmaker specializes in using interlocking parts secured by adhesives and the cut joint. The cabinetmaker constructs what is called case furniture—cabinets, desks, cupboards, chests, and so on—as opposed to the construction of framework furniture, such as chairs."

"Yes, sir. I understand," Daniel said, perched stiffly on the edge of his chair.

"Joinery, or the technique of joining together pieces of wood, applies to the work of both carpenters and cabinetmakers. But cabinetmaking differs from carpentry in that it requires greater precision and an understanding of the strength and placement of joints."

Judson stood up from his chair and walked over to the chest he was building for a new client. Daniel rose, too, and followed him.

"Take this chest, for example." Judson gestured to the unfinished article of furniture. "The first step in constructing any piece of case furniture, such as this chest, is to make a drawing or pattern of the item to be built with its dimensions, design, and decorative motifs. Then the designer chooses the appropriate wood for the article. The assembly of the product requires skilled handwork. After that comes the finish work. The product is then completed with applications of oil, varnish, or paint and hand rubbed to a shine. This process of applying a coat of oil and then hand rubbing it in is repeated several times more to create a smooth finish."

Daniel studied the framed panels and joints that Judson had already completed on the chest. He pointed to one of the joints. "Here is where the greatest stress occurs?"

Judson smiled. "That's right. That's a primary joint, called a mortise joint, or a mortise-and-tenon."

Daniel bent down to get a closer look at the joint and rail.

Judson pointed out the grooved joints used to secure the side panels to the top and bottom frames of the desk and the dovetail joints in the corners of the single drawer. They discussed the different types of wood used in cabinetmaking, and Judson outlined the strengths and weaknesses of each variety. Judson introduced his new assistant to the tools he used in cutting and shaping the wood, and the two of them talked about the differences between commercially mass-produced wood furniture and that crafted by hand.

"The handmade, or custom, product is largely put together by one man working at a bench. Skilled handwork is scarce and costly, but it is better made and more attractive than that produced by the factory process," Judson explained.

Daniel walked about the shop, studying each piece Judson was in the midst of constructing for his clients. "How did you get started in this business?" he asked, pausing to study the Victorian chair Judson had just completed the evening before. "Have you always been interested in woodworking?"

Judson chuckled. "No. Actually, I just fell into it. I was about your age, 16 or 17, and living in Michigan where I grew up, and needed a job. One of my friends was employed at a trunk-making factory and suggested I apply. I did and was assigned the job of building the wooden frames for the trunks. I took a liking to it and discovered I was fairly good at working with the wood. Later on, I was promoted to designing trunks." Judson smiled, remembering his experiences at the factory.

"What about this chair?" Daniel asked, eyeing the curved, slatted back of the ornately carved Victorian chair. "This is not the typical cabinetmaker's work, is it?"

Judson approached the chair and ran his fingers along the top rail of it. The wood was smooth and even under his touch. "That's true. Chairs fall into the category of framework furniture. But an acquaintance of mine wanted a custom-made chair for his law office and agreed to pay me a handsome price for making it. So I consented." Judson smiled. "The construction isn't too different from cabinetmaking in a lot of ways. The main factors are strength, proportion, and style of design. Like cabinetry work, the adhesives at the joints prevent the parts from moving."

"I see."

"Have you had any experience in woodworking other than the piece you wear around your neck?"

Daniel glanced down at the carved wood representation resting against his chest. "I have carved many things out of wood and bone."

"May I take a closer look at that?" Judson asked, gesturing to the piece cut into the shape of a wolf.

Daniel removed the necklace and handed it to Judson. Three brightly colored beads were strung on the leather strand on either side of the wolf. Judson turned the carving over to look at the reverse side and then studied the edges. "This is well done, Daniel. I doubt I could produce anything as fine. When did you make it?" he asked, handing the necklace back to him.

"About a year ago."

Judson hoped he'd add some explanation about why he had carved that particular animal or what it represented, but Daniel didn't elaborate further. Judson decided to press him for details concerning his background. "What else have you carved? Other animals?"

Judson could see him hesitate before answering. "When I was younger, I carved a wolf for my mother."

Here was a topic Judson could build on. "Is your mother Native American?" he asked, trying to be tactful.

Daniel nodded. "She is Ute."

"Have you and your family been living on the Ute reservation?"

Daniel's fingers twitched at his side. "I have not been there for some time."

Judson chafed at the boy's evasive answer. With reluctance, he abandoned the subject, hoping Daniel would divulge more when he became better acquainted with Judson and trusted him. "We can put your skill with wood carving to good use here. I'll give you some wood scraps to practice with, and then you can take over the job of carving. Does that sound satisfactory to you?"

Daniel nodded and his eyes shone with eagerness.

"I'll pay you weekly, and when you've learned the trade and are able to carry your weight, the pay will increase."

"Thank you, Mr. Carter."

"It's Judson. If we're going to be working together, there's no need for formalities."

"Yes, sir."

Judson smiled to himself. He had a good feeling about this young man and the direction the apprenticeship was taking. "Very well. Let's get started. Hand me that section of pine and the plane to smooth it."

CHAPTER SIX

Throughout the following week, Judson worked with Daniel at the shop, teaching him the rudiments of the cabinetmaker's craft. They began work together on a chest of drawers, starting with the boxed frame. Judson taught him how to select the wood, cut it, and prepare it for assembly. He demonstrated the tools used—the lathe for shaping turned parts such as posts, spindles, rungs, and legs; the vise for gripping and holding a section of board; drawknives, scrapers, and shavers for cutting; planes for smoothing the wood; frame saws and hand sanders; folding rules and adjustable squares for measuring; chisels and awls. He found Daniel to be a quick learner and unafraid to try his hand at each new task. During breaks when Judson was busy with a customer or out of the shop on an errand, Daniel practiced using the trammel, a drawing tool for scribing ovals, and the other implements for carving designs into wood. During lunch breaks, he ate a simple meal that he brought with him to the shop. Judson noticed that while he ate, Daniel read from the same brown, hardbound book each day.

The friend who had commissioned the Victorian chair came to the shop at the end of the week to collect it. Pleased with the finished product, he complimented Judson on his skill and paid him an additional three dollars beyond the agreed upon sum as a token of his satisfaction with the work. On Friday evening, Judson dined out alone and then paid a visit to the Blue Fly. Lorin Stotts was tending the bar and had some good news to share—his wife was pregnant with their first child. Judson congratulated him and then the two of them shared a toast to the unborn baby. He spent most of the evening at the saloon, playing cards and visiting with acquaintances. When he returned home, he read for a while under the fuzzy glare of the electric lamp, and then went to bed and promptly fell asleep.

On Saturday afternoon Judson called on Rachel. He took her for a buggy ride into the canyon and they sat down to eat a picnic lunch beside a lazy stream. The day was sunny, and the fragrant smell of pines carried on the breeze. Rachel seemed relaxed and happy. "Have some more chicken," she invited. "I brought plenty."

Judson chose a leg of fried chicken from the plate she held out to him. "I'll have another biscuit to go with it," he said, smiling.

"Do you like those biscuits? I made them this morning." She teased him by offering the basket of biscuits, then snatching it back as he reached for one. She laughed, and the sound of it was like a trilling bird. As she sat beside the stream with the sunlight dappling her heart-shaped face, Judson felt a strong pull of attraction and began to re-examine his feelings for her. With her dusky hair and emerald eyes, Rachel was beautiful as well as enchanting. She seemed to enjoy the domestic duties of cooking and sewing, and she possessed a natural grace and style. She would make any man a desirable wife. As he took a bite of chicken, he once again dallied with the thought of asking her to marry him.

"Have you finished the Victorian chair you were telling me about?" Rachel asked, dipping her fingertips into the slow moving stream murmuring at their side.

"Just last week, as a matter of fact. The buyer picked it up yesterday."

"Did he like it?"

"I believe he did." Judson remembered the extra three dollars his friend had given him. That, together with money he had put away as savings, could easily go toward the purchase of a wedding band.

"Do you have other pieces you're working on?" She glided her hand across the top of the water.

Judson followed the movement with his eyes, almost mesmerized by the motion. The water lapped around her fingers, droplets reflecting the sunlight and sparkling like beads of crystal. With effort, he pulled his gaze away, gathering his thoughts. "Yes. I have several new orders. I've been so busy that I've had to hire an assistant."

"Oh?" Rachel withdrew her hand from the water and playfully flicked a few drops in Judson's direction before drying her fingers on a napkin. "How does he seem to be working out?"

"Very well. He's a young man, about seventeen or so, but he has a knack for woodworking. I've been training him, and he's grasped the basics quickly." Judson thought about how well Daniel was progressing. Yesterday, he'd been surprised with the quality of Daniel's workmanship on a dovetailed joint. When completed, the joints had fit together smoothly and snugly.

"What's your new assistant like?" Rachel asked, nibbling on the corner of a biscuit.

"He's quiet. Keeps his thoughts to himself. His eyes are brown and intense, and his voice is mild." Even though Daniel's grammar and diction were flawless, Judson mused, there remained an unusual cadence to his speech, as though the rhythm of it retained the last vestige of his native language.

"Well, I hope he'll be of some help to you. Perhaps you can get away from the shop a little more now than you have in the past."

Judson leaned back on his elbows and gazed toward a stand of quaking aspens on a hillside. Their leaves fluttered in the breeze like the wings of butterflies. A little higher up the hillside grew green pines and juniper.

"I've been wanting to visit my sister at the ranch," Rachel said, dusting a crumb off her skirt. "I'm planning to go out to the Double K next weekend if Mrs. Howells doesn't need me at the shop."

Judson hadn't given Rebecca Kade a thought for quite some time, but Rachel's mention of her brought Rebecca's pretty face sharply into focus. He wondered how she was managing with her responsibilities at the ranch and if her grief had eased over the death of her father.

"Would you like to go with me?"

Judson focused his attention on her. "I don't know. I'm not sure I can get away from my work."

Rachel leaned forward and gave him a beguiling smile. "What about your new assistant? Can't he take over for you for just one day?"

Judson considered her suggestion. He didn't really want to take time away from work to go with Rachel to the Double K. He was in the middle of educating Daniel about the business; and it was now mid-August, his busiest season. "I'll have to take a look at my work load to see if I can leave for a few days at the end of next week. I'll let you know, all right?"

Rachel placed her hand lightly on his arm. "I hope you'll be able to come with me. It will take the dreariness out of having to stay at the ranch."

Judson pulled back a little to look at her. "I thought the reason for your going was to visit your sister."

"Oh, it is. But having you there, too, will make it a much more pleasant trip."

Judson frowned as he watched Rachel begin to clean up their lunch dishes and pack them back inside the picnic basket. He disliked that streak of selfishness that occasionally surfaced and marred Rachel's polished deportment. He tried to look past her faults as he helped her gather the leftover food and fold up the blanket they'd been sitting on. The breeze was growing stronger, threatening to turn into a whipping wind, and the sky was becoming overcast. Judson hurried her along, wanting to get back down the canyon before the weather turned nasty.

On Wednesday of the following week, Judson sought out Daniel during the lunch break while he was eating. As he approached, Daniel set aside his book and looked up expectantly. "I'm planning to be away from the shop on Friday. Do you think you can handle things here by yourself?" Judson asked.

"Yes, sir."

"Mr. Jacobsen will probably be coming in Friday morning to check on the progress of the sideboard I'm building for him. He generally stops by once a week to make sure I'm working on it," he added jokingly.

Daniel nodded without smiling.

"In the afternoon, Mr. and Mrs. Cobb mentioned they might come by to place an order. Write down all the particulars as they give them to you so that we can construct the piece to their specifications."

"I will, sir."

"I'll give you the key to the shop so that you can open it Friday morning and close up in the evening." Judson paused, trying to think if there were any other instructions to relay to his new assistant. "Do you have any questions?"

"None I can think of right now, sir."

Judson smiled tolerantly to himself. No matter how many times Judson had reminded him that formality was not expected at the shop, Daniel still continued to address him as "sir." He'd also continued to keep his personal life private. He'd evaded Judson's gentle probing, keeping his responses short and generalized. He hadn't revealed anything more about his past other than what he'd told Judson earlier about his mother. He'd never mentioned his father. Judson hadn't learned where the young man was born, if he had any family, or why he'd come to Salt Lake City. He knew only that Daniel rented a small, attic room at a boarding house in town and that he'd been residing in the city for only a few days before Judson had met him at the saloon.

But now, if Judson intended to leave the youth solely in charge of the shop, he felt it necessary to obtain a few answers from him first. Nodding toward the book Daniel had put aside and from which he so often read, he said in a casual tone, "You seem to be enjoying that book. What's it about?" He accompanied the question with what he hoped was an innocent smile.

Daniel picked up the volume and held it out to Judson to see for himself.

Taking the book from his hand, Judson glanced at the title stamped on the spine. He started in surprise when he read it. "Where did you get this?"

"It belonged to my mother. Two missionaries gave it to her while we were living on the reservation."

Judson had not expected this particular book to be in the young man's possession. He stared at it without speaking.

"My mother often asked me to read from the book to her. She had never been taught to read the white man's language for herself."

"Is your mother still living on the reservation?"

Daniel shook his head. "She died a few months ago."

"I'm sorry to hear that." Judson handed the book back to him. "Were you raised on the reservation?"

Daniel rested a palm on the cover of the book. "Yes, until I was ten. Then I was sent to Denver to attend the white man's school."

"Denver? Were you living on a reservation in Colorado?" Judson had little knowledge about the subject of Indian tribal grounds or the government's relocation policies. He was aware of the Ute reservations established by Congress in the 1860s, but he had no clear idea of their boundaries.

"I was born on the Consolidated Ute Reservation in Colorado. My mother was sent to this reservation along with her band of Tabeguache Utes before I was born."

Judson noticed that his voice held a trace of bitterness. "What about your father?" Judson asked carefully.

"I have never met my father." His face hardened with the words.

"Your father is a white man, I'm guessing?"

Daniel nodded, carefully erasing any trace of emotion from his eyes. He set the book on the floor next to his chair. "That is part of the reason why I am in this place. I have been searching for my father to tell him of my mother's death. And to give him this." He lifted the ornament, carved in the shape of a wolf, from his chest and then let it fall back into place.

Judson said nothing for a moment, trying to read between the lines of Daniel's explanation. There was more the youth was not telling him. "Do you have reason to believe your father is here in Salt Lake City?"

"I have learned that he may be living here."

"Perhaps I've heard of him in the course of my business dealings. What is his name?" Judson asked.

"Solomon Curtis. Do you know of him?" Daniel's expression held a curious mixture of hope and disdain.

"Solomon Curtis. No, I'm sorry. I don't believe I've ever met anyone by that name."

The look on Daniel's face did not change. "That is all right. I will ask the Mormon leader who wrote this book. He will be able to tell me where my father is."

Judson shook his head, smiling slightly. "I'm afraid the Mormon leader who wrote that book is dead and has been for quite some time."

Daniel stiffened in his chair. "I was told that the Mormon chief lives near the great temple. I was told he is not dead."

"Oh, you mean the old gentleman, Wilford Woodruff," Judson said. "He's the current president of the Church. Yes, he lives here in the city."

"I will go to him and ask him to inquire of his God about my father. God will listen to him."

"I imagine that's true. But you may have some difficulty gaining an audience with President Woodruff. He's a busy man."

"I will wait."

Judson was surprised by this whole story. If he had tried to come up with an explanation about Daniel's past, he would never have imagined this one. "There's still one thing I don't understand, Daniel," he said, frowning. "What were you doing in the saloon that night we met? You're a bit young to be frequenting an establishment like that."

"A stranger I met on the street told me I would find the Mormon leader inside," he said simply.

"What!" Judson exclaimed. He started to laugh, but then quickly stopped himself on seeing Daniel's indignant expression. "That person was joking with you or deliberately misleading you. President Woodruff is a teetotaler."

"Teetotaler? I do not understand this word."

"It means a person who does not drink liquor. The Blue Fly saloon is the last place you'd find a Mormon prophet."

Just as Judson was about to explain further, the door to the shop swung open. Glancing over, Judson was surprised to see Rachel Kade standing in the doorway. He stood up from his chair and hurried over to her. "Rachel, I didn't expect to see you this afternoon. Come in."

"Hello, Judson." As she stepped inside, her eyes swept through the room. She spied Daniel at the rear of the shop, and her dark brows rose in question.

Seeing her expression, Judson said, "That's my new assistant, Daniel Briggs." He motioned to Daniel to join them and then introduced him to Rachel.

"How are you enjoying your work here?" Rachel asked him with a stiff smile.

"Very well, thank you," Daniel returned.

"That's good."

"Daniel has been doing an excellent job," Judson said. "I've appreciated his help."

"Indeed," Rachel responded, glancing again at the young man. "I'm sure Judson has found your assistance invaluable."

"I hope so." Daniel's demeanor was respectful, but his dark eyes narrowed slightly.

Rachel turned to Judson. "I want to speak with you if you have a moment."

"All right."

"Would you excuse us?" Rachel asked, nodding to Daniel. Although her voice was friendly, Judson detected a condescending note in it. He watched Daniel return to the back of the shop and resume his work.

After he was out of earshot, Rachel said in a hoarse whisper, "Judson, you didn't tell me that your new assistant is an Indian!"

Judson frowned at the tone of her words and the supercilious gleam in her eyes. "I didn't think it was relevant."

Rachel cupped one gloved hand to the side of her mouth to prevent Daniel from hearing her. "Of course, it's relevant. How could you possibly hire an Indian? The whole race are thieves and troublemakers."

Judson bristled, offended by her bigotry. "That's a rash statement, Rachel. And completely untrue."

Rachel didn't seem to be even listening to him. "Aren't you afraid he'll steal from you?"

Judson's annoyance was quickly turning to anger. "What did you want to discuss with me, Rachel?"

She dropped her hand to her side. "I came in to say that I won't be able to go to the ranch this weekend as we planned."

"All right," Judson said, still irritated by her previous comment.

"Mrs. Howells has received a rush order from a wealthy client and has asked me to work through the weekend."

"That's fine. I need to be here at the shop anyway."

"Oh, I was hoping you would still go," Rachel said, pursing her lips. "I'm worried about Rebecca and want her to have some company."

"You want me to go to the Double K without you?" Judson asked in surprise.

"Yes, if you could; just for the day. You can tell her that I planned on coming for a visit, but at the last minute couldn't get away."

Judson shook his head. "No, I'm sorry, but—"

Rachel cut in before he could complete his thought. She stepped closer and placed a hand on his arm. "Oh, please do it for me, Judson. I'd be so grateful. I don't know when I'll be able to get out to the ranch again."

Judson blew out his breath in frustration. "What about waiting until next weekend?"

"I don't know if we'll be finished making the hats by then." She gently squeezed his arm. "Please go in my place, won't you?"

"All right," he answered, shaking off her hand. "But I don't like the idea."

His curt reply didn't seem to bother her. "Thank you. I know Rebecca will be happy to have a visitor." She leaned over and pecked his cheek.

Judson drew back, resisting her kiss.

"Will you be coming to the boarding house this evening?" she asked with a smile.

"I don't know yet."

"If not, then I'll see you in a few days." She turned and cast a suspicious glance in Daniel's direction. "And be careful around that Indian."

CHAPTER SEVEN

Rebecca had renewed her efforts as the weeks passed, working from sunup to sunset. She'd dropped into bed each night exhausted but unable to sleep, nagged by the thought that the ranch was slipping from her grasp despite all her hard work. It had been six weeks since her father's death, and in all that time not a day had passed that she did not mourn him.

Her father's younger brother, Samuel, had come out to the ranch to see her and had stayed for several days. She'd been comforted by his presence and for the first time since her father's passing, she had felt her burdens lighten. After Samuel returned home, she'd set about her tasks with renewed optimism. The ranch was operating reasonably well under Micah's able supervision, and a series of late summer showers had invigorated the grasses on the range.

With the cooler temperatures of September not far away, the cattle would begin to fatten and grow strong.

On a sultry Friday afternoon as Rebecca lugged firewood from the shed to the front porch of the house, she spotted a horse and rider coming up the ranch road. Setting the wood on the porch and shielding her eyes against the sun's glare, she stared at the man on horseback. It was only when he was within a few yards of the house that she recognized him. She drew a tight, quick breath, then smoothed her hair and straightened her blouse, tucking it more neatly into the waist of her riding skirt. An instant later, Judson Carter reined in his horse.

"Hello, there," he said, offering her a smile.

She pushed a lock of hair away from her eyes. "Good afternoon, Mr. Carter. What brings you to the Double K?"

Judson dismounted and tied the reins to the hitching post near the porch. "I came to see how you're getting along, Miss Kade," he said, walking over to her. "I hope you don't mind the intrusion."

"Of course not." Rebecca couldn't help but notice how striking he looked in his smartly tailored trousers and matching high-buttoned frock coat. The white shirt he had on was coupled with a starched collar and knotted tie.

He planted one booted foot on the porch step. "Rachel planned on coming to the ranch to visit you and asked me to come along. But then the hat shop where she's employed received a rush order and she had to stay in town to work. So you're stuck with just me."

"I hope she's not working too hard," Rebecca responded, purposely avoiding his charming smile.

"No, I think not." His eyes swept the yard. "Is everything well here?"

Rebecca nodded. "We're getting by."

She watched his glance fall on the chopped logs on the porch at her feet. "Haven't you a man to help you with that?" he asked, pointing to the firewood.

"I can manage by myself."

"I've no doubt that you can. But let me give you a hand with it."

Before she could reply, he began stacking the wood in his arms. "Where do you want this?"

"Right in here," she answered, holding open the porch door for him. She led the way into the kitchen and motioned for him to set the firewood in the bin beside the stove. "Thank you."

"It's my pleasure. I'll bring in the rest."

She waited while he made another trip from the porch to the stove. When he'd placed the wood inside the bin, he turned to her. "Would you like more wood brought in from the shed?"

"No. That's enough for now."

They stood together in the kitchen, an awkward silence falling between them. "I guess I've forgotten my manners," Rebecca said hastily. "Won't you have a seat?" He took a chair near the table and Rebecca seated herself across from him. She bit her lip, unsure what to say. "Can I get you a glass of lemonade? I made some this morning."

"Thanks. I'd like that."

While she poured the lemonade into a glass, she glanced over her shoulder at him. His eyes were taking in the details of the spare, small room. She carried two glasses of lemonade to the table and set them down, then took her seat opposite him.

His fingers drummed against the glass, sounding like a steady rain against a window pane. "Rachel's been worried about you. She wanted to make sure you're all right and made me promise to give her a full report."

"You can tell Rachel that we're getting along fine." She avoided his gaze as she lifted the glass of lemonade to her lips.

"She'll be glad to hear that." He took a swallow from his glass. "This tastes good. Just the right balance of sweetness and tartness."

Rebecca clamped her hands together in her lap. She felt nervous and awkward in his company and was sure he sensed it. As he leaned back in his chair and let his eyes wander the room, she watched him silently.

"That's a handsome piece," he said after a moment, nodding toward the fireplace mantle.

Her gaze followed the direction he'd indicated. "What?"

"That carving on the mantelpiece. Did that belong to your father?"

Rebecca glanced at the walnut carving of a steer in full gallop, its nostrils flaring and its legs in motion. "Yes.

My father carved that. He enjoyed working with wood when he had a few moments to spare."

Judson studied the piece from his chair. "It's very good. He's captured the spirit of his subject."

"Are you interested in art, Mr. Carter?"

"In a certain sense, it's my line of business," he replied, smiling at her.

"You're an artist?" Rebecca asked in surprise.

He laughed. It was a deep, melodious sound that Rebecca found attractive. "Not exactly. I'm a cabinetmaker. I build furniture—cupboards and the like."

"Oh, I see." She would not have guessed that about him. From his stylish dress and impeccable grooming, she assumed he was a professional man such as a lawyer or a banker.

His eyes returned to the carving of rich, dark walnut resting on the mantle. "Have you inherited your father's talent?" he asked with interest.

"Heavens, no. I can hardly draw a straight line, much less carve one."

"No? Then I'll bet you have a lovely singing voice," he said with a playful grin.

She shook her head, smiling at the absurdity of his words.

"An accomplished violinist?

"Not at all."

"How about a poetess?" He raised his brows in question.

"Absolutely not," she smiled.

He leaned forward in his chair, his eyes sparkling. "Then tell me what you like best to do with your spare time."

She thought about his question. "Gallop Onyx through a field of wildflowers after a spring rain."

"Onyx?" he repeated, one brow hooking up quizzically.

"My horse. He's black and shiny as polished stone with a white blaze down his face."

"Did I miss seeing this magnificent animal when I was here before?"

"If you did, I can show him to you now. He's in the corral." She was glad to have an excuse to leave the confines of the room and put some space between Judson and herself.

They finished their lemonade, then went outside. Onyx was one of four horses pastured in the fenced corral. His ears pricked forward when he heard them approaching, and he whinnied shrilly.

"There he is," Rebecca said, nodding toward the black gelding.

Judson let out a low whistle. "He's a beauty, all right."

Rebecca opened the gate to the corral and they walked over to the horse. She slid an arm around his neck and stroked the strip of white on his forehead.

"He has nice conformation," Judson observed, circling the animal.

"He's part mustang. His grandfather was a mustang named Dynamite owned by my father's cousin. It was her favorite horse, given to her by her husband when they were courting."

Judson ran his hand over the horse's hindquarters. "I'll bet he's as swift as the wind."

"He is. And he'd run until he burst, if you let him." She noted with pride the gelding's sleek coat, broad chest, and handsome markings.

"Have you ever entered him in a race?"

"No, he's not trained for racing."

"It wouldn't take much training if he's as fast and strong as he looks. There's a half-mile race taking place in Salt Lake City in October that a few of my friends are putting together. I've a five-year-old Morgan I'm entering. Would you be interested in racing your gelding?"

"No, not at all," Rebecca replied, running her fingers through the horse's thick mane.

"The winning purse is $50.00," he said, dangling the words in front of her like a carrot on a stick.

She rubbed the gelding's neck. "I can't spare the time to train him—not my time or his."

"Then perhaps you'll come to Salt Lake to see the race. We're planning to hold it in connection with the celebrations for statehood."

"I don't believe so, Mr. Carter."

Judson smiled at her from across the horse's neck. "Why not?"

"Well, I'm not planning to go to Salt Lake City, for one reason."

He bent closer. "Not planning to come to the city for the statehood celebrations? Come, come, where's your patriotic spirit?"

Rebecca knew he was teasing her, but his words carried a genuine trace of surprise. "I can't leave my work here at the ranch. I'll read about the celebrations in the newspaper."

"Read about it!" Judson exclaimed, his eyes wide with mock horror. "You have to experience it. This is an extraordinary event, Miss Kade. It will be something to tell your grandchildren about."

Rebecca gave her horse a final pat on the nose, then started for the gate with Judson following beside her. "Perhaps there won't be any celebration," she said, glancing at him as they walked. "This attempt at statehood may turn out like the others before it."

They passed together through the gate of the corral. "We'll be successful in achieving statehood this time. President Cleveland's signature on the Enabling Act guarantees that," Judson replied, nodding confidently.

She glanced at his face as they walked toward the house. The brightness of the sun defined his every feature—the wide, brown eyes enlivened with specks of green; a thin, straight nose; expressive lips. He cut a handsome figure, striding along beside her.

"I have a friend who was a delegate to the Constitutional Convention held last March. He told me that it took 66 days for the delegates to frame Utah's constitution, and the resulting document meets all the requirements set forth by Congress."

"But will it be ratified by the people of Utah?" She posed the question primarily to keep him talking. She liked the sound of his voice and his self-assured manner.

"I don't think there's any doubt of that. Nearly everyone in the Territory is in favor of statehood, knowing the advantages it will bring."

Rebecca swiped at a strand of hair blowing against her cheek. The wind had come up, kicking dust into the air. A dry tumbleweed cartwheeled past her feet. "What do you see as the benefits of statehood, Mr. Carter?"

His answer was quick and decisive. He listed the opportunities that would come with statehood, starting with the right to local self-government through elected state officials. Rebecca asked him if he would be voting the Democratic or Republican ticket at the general election in November, to which he replied with a chuckle, saying that it depended on the candidate.

By this time they had reached the cattle pens nearest the house. Dust and flies swirled around the cattle, and their bellowing created a constant din. The roan calf Rebecca had been nursing back to health bawled plaintively inside the holding pen. She paused to study it. "Do you see that white-faced calf standing beside its mother?" Rebecca asked, pointing to the smallest calf in the pen.

Judson followed her gaze and nodded.

"Less than a month ago that calf was attacked by a cougar while grazing in the pasture. I stumbled across her right after it happened. We carried her off the mountain and kept her in a stall in the barn for two weeks, where I tended to her every day. To my surprise, she survived the attack and the infection that set in afterward and is just now beginning to eat on her own and starting to regain her strength."

Judson nodded again, his expression sober.

"When I think about statehood for Utah, Mr. Carter, I see that calf and wonder how state representation will better my circumstances when it comes time to sell my cattle at market."

"I understand your point," Judson said, his eyes still on the cattle in the pen.

Rebecca chased a fly away from her face and frowned. If Utah's induction into the Union did not improve the economic outlook, then statehood had little relevance for her personally. She was about to comment further when she spied Micah Grant on his roan gelding coming up the trail at a canter. From his posture, she immediately knew something was wrong.

He reined in his horse when he reached her.

"What is it?" she demanded as soon as he'd dismounted.

Micah glanced briefly at Judson, barely acknowledging his presence. "We've got some cattle down in the east pasture, Miss Rebecca. The boys and I found four of 'em this afternoon."

Rebecca's breath turned cold, and a chill ran down her spine. "What's causing it?" She felt Judson tense at her side, but she was too focused on Micah's report to pay him any heed.

"Looks like it could be an outbreak of blackleg."

"Blackleg? Are you sure about that, Micah?" She tried to keep her voice calm, but her heart was hammering so violently that her body shook.

"I've seen the disease before," Micah grunted. "The symptoms are the same."

"Can you separate the sick animals from the herd?" Judson asked, glancing from Micah to Rebecca.

Rebecca shook her head, quickly explaining how it was usually too late to do anything to prevent the disease from spreading once the symptoms appeared. "I need to attend to my cattle, Mr. Carter," she said. "You're welcome to stay the night. There won't be another train back to Salt Lake City until morning."

"Is there anything I can do to help?"

"Not unless you know how to cure blackleg," she answered brusquely. In light of this grave new development, Judson Carter's presence at the ranch had become an unwelcome intrusion. She banished every other thought as she saddled and bridled her horse, conscious only of a sense of impending disaster. Blackleg could wipe out an entire herd. She mounted the gelding, and with Micah beside her galloped her horse out of the yard, not once turning back to glance at Judson.

Rebecca spent the rest of the day in the east pasture with the cowhands. As they rode among the herd scattered on the hillsides, they counted six dead or dying cattle;

Rebecca knew, however, that many more could be infected before the disease ran its course. Overhead, she spotted a trio of vultures circling. Their strong, dark wings beat ominously as they swooped over the dead cattle on the ground. She fired a shot from her rifle to frighten them away. Seated in her saddle, she pulled a handkerchief over her nose and mouth to cover the stench of burning flesh as the cowhands torched the carcasses. She watched curling plumes of smoke rise into the sky, looking like black smudges on a canvas of blue. The sight of the carnage filled Rebecca's heart with despair. She felt as if she were trapped in a dark nightmare from which she couldn't awaken.

As the sun began to lower, casting a red glare onto the hillsides, Rebecca and Micah started back to the ranch house, leaving the other cowhands on the mountain to keep watch over the cattle. They had gone only a short distance when Rebecca spotted movement in the brush off to one side. She reined in her horse, her eyes trained on a quivering bush. A second later a steer emerged from the underbrush, reeling drunkenly. His swollen legs failed him and he toppled over with a mournful bellow.

A shot rang out and the sharp sound ricocheted against the mountain slopes. Rebecca saw the steer lurch, then lay still. She turned toward Micah. In his hand, he gripped a smoking rifle.

"Burn the carcass," she ordered, turning away so Micah wouldn't see the tears welling in her eyes.

Rebecca returned alone to the house. Her clothes and hair smelled of smoke, and dirt streaked her face. After she'd rubbed down her horse and put him in the corral, she started for the house—hungry, upset, and tired. She found Judson on the porch. He stood as she approached.

"How bad is it?" he asked.

"We've lost seven head so far. Maybe more. The boys are still out." She sank onto a porch chair, wiping the dust from her hands onto her dirt-stained skirt.

"I saw the smoke," Judson said, pulling his chair beside hers.

She glanced over at him, but didn't reply.

The two of them sat in silence for a moment, staring out at the hills. Shadows were beginning to fill the canyons and gullies, veiling them in black.

"There's stew on the stove from this afternoon," Rebecca said. "You probably haven't had anything to eat yet. Would you like to have some with me?"

"Let me get it," Judson responded, rising quickly to his feet. "You stay right there. Just tell me where the bowls are."

She was grateful for his offer. She didn't feel like stirring from her chair because she was so exhausted. "In the cupboard to the right of the door."

After he disappeared inside the house, Rebecca leaned back in her chair and sighed. Her back hurt from being in the saddle all afternoon riding over rocky terrain. She'd skinned the back of her hand, too, on a sharp branch. The sight and smell of dying cattle was etched in her mind. Once again, for the umpteenth time, she wished her father were alive to direct matters on the ranch.

While she waited for the stew, she began to unwind her braided hair. The single braid tumbling down her back had loosened during the day's ride and locks of hair fell onto her neck. When she'd finished untangling it, she ran her fingers through, trying to tame and smooth it. Flecks of brush and grass were caught in the curls, and she combed them out with her fingers.

Before she could get it neatly braided again, Judson returned to the porch with two bowls full of steaming stew and two thick slices of bread smeared with jam. "Here you are," he said, handing her a tray.

Hastily tying back her hair, Rebecca took the tray and set it on her lap. An aroma of spices drifted up from the bowl.

"It smells good," Judson said, sitting down beside her.

"You'd better reserve judgment until after you've tasted it," she replied with a faint smile. She dipped her spoon into the thick soup and scooped it into her mouth.

Rebecca ate without making further conversation. She concentrated on the meal and tried to block out for the time being the trauma of the day's events in the east pasture. Judson started on his own bowl of stew, complimenting her on the flavor after the first bite.

After a moment, he leaned forward in his chair. "You're getting the ends of your hair in the soup," he said, smiling.

"Here, let me help you." He pushed aside a strand of hair from her cheek, tucking it behind her ear.

His unexpected touch made her quiver.

"There. That's better." His eyes lingered on her face. "Your hair looks almost red in this light. It's very pretty."

She felt her cheeks flush. Keeping her eyes lowered, she bit into the slice of bread and jam.

She sensed, rather than saw, Judson ease back into his chair. He finished the last spoonfuls of stew and set his bowl on the porch. "That was the best stew I've ever had. And I make a pretty good stew myself."

Rebecca laughed at his remark.

He stretched out his legs and crossed one booted foot over the over. "I took the liberty of walking the grounds while you were gone. You're running a nice outfit here."

Rebecca glanced up. His eyes were focused on something in the distance. She stared at his face for an instant, and her breathing quickened. "It's the same as when you were here with Rachel," she said. He turned to look at her, and something about the intensity of his expression made Rebecca's heart skip a beat.

"Yes. But I failed then to notice its appeal." He smiled, then slowly got to his feet. "You must be tired. I'd better let you get some rest."

He started down the porch steps, and Rebecca felt a glimmer of disappointment. "I hope you'll be comfortable for the night in the bunkhouse," she murmured.

"I will. I'll be getting an early start in the morning. Good night."

"Good night." Rebecca watched him walk away. She sat on the porch in the gathering dusk, her unfinished bowl of stew in her lap, wishing he'd stayed longer to talk.

CHAPTER EIGHT

The next morning when Rebecca went outside to saddle her gelding, she saw at a glance that Judson's horse was gone from the corral. Even though she'd been up early, she hadn't heard him leave. She'd spent a restless night; when she'd closed her eyes, she saw dead cattle with flames leaping from the fires consuming their carcasses. And then sometimes, she thought she saw Judson's face flickering through the flames. She frowned, annoyed with herself for thinking about him. Last night on the porch, she had let her emotions run unchecked. Perhaps it had been because she was tired and upset, and that had made her vulnerable to his charms. In the harsh morning light, she was embarrassed about her giddy feelings the evening before.

She saddled Onyx and set out for the east pasture where most of the infected cattle had been grazing. There she met Andrus and Hernandez, and spent the day checking on the herd. A half dozen more cattle had died during the night, and these had been among the healthiest yearlings in the herd. She knew the outbreak might last as long as ten days before running its course, and the loss to the herd could be catastrophic. As she rode among the cattle grazing on the hillsides, she felt worn down with worry and fear.

"We've lost over 90 head of cattle to the blackleg," Micah reported a week and a half later, "but I think that's the end of it. I haven't seen any more cattle down for the last day or two."

"At least that part is good to hear," Rebecca replied glumly. She glanced from Micah to Jake Baxter. The cowhand stood in the yard with his hands shoved in his pockets and his creased, dirt-stained hat pulled low over his forehead to shade his face from the glare of the afternoon sun. Tucked into the rawhide band of his hat was the small hawk feather he always wore there. "You haven't seen any sign of the disease returning, have you, Jake?"

"No, Miss Kade. I ain't seen any cattle with the fever in the last few days, like Micah said."

Rebecca ran a restless hand through her hair. "I received a circular in the mail a few weeks ago advertising yearlings for sale at auction. Do you think we ought to buy more stock and hope we can fatten them up before market?"

"Do you have money for that?" Micah asked, taking off his hat and scratching his head.

"My father had some money put away for emergencies."

"How much you got tucked away?" Micah asked.

"I'm not sure of the exact amount. Let's go into the house and see."

The two men followed her and stood just inside the doorway of the house. Rebecca went to her father's desk and opened the bottom drawer. Moving a few items aside, she withdrew a quart jar filled with paperbacks and coins and set it on the desk top. She unscrewed the lid of the jar and dumped out the money onto the desk to count. Her lips moved silently as she thumbed through the cash.

"Along with what savings I have in the bank, I may have enough for 30 or 40 head, if you can negotiate a good price for them, Micah," she said, looking up at the two men in the doorway. From where they stood, they could just see her at the desk beside the hearth.

"I can start bidding at the low end of the scale, if that's what you want to do, Miss Rebby."

"All right." Rebecca's gaze moved from Micah to Jake. His eyes were fixed on the pile of greenbacks lying on the desk. "Jake, when Micah leaves, you carry out whatever instructions he gives you with regard to the ranch while he's gone."

Jake quickly lifted his eyes from the desk, and Rebecca thought she saw a greedy gleam in them. "You bet, Miss Kade. Whatever Micah says," he answered, nodding.

"The auction takes place in Ogden in about two weeks," she said, scooping up the money and placing it back in the jar.

"I'll take a look at the stock for sale a day or two beforehand," Micah responded. "Come on, Baxter. Let's get back to work."

After the two men had left the house, Rebecca stared at the money stored in the quart jar. The bills were crinkled and worn, and the coins gleamed dully in the light coming from the window. It would take every penny of it, plus most of what she had in savings, to buy the cattle. She felt her stomach begin to churn. Should she spend her emergency fund on purchasing more cattle? What if she needed the money later for something else? She struggled with the decision. Then as she put the money jar back into the drawer, her heart skipped a beat as another unsettling thought struck her. Had she been careless in displaying the jar of money and where it was kept in front of the two ranch hands? Surely, she had no need to worry on that account; the men worked for her and wouldn't do anything to jeopardize their jobs. She put the jar firmly in the drawer and closed it. But as an afterthought, she took the key to the desk and locked the drawer. Then she put the key in the pocket of her skirt.

When she went back outside, Micah was in the yard waiting for her. "Is there something more you wanted to discuss, Micah?" she asked.

"There is. You're going to crack, Miss Rebby, if you don't get a bit of rest and recreation. You're up 'afore the ranch hands and the last one to bed at night."

"I'm fine, Micah. Really."

"Your pa would shake the daylights out of me if he knew I was lettin' you work as hard as you do. No, Miss Rebby. You need a day off."

"Oh, all right. I'll stay in bed late tomorrow, if that will suit you."

"You do that. But it's not enough. A young gal like yourself needs some diversion. You should be havin' young men callin' on you. Attendin' parties and such. Not wearin' yourself out day and night here at the ranch."

She rolled her eyes, suspecting that this idea sprang from Judson's visit to the ranch.

"I heard the boys talkin' about a dance this weekend at the Rideout Hall. You should go. Get dressed up and go enjoy yourself for an evenin'."

"In Draper?"

Micah nodded. "I'll drive you there and back in the buckboard so you're not travelin' alone."

The idea of attending a dance did sound appealing, Rebecca thought. Nearly every Friday night, a ward dance was held at the Rideout Hall situated on the upper floor of the mercantile. But Rebecca hadn't attended one in months. "All right, Micah. I'll think about it."

As the weekend approached, Rebecca's enthusiasm for the idea grew. Directly after supper on Friday, she changed into a blue cotton dress trimmed with orange cording at the neck, cuffs, and hem; then she opened her bureau drawer and removed a small, fabric pouch. Untying the drawstring, she turned the pouch upside down into her hand and a cameo pendant, attached to a black velvet ribbon, tumbled out. The cameo, made of polished coral and carved with the figure of a woman's face in profile, glistened in the palm of her hand.

The necklace had belonged to her mother, along with a matching pair of earrings. Ethan had purchased the set of jewelry for Susannah as a gift to commemorate their tenth wedding anniversary. Susannah had treasured the jewelry not only for its beauty, but because of the sentiment attached to it. Occasionally, she'd allowed Rebecca or Rachel to try on the necklace. Rebecca had a memory of standing in front of the mirror as a child admiring the gleaming, coral pendant resting against her blouse. She remembered looking at herself in the mirror and hoping some day that she would be as beautiful as her mother.

Now as Rebecca gazed into the mirror, fastening the ribbon around her neck, she took pleasure in noting how the polished cameo fell softly against the neck of her dress. The contrast of glistening orange on the field of blue was lovely. But the necklace was more than an object of beauty—it was a precious legacy connecting Rebecca to her mother.

Micah was waiting for her in the front yard with the buckboard and issued a low whistle when she stepped out the door. "Whooie, Miss Rebby. Hearts are goin' to be broken tonight."

Rebecca blushed, though she felt foolish for it. "You're a silly old man, Micah," she teased him.

He helped her up into the wagon, then settled on the seat beside her. He snapped the reins, and the horses hitched to the buckboard started forward at a trot.

Rebecca smoothed her dress, smiling with anticipation.

"Yes, siree. You look real pretty," Micah said, gazing ahead. "The picture of your mama."

"Why, that's the nicest thing you could say to me, Micah."

The ride into Draper took a little more than an hour. Rebecca sat with her hands folded in her lap, careful not to wrinkle her dress. The dust churned up by the turning wheels of the wagon collected along the hem of her skirt, and she brushed it off several times as they rode. When they arrived in Draper, Micah dropped her off at the door of the Rideout store, telling her he'd take "a bit of refreshment" at the saloon while he waited for her.

Her heart feeling lighter than it had in weeks, Rebecca climbed the flight of stairs on the outside of the building to the upper story. The room over the store was used not only as a dance hall, but also for theatrical productions, concerts, lectures, and many other community events. When she stepped inside the hall, a whirlwind of sound and motion greeted her. Couples swayed on the dance floor in time to the music of the Draper Band. Around the room, people were gathered in groups talking and laughing or lingering over refreshments set out on a long table. The coal-oil lamps hanging from the ceiling gave off a warm glow. Rebecca spotted a couple of young women she knew and started toward them. Among the group was Lettie Miller, and when Lettie saw her she called out, "Rebby! Over here!"

Rebecca waved and made her way to the group of friends.

"Oh, I'm so glad to see you!" Lettie exclaimed, giving Rebecca a hug. "I haven't talked with you in ever so long. Tell me everything that's been going on."

Rebecca smiled at her friend's enthusiasm. Lettie's brown curly hair was swept up into a bun, and her blue eyes sparkled with excitement. She'd tried to cover her sprinkling of freckles with face powder, but the freckles still shown through, as bright and sunny as her smile. The other girls, too, crowded around Rebecca. Encircled in the warmth and companionship of her friends, Rebecca realized that this was exactly what she had needed to regain her perspective and restore her spirits. She eagerly exchanged news with Lettie and the other girls, the conversation sweeping along like a rushing stream, twisting and turning at every bend into a new topic. As they talked, Rebecca glanced around the hall. She was acquainted with a few of the young men present at the dance. As she looked over the crop of them, she decided that none of the boys were as handsome or as sophisticated as Rachel's new beau. She recalled Judson's visit and his kindness toward her after she'd come back from tending to her sick cattle. If his ambition had been to impress and charm her in preparation for becoming her future brother-in-law, he had certainly succeeded.

While her thoughts lingered on Judson, a young man with sandy hair and sunburned cheeks stepped from the crowd and invited her to dance. He was a fellow from town whom Rebecca had known for some time; she was happy to take his arm and accompany him to a spot on the dance floor where couples were forming a line for a Virginia reel. The dance was lively and quick, and the young man was adept at leading her through the fast-paced steps.

After the reel, another fellow offered his arm and then another. Rebecca had nearly forgotten how enjoyable it was to socialize with her friends. Lettie and a couple of the other girls started a square with their dance partners and motioned Rebecca to join them. As she and her partner hurried to take their places for the square dance, she was startled to see Jake Baxter saunter into the dance hall. She only had time for a moment's glance, however, before the music started and the caller began directing the steps for the dance. As she curtseyed to her partner, she was glad Micah had insisted she attend the dance because she was having a grand time.

She and Lettie giggled together as they went through the dance steps with their partners, and when the square dance ended, they stood aside talking. A new tune started up. The flutes trilled, the trumpets and trombones blared, and the drums boomed out the rhythm. Rebecca continued conversing with her friend, tapping her toe in time to the music and hoping another young man would ask for the next dance. But instead of one of the fellows from Draper, Jake Baxter approached her and executed a clumsy bow. "Miss

Kade, would you give me the pleasure of this dance?" Jake asked, his speech slurred.

Rebecca was taken aback by his request. In spite of her dislike for him, she accepted, hoping her response would temper the ill will existing between them. "Thank you, Jake," she replied, trying to inject some enthusiasm into her voice.

The touch of his hand was unpleasant as he ushered her onto the dance floor, but she tried to put aside her feelings for the sake of diplomacy. As he drew close to begin the reel, she noticed with a jolt that his breath smelled of alcohol. The music started, and he took her hand. She didn't often see him without his hat, and he looked more disheveled than usual, his hair hanging limp and stringy against his neck. When they hooked elbows for a spinning step, he flashed her a leering grin. "You step as lightly as a feather, Miss Kade."

The compliment did not please her. His words had a coarseness to them that repulsed Rebecca. As they whirled together, elbow in elbow, his eyes burned with a reckless glow. She was relieved when the dance routine called for partners to separate and form a line. Glancing across at him, she forced a cordial smile. His brow glistened with perspiration, and his normally sallow complexion had taken on a ruddy hue. When it was their turn to join hands and sashay down the aisle between the line of dancers, she felt herself cringe at his touch.

As they promenaded hand in hand around the circle, he leaned close. "You look like a Christmas ornament—all glowing and rosy," he breathed in her ear.

Rebecca was repelled by his whispered words. Both his speech and his manner were offensive to her. They separated into their respective places in the line, then came together for a final whirl as the music mercifully ended.

She moved away from him quickly. "Thank you for the dance," she mumbled.

"It was my pleasure. Will you favor me with the next dance also?"

"I'm sorry, Jake. I'm quite out of breath. I believe I'll sit the next few dances out."

She turned and began walking away, but he trailed after her. He tapped her shoulder. "Perhaps later, after you've rested?" he asked, giving her a persistent smile.

"I don't think so. But thank you." She continued moving away, hastening her step, but he stayed at her side.

"I been meanin' to speak to you, but I thought it best to wait 'til you got over the shock of your Pa's death," he said more insistently. He pulled on her arm to capture her attention.

"Talk to me about what?" she asked curtly.

"I don't know that this is the proper place. Why don't you and me step outside for a minute where we can talk in private."

"Whatever you have to say to me can be said right here."

He rubbed one bleary eye and smiled, showing crooked teeth. "Aw, come on, Rebecca," he said in a syrupy tone, "don't make me say it outright."

He had never addressed her by her given name before, and the sound of it coming from his lips sullied the name.

He took a step closer, his eyes narrowing in concentration. "I've had a hankerin' for you ever since I stepped onto the ranch. You're about the prettiest gal I ever laid eyes on." A frown darted across his face. "But also the most feisty."

"This conversation has gone far enough. You're an employee of the Double K Ranch, and your behavior here is inappropriate."

"You can't dismiss me like some whimpering pup," he said in a sudden flare of anger. "I'm fit as any man to declare my feelin's for you."

Rebecca turned her back to him, ignoring his protests, and this time he did not follow her. She deliberately lost herself in the crowd, trying to slip out of his sight. His brazen words and coarse behavior repelled her. She went out of her way to avoid him, and the effort nearly ruined what was left of the evening. At times, she felt his eyes on her and turned to find him staring at her from across the hall. She stayed for another half hour, but Jake's continuing presence upset her. Even though it was still another fifteen or twenty minutes until Micah was scheduled to meet her outside in front of the store, she could bear the strain no longer.

She sought out Lettie to bid her good night, then casting a glance over her shoulder to be sure Jake was not watching, she left the dance hall. Once outside the building, she breathed a deep sigh of relief. She hurried down the flight of stairs to the ground below. Finding herself alone, she leaned against the brick and looked up at the stars winking in the night sky. They looked like tiny lanterns, lighting a meandering pathway in the dark. She relaxed her shoulders and focused on the beauty of the evening. It was warm, and the moon cast a bright beam of light. Closing her eyes, she breathed in the night smells.

"I thought I saw you leave the dance."

Rebecca jerked abruptly, and her eyes flew open. When she saw Jake Baxter descending the last few steps of the stairwell, she felt a thread of fear tighten inside her.

"I didn't mean to startle you. I just want to ask you a question," he said. In the dim light, he looked like a looming shadow.

"What is it?" she rasped.

He moved closer, and a beam of moonlight struck his face, revealing a hungry gleam in his eyes. "Why do you always have to act so high and mighty? It's irritatin' to a fellow."

Rebecca's heart began pounding. The building blocked any retreat to her rear, and Jake stood firmly in front of her.

"If you'd treat me with a little respect, I'd be appreciatin' it," he growled.

"Stay away from me, Jake," she said, sounding more calm and controlled than she felt.

He gave a short, harsh laugh. Rebecca cried out as he grabbed her roughly around the waist and pulled her to him. His lips grated against hers.

"Stop it!" Rebecca shouted, wrenching out of his grasp.

He gripped her by the back of the neck, trying again to force her mouth to his. In the struggle, his hand dislodged the velvet ribbon tied around her neck, and the ribbon and cameo pendant slid to the ground. Rebecca wriggled free from his hold.

He glared at her. "Always the one wantin' to take charge, aren't you?"

Rebecca was breathing so rapidly she couldn't reply.

"Someday we'll see which of us has the last say." He gave her an ugly stare, then turned and stalked away.

Rebecca sagged against the side of the building, tears surging to her eyes. She lifted her necklace from the dirt and clutched it in her fist. Through blurry eyes, she stared at the oval-shaped pendant winking in the moon's light and discovered that an edge of it was scuffed and scratched. The black, velvet tie was sullied, too; in the scuffle, Jake's heel must have ground the necklace into the gritty dirt. With tears spilling down her cheeks, she cuddled the damaged cameo in the palm of her hand.

A couple exited the building and glanced at her curiously. She turned away from their stares, dashing the tears from her eyes. With trembling fingers, she retied the black velvet ribbon around her neck and adjusted the cameo against her dress. Ten minutes later, Micah arrived with the wagon. By then, Rebecca had regained her composure, and to Micah's unsuspecting eye, she appeared unruffled. As she seated herself in the buckboard, she resolved to say nothing about the attack. She would find a way to deal with Jake Baxter.

CHAPTER NINE

The following morning Rebecca strode out to the corral where Jake Baxter was slitting open a sack of feed with his folding knife for the horses. "I'd like to speak with you," she said to him in a sharp tone of voice.

A flicker of apprehension crossed his eyes, but then was quickly replaced by his usual surly expression. He put his knife into his shirt pocket and sauntered over to the fence where she stood waiting. His sweat-stained hat with the hawk feather jutting from the rawhide hatband sat low on his forehead.

She swallowed, nervous about initiating a confrontation between them, but determined to speak her mind. "I'm willing to forget your despicable behavior of last evening, Jake. Nothing more needs to be said about it—except your promise to me that it will never happen again."

He stared at her, looking neither ashamed nor embarrassed. "I'm real sorry about that, Miss Kade. I had a little too much whiskey 'afore I went to the dance hall."

She stood silently, waiting for more of a heartfelt apology from him.

"To tell you the truth, I can't rightly remember what I said to you last night. If I was rude or a little rambunctious, I sure didn't mean nothin' by it."

Rebecca knew he was lying. He remembered what had occurred between them as clearly as she did. "Your word, Jake," she said, unmoved.

"Sure. You have my word. I wouldn't dream of offendin' you, Miss Kade."

The words were so shallow that Rebecca nearly scoffed at them. "Good. Then we can continue working together in a common cause to keep the ranch operating smoothly."

"You mean as boss and hireling?" He didn't bother to hide the scorn in his voice.

"Yes. If that's how you choose to term it."

Jake shrugged his shoulders, but his eyes smoldered with resentment.

"All right. That will be all." She dismissed him in a tone sounding more imperious than she'd intended.

He glowered at her, then turned and started to walk away.

"And Jake," she called, unable to resist the impulse to make him feel accountable for his actions, "from now on when I'm bathing in the pond near the house, I'll thank you to keep your distance."

His eyes narrowed into a slit, but he said nothing and stalked away to continue his chores.

Rebecca returned to the house. Her heart was beating hard from the uncomfortable exchange with the cowhand. She went to her room and closed the door behind her. Taking the cameo necklace from her dresser drawer, where she'd placed it the night before, she rubbed the pendant with her thumb. In the morning light, the scratches along the edge shone starkly. It was all she could do to hold back tears as she examined the damage done to the coral cameo. Wetting the corner of a cloth in the basin of water resting on the washstand, she carefully dabbed at the deep scrapes, then dried and polished the pendant with her cloth. Her attention did little to erase the marks. In addition to the scratches scoring the edges, Rebecca found a chip on the face of the stone. Her heart heaved with sorrow. Her mother had cherished the necklace and taken special care of it; and now while in Rebecca's charge, the cameo had become marred. The stone seemed a tangible symbol for her own bruised heart, a reminder of the guilt she carried from the circumstances surrounding her mother's death.

With the necklace in her hand, she curled up on the patchwork quilt covering her bed and closed her eyes, wanting to blot out the image of the blemished stone. The quilt was soft and comforting. She'd gotten little sleep the night before because of the encounter with Jake, and now as she lay with her eyes shut tight, her mind wandered somewhere between wakefulness and sleep.

"Rebby, go pick some wildflowers for the supper table, will you?"

"All right, Mama." Rebecca put aside the picture she'd been drawing of a wild mustang drinking from a stream. "Can I take my horse? Yesterday while I was out riding, I saw a meadow full of wildflowers just on the other side of a gully not far from the house."

"That will be fine," Susannah answered. She glanced over her shoulder at Rebecca while stirring a pot of soup on the stove. "But don't be gone too long. Your father and the ranch hands will be in for supper soon."

Rebecca went to her mother's side and sniffed the contents of the pot cooking on the wood-burning stove. "Mmm, corn chowder. How much longer does it have to cook before it's ready?"

"For a little while more." Steam rose up out of the pot, and Susannah wiped away the perspiration glistening on her brow. A muslin apron covered her white, high-necked blouse and red calico skirt.

"Will you come with me to the meadow while supper cooks?" Rebecca asked. "I want to show you how pretty the wildflowers look on the hillside."

"Not now, Rebby. I'm busy."

"Please. We can pick the flowers together."

Susannah leaned over to give her a quick hug, and Rebecca caught the scent of lavender in her mother's dark hair.

She wore it done up in a bun, but part of it had loosened and strayed onto her neck.

"Please," Rebecca pleaded. "Rachel's been gone all week to Grandma's house, and you promised to go riding with me while she was away."

"Oh, all right," Susannah said, setting down the long-handled, wooden spoon and untying her apron. "I guess we can let the soup simmer for a while." When she smiled at Rebecca, her dimples shone and her green eyes sparkled, reminding Rebecca of the dappled, sunlit grass in the pastures.

"I'll saddle your mare for you, Mama."

Rebecca jerked in her sleep, and her eyes fluttered open. She blinked, then slowly closed her eyes again.

"There's the place," Rebecca said, pointing with her finger. "Have you ever seen so many wildflowers in your whole life?" Rebecca's eyes roamed the dazzling array of flowers. Blossoms of scarlet, lavender, pink, and yellow dotted the meadow, looking like embroidery on a silken cloth. She kicked her brown gelding with her heels to urge him forward. "Come on, Prince. Gid up."

Susannah was riding on her gray mare a few horse lengths behind. "They're breathtaking," she said, reining in her horse so she could gaze at the field of flowers. "Every color of the rainbow. You're right, Rebby. This is the perfect spot to pick wildflowers."

"I told you so." Rebecca knew her mother liked pretty things—colorful flowers; brilliant sunsets; glistening pebbles resting in a crystalline stream. She enjoyed being surrounded by objects of beauty, both outdoors and at home. Their adobe home was simple, but tastefully adorned. The rooms were plain compared to the cluttered interiors typical of the popular Victorian style. Susannah preferred a theme of quiet grace and elegance, soothing to the eye, but sensible, and easy on her husband's pocketbook. Although she appreciated pretty clothes, sparkling jewelry, and fine furnishings, her family was the most important thing to her. Rebecca had often heard her mother say how Ethan and the children were her most precious treasures.

"Won't your father be surprised when he sees the vase full of these beautiful flowers?" she asked, smiling at Rebecca.

"I'll race you to the meadow," Rebecca challenged. "The first one to cross the hollow and reach the meadow wins." She hammered her horse in the sides and started off, the wind catching her long, single braid and sending it flapping against her back.

"No, wait, Rebby," her mother called out.

"Come on, Mama. You'll lose the race for sure if you don't hurry that slowpoke mare of yours," Rebecca shouted, turning to look over her shoulder. She saw her mother give the reins a shake. Rebecca bent forward, intent on reaching the meadow before her mother. As she started into the rocky gully, she heard Susannah's mare break into a trot behind her. She laughed, caught up in the excitement of the competition with her mother. It wasn't often that Susannah agreed to go riding.

She was a capable horsewoman, but she preferred the carriage to horseback riding. The gray mare Ethan had purchased for her was dependable and had a smooth gait, and when she accompanied Ethan on an occasional afternoon ride, it was the mare he saddled for her.

"I'm gaining on you," Susannah called. Her voice floated across the hollow as light as a butterfly's wing.

"You'll never catch me!" Rebecca cried as her horse began scrambling up the far side of the gully. She turned to gauge the span of distance between herself and her mother. Susannah's mare was just entering the hollow at a canter. Rebecca lashed her horse with her heels. "Gid up, Prince," she clucked.

She'd just turned her head to look back again when she heard the gray mare whinny frantically and then saw the horse go down. Rebecca caught sight of a tangle of flying hooves and a flash of red calico, and then a wall of dust churned up, screening her view.

"Mama!" she screamed. She yanked on the reins, halting her horse so abruptly that the gelding's hooves slid in the loose dirt. Jerking the reins sharply against the horse's neck, she turned him and wildly kicked him into a gallop. It took only a moment to reach her mother. She found Susannah lying on the stony ground, her dark hair loosed from its bun and flung across her face like a black veil. The mare was whinnying shrilly and struggling to get to its feet. Rebecca jumped off her horse. "Mama! Mama!" she shrieked.

Rebecca awoke with a gasp. Her eyes were moist, and her breath was coming in heaving sobs. "Mama!" she cried out.

The vivid images in her mind's eye caused her to tremble with emotion. She'd been half asleep and wasn't sure if she'd been dreaming or simply remembering the horrifying event from the past. Bolting off the bed with the cameo necklace still clutched in her hand, she paced the room, trying to clear her head and regain control of her emotions. It took several minutes before she was calm enough to think objectively. Finally, she let go of the necklace and replaced it in its pouch, then tucked the pouch into the drawer of her dresser. The window above the dresser poured sunlight into the room. Rebecca stared out of the pock-marked glass pane. The sun was high in the sky; she should have been outside tending to her chores and her cattle, instead of locking herself away in the bedroom. Giving the dresser drawer a last glance, and thinking of her mother's ruined necklace resting inside, she drew a sharp breath and hurried out of the room.

Late in the afternoon the sky darkened and thunder began rumbling in the distance. Rebecca stood outside on the porch, studying the horizon. Black clouds were rolling in, but the air was hot and humid and no rain fell. She worried about lightning striking the dry, withered grass and starting it on fire. She'd seen a grass fire caused by lightning once before. The strike had boomed across the hills like a rifle shot, and Rebecca had felt the electricity it generated in the dry, stale air. The grass had caught fire, and the wind had whipped it into a frenzy; before it had burned itself out, the flames had scorched the entire hillside.

Anxiously eyeing the sky for any sign of rain, Rebecca paced the length of the porch. The grass needed rain desperately. The streams were low and the earth parched. The cattle required moisture in order to survive on the hillside pastures. She paused to stare up again at the sky and sighed. Then she went back into the house and started supper for herself.

After she'd eaten and put away the dishes, she went outside to find Micah and give him the advertisement she'd received in the mail for the cattle sale. He was working at the cattle pens, filling the troughs with water. The sky was still overcast, and the wind had increased in strength. It whipped Rebecca's skirts around her legs as she walked over to the cowhand. "How is everything here?" she asked him, resting her arms on the top rail of the fence.

Micah emptied a bucket of water into the trough, then joined Rebecca at the fence. "Looks like the cattle are gettin' along," he answered. "That calf you brought down from the mountain is gainin' weight."

Rebecca focused her gaze on the white-faced calf milling among the cattle penned in the corral. It was still underweight and weaker than its fellows, but it was growing stronger day by day. She was happy with the calf's progress; it gave her a reason to be optimistic about the future. She tucked a strand of hair behind her ear to prevent it from blowing against her cheek. "Here's the ad for the cattle, Micah," she said, handing him the paper. "The auction takes place on the 29th of this month."

Micah studied the circular. The broadside featured a drawing of a steer and the words "CATTLE AUCTION" printed in big letters.

"You can take the train up to Ogden a day or two before, spend some time looking over the stock for sale, then acquire what you can for the best price possible. I'll wire the money after the sale."

"All right. I'll make good use of your funds."

"Thanks, Micah." Rebecca stared out at her penned cattle. Dust boiled up inside the corral, and the wind fanned it into a cloud through which could be seen only a jumble of hooves, horns, and hide.

Micah squinted up at the dark clouds scudding across the sky. "I'll help out in any way I can. Mr. Kade was a fair and generous man. I had great respect for him."

"I know you did, Micah."

"If that's everything for now, I'll be gettin' back to my chores," Micah said, tugging his hat over his forehead.

Rebecca watched him pick up his bucket and carry it to the water pump to refill, then she went back to the house.

The rain finally came during the night, accompanied by deafening crashes of thunder and streaks of lightning that lit up Rebecca's room brighter than at noon day. Rebecca lay in bed listening to the thunder and the rushing wind, and flinching whenever the lightning split through the sky. She worried about her cattle out on the range, fearful of them stampeding in the storm and concerned about them getting struck by lightning. She barely slept and was up and dressed at first light. She spent most of the day in the hills and was relieved to find that none of her cattle had been injured from the effects of the storm. After returning to the house in the late afternoon, she changed into a fresh skirt and blouse and then sat down at her father's desk to write a letter to Rachel.

Removing a clean, smooth sheet of paper from the desk drawer, she dipped her pen into the ink bottle and began to compose a letter to her sister, explaining about the outbreak of blackleg and her decision to purchase more cattle. Her thoughts were difficult to form into words, and she tapped the pen against the desk, considering exactly what to say. She wished Rachel would come out to the ranch so they could discuss these matters together. Outside the window the sky was clearing and the sun beginning to peep out from the curtain of clouds, but a few spatters of rain still fell against the pane. She stared out the window, her pen idle. She could see Andrus outside working, his shoulders hunched up against the rain. In two weeks, Micah would be leaving for Ogden, and Rebecca was still unsure about her decision to buy more cattle to replace the ones she'd lost. Perhaps she should wait until after market in the fall and assess her situation then. She gripped the pen tighter and pressed the tip to the paper, as if hoping the words that would flow from it would give her the answers she needed.

CHAPTER TEN

It had been more than two weeks since Judson's trip out to the Double K Ranch, and in all that time he hadn't been able to get Rebecca Kade off his mind. He pictured her face, dirt-streaked and tired, when she'd come in from the range after tending to her sick cattle. At night, when he closed his eyes before sleeping, he remembered her sitting across from him on the porch, her cheeks sunburned and her hair red in the dying light. He found himself wanting to see her again, and his thoughts flirted almost daily with making another visit to the ranch.

His days had been taken up with work at the shop. His new apprentice was learning the trade quickly, and Judson was able to trust him with more of the details. Daniel arrived early at the workshop each weekday morning, usually ate his lunch there while reading from his book, and often stayed until after hours to practice his woodcarving skills. He seemed to be enjoying the job, and Judson was glad to have his help. He'd received three new orders for furniture and would have been hard pressed to keep up with them without Daniel's assistance.

On Wednesday afternoon one of Judson's new clients, a wealthy man named Henry Addams, was scheduled to come into the shop to discuss an order for some furniture. Judson had never met the man before, but knew of him from reading his name in the newspaper. Addams was a prominent philanthropist and a shrewd businessman who'd made his money in railroading and banking. Judson alerted his assistant to the fact that Mr. Addams would be arriving shortly. He directed Daniel to sweep the sawdust from the floor and clear the clutter of discarded wood, tidying up the shop in preparation for Mr. Addams' visit.

In the late afternoon, shortly before Judson was ready to close the shop for the day, the door rattled open and a middle-aged man accompanied by an attractive young woman, stepped into the workshop. Both were handsomely dressed. He sported a stylish coat and top hat and carried a cane with a gold knob; she had on a striped lavender and cream dress, and a fringed handbag swung from her wrist. The girl wore a pleasant expression on her face, but the man's face betrayed a harsh and critical character.

"Are you Carter?" the man demanded, stalking to Judson's side.

Judson could tell from the man's tone of voice and his stern brow that Addams was accustomed to being the one in charge. "Yes, I'm Judson Carter. You're Mr. Addams?"

"That's right. This is my daughter, Louisa," he said, gesturing to the young woman standing beside him.

Judson politely nodded his head. "How do you do, Miss Addams?"

"Very well, thank you," she replied, accompanying her greeting with a warm smile.

"It's my daughter's seventeenth birthday in a few weeks, and I've promised her a matching set of furniture for her sitting room," Addams said, dispensing with pleasantries.

Judson's eyes returned to the daughter. "Congratulations on your upcoming birthday," he said to her.

"Thank you, Mr. Carter."

Her response seemed genuine. "What can I do for you?" Judson asked, his eyes moving from the girl to her father.

"Louisa has her heart set on a bureau and matching side table. She's quite particular about the design. Are you qualified to carry out her wishes, Mr. Carter?"

Judson ignored the arrogance in the older man's voice. Instead, he turned again to Louisa. "Perhaps you can tell me what you have in mind, Miss Addams."

"I shall try to explain," she answered, accompanying her words with an apologetic smile as if embarrassed by her father's rudeness.

She went on to describe a five-drawer bureau, which she wanted built out of mahogany, with fancy knobs and elaborately carved legs. The detail on the chest of drawers was to match that on the side table, and she outlined the design for both. When she finished, Judson motioned to Daniel to join them. Daniel had been quietly working at the back of the room. When he approached the group, Judson said, "This is my assistant, Mr. Briggs. He's especially skilled at carving decorative ornamentation. I'll have him draw out several designs on paper for you, Miss Addams, based on what you have told me. Then you can look them over, and we can discuss any changes you want made."

"I shall be pleased to see your designs, Mr. Briggs," the young woman replied, turning her gaze on him.

Judson saw Daniel blush under the girl's pretty smile; but it was her father's expression that caught Judson off guard. As Henry Addams got his first full look at Daniel, Judson saw his brows lower and his mouth harden into an unyielding line.

"When can we expect the first set of plans from you, Carter?" the older man asked brusquely, failing to even acknowledge Daniel's presence.

"I'll draw up the design for the bureau and matching side table, according to Miss Addams' specifications and have them ready for you in a week," Judson responded. Addams' supercilious attitude was beginning to annoy him.

"That will be satisfactory," Addams said curtly. "Come along, Louisa." He took his daughter by the arm and steered her toward the door.

Judson followed Addams and his daughter to the front of the shop, but Daniel remained standing where he was.

As Addams opened the door for his daughter to exit, he turned to Judson and said in a low voice, "My arrangement is with you, Carter. Not your assistant." Wearing a scowl on his face, he followed his daughter out of the workshop.

Judson stood still for a moment beside the door. He understood exactly Addams' meaning, and the man's remark infuriated him. Judson had no intention of taking Daniel off the project just because Addams objected to the young man's race. He walked back to Daniel, silently fuming. "After we've finished the cupboard we're working on, we'll get started on this new job," he said.

Daniel glanced down at the floor, then opened his mouth to say something. But he closed it again without speaking.

"Is there something on your mind?" Judson asked him sternly. He was perturbed with Addams' attitude, and his annoyance surfaced in his tone with Daniel. From the young man's expression, he knew that Daniel had sensed Henry Addams' dislike for him, and that fact filled Judson with indignation.

"No, sir."

"Then let's get back to work."

After closing the shop that evening, Judson visited the Blue Fly for a drink. Lorin was behind the counter and poured Judson a shot of whiskey and slid it in front of him.

"How's Catherine doing?" Judson asked as he took a swallow from his glass.

"The pregnancy is going well. She's been a little sick to her stomach at times, but I think everything is progressing as it should," Lorin answered, giving the counter a swipe with his cloth.

"That's good to hear. Are you hoping for a son or a daughter?"

"Either way," Lorin replied, smiling. "Just so the baby arrives healthy."

Judson saw the look of anticipation in his friend's eyes. "I'm happy for you, Lorin. I hope things continue to go well for Catherine."

"Thanks. What about you? What have you been up to this week?"

"Just working at the shop." Judson took another swallow of his drink.

"I heard you've hired a new assistant."

Judson squinted at the bartender over the rim of his glass.

"Word gets around in a place like this," Lorin said, shrugging his shoulders.

Judson set down his glass. "That's right. He's been assisting me at the shop for about four weeks now."

"An Indian boy, isn't he?"

Lorin's question wasn't judgmental, but Judson knew there were plenty of others who would find fault with him for hiring an Indian. He thought about Henry Addams and frowned. "He's half Indian. His mother was a Ute."

Lorin nodded without commenting.

"You don't happen to know someone by the name of Solomon Curtis, do you?" Judson asked after a moment's pause.

Lorin thought about the question. "No, I don't think so. Should I?"

Judson shook his head. "No. Someone mentioned that Curtis had passed through town a couple of months ago and asked if I knew him."

"I'll keep my ears open," Lorin said.

"Thanks." Judson finished his drink in one last gulp and plunked down the glass.

"Want another?" Lorin asked.

"No, thanks. I'd better be going."

"You haven't changed your mind about entering that gray of yours in the half-mile race next month?"

"No, I'm still planning to run him."

"I've decided to enter my bay. He's temperamental and contrary, but he has a fast sprint."

"Then I'll probably bet my money on the bay," Judson said, smiling.

"Your Morgan is fast, too. He beat Joe Johnson's stud by two lengths when the two of you raced a few months ago."

Judson chuckled. "That was just two fellows bragging about their horses after having had a few too many whiskeys. We raced on an empty stretch of road for the sport of it."

"But your horse won."

Judson nodded, still smiling. "That's a fact."

"Between your Morgan and my bay, one of us should be fortunate enough to come away with the prize money."

The other man's words triggered a thought that had been bouncing around in Judson's head. If he could persuade Rebecca Kade to enter her black quarter horse in the race, she'd have a good chance of taking the purse. And the money would go a long way toward helping her with the ranch. "It's an open-ended race, right? No limit on the number of competitors?"

"That's my understanding."

As they continued to discuss the horse race, the door to the saloon opened and two men walked inside. Glancing over, Judson recognized them at once and a frown settled on his face.

Lorin, too, saw the men enter. "Here comes a pair of troublemakers," he said quietly to Judson.

Judson tapped his forefinger on the rim of his empty glass, saying nothing. Although Murdock was not with them, these two were the same men who had been with Murdock in the saloon the night they'd heckled Daniel. Judson had become personally acquainted with their sour dispositions then and their penchant for stirring up trouble. He ignored them as they chose a table at the rear of the room and called for Lorin to bring them whiskeys.

After Lorin had served the two men, he and Judson resumed their conversation about the horse race. They'd only been talking a few minutes when one of the men from the table called out. "Hey, carpenter. How's that half-breed doin' you got workin' in your shop?"

Judson's skin prickled. As he slowly turned toward the men at the table, he felt Lorin's hand on his arm, cautioning him. Ignoring the bartender, he stood up from his stool and walked to the table where the pair of men sat. They had an open bottle of whiskey between them and two glasses. "Do you want to repeat that?" Judson growled, addressing the one who had made the remark. The man's straggly hair hung nearly to his shirt collar, and his chin bristled with a day's growth of whiskers.

"Sure do. I said it ain't good practice to hire a red man and set him workin' on white folks' belongin's."

Quick as lightning, Judson grabbed the man around the shirt collar and jerked him out of his chair. "You got a big mouth, do you know that?" Judson snarled.

"What you gonna do about it?" the other man spat back.

Just as Judson doubled up his fist ready to strike him, Lorin stepped to his side. "You know I don't allow fighting in here, Judson."

Judson glanced at the bartender. Lorin's mouth was pinched, and a frown knotted his brow. In deference to his friend, Judson unclenched his fist and shoved the man back into his chair, but it was hard for him to swallow his anger. "My advice is to mind your own business," Judson said to the man in a threatening voice.

The man glared at Judson but said nothing more. His partner at the table also remained silent. Judson walked back to the bar with Lorin following him.

"He isn't worth the trouble," Lorin said, nodding toward the table where the two men sat.

Judson didn't reply. He had wanted to knock the man off his chair, and he was still seething with anger. He could hear the two men at the table snickering between themselves and knew that eventually he would have to settle his differences with them using his fists. He nodded at Lorin and left the saloon. The night sky was drizzling rain. As he stepped into the street, he pulled down the brim of his hat and turned up his shirt collar. The walk back to his house was wet and cold, and the dirt road had turned to mud, sullying his boots. By the time he reached his door, his temper had cooled, but the altercation at the saloon left him in a dark mood.

Judson worked long hours at his shop the rest of the week; the following Tuesday he called on Rachel. Before the evening was out, they had argued bitterly, sparked by some trivial comment Judson had made. He spent a restless night examining his feelings for Rachel and came to the conclusion that he was not in love with her. This realization disturbed him at first, but after giving it considerable thought, it came almost as a relief to finally reach a decision regarding his relationship with her.

After work on Friday, Judson rode his gray to the boarding house where Rachel was living. It was an uncomfortably warm night and sultry from the day's sprinkling of rain. His shirt clung to his skin and perspiration collected underneath his collar. He took his handkerchief from his pocket and wiped his brow with it before dismounting in front of the brick boarding house.

The woman operating the rooming house let him inside and invited him to wait in the parlor while she went to summon Rachel from upstairs. As he waited he paced the room, trying to collect his thoughts. The windows were open to admit the night air, but the room still felt stifling. He sat down on the worn upholstered chair, tapping his fingers together nervously, then quickly got to his feet again as Rachel glided down the staircase and swept into the room. When she came to his side, he smelled the cloying scent of perfume.

"This is a pleasant surprise," she said, resting her hand on his arm. "I'm always happy to see you, Judson, but I wasn't expecting you to call this evening."

Judson swallowed and passed a hand over his chin. In spite of Rachel's calm demeanor, he knew she was still upset with him because of their argument three nights before. "Sit down," he offered, indicating the chair next to his.

She gathered her skirt and seated herself on the chair. "It's warm tonight, isn't it? My room is like an oven."

"Yes. We could use a hard rainstorm to cool things off."

She smoothed the folds of her skirt. "Rain keeps threatening, but all we ever get is a drizzle."

The palms of Judson's hands were sweating. He wiped them on his trouser legs. "Rachel, I've been doing some serious thinking lately and have come to a decision."

He saw her eyes brighten as she lifted her face to meet his and was disconcerted by her reaction. Then, with a sinking heart, he realized that she thought he'd come to ask for her hand in marriage. "Yes?" she said, almost in a whisper.

He took a gulping breath. "What I have to say is probably not what you're expecting." He glanced at her and saw her brows rush together. "I don't believe our relationship is working out in the way we both would have liked it to."

Her face paled. "Go on," she said.

"I'm afraid my feelings for you are not what they should be in order to propose marriage. With that being the case, I think the best thing to do is relinquish all ties."

She looked as if he had struck her. She sat rigid in her chair, the color vanishing from her cheeks.

For an instant, he was sorry for his words and wished he could recall them. Seeing her stunned expression pained him. "I'm sorry," he said hastily. "I didn't intend to hurt you."

Her lips quavered when she spoke. "I see. And just how long have you been dishonest in your feelings toward me?"

"I've never intentionally been dishonest with you, Rachel," he replied earnestly. "As soon as I realized my feelings for you were not what I had hoped, I've been looking for a way to tell you."

Her expression changed from shock and dismay to a cold fury. "You've certainly accomplished that."

"Rachel, please, I . . ."

She stood up abruptly before he could finish the sentence.

Judson rose to his feet, too, anxious to find a way to soften the blow he had dealt her. "I hope in time you can forgive me and we can remain friends."

"Friends?" She arched her brows, clearly indicating her disdain for his suggestion. "I doubt that. I never want to see you again." With that declaration, she brushed past him and started toward the stairs.

"Rachel, wait!" he called, hurrying after her.

She turned to look over her shoulder. "Don't ever speak to me again, Judson."

He watched her march up the staircase, her spine stiff, and then heard the door to her room slam. Clutching the banister, he stared up at the empty hallway above. He had mishandled the breakup and was sorry he had not prepared more carefully to take the sting out of his words. When he turned toward the door, he saw the woman who ran the boarding house standing in the doorway to her private quarters frowning at him. Nodding slightly to her, he hastily let himself out the front door.

He began sweating as soon as he stepped out into the hot, humid night. Mounting his horse, he reined the gray away from the rooming house, and as soon as he'd turned the corner of the street, he spurred the gelding into a canter. When he reached his place, he pastured his horse in the corral behind the shop and went inside. Without turning on any lamps for light, he slumped onto a kitchen chair. He mulled over the action he'd taken, unsure whether he was happy about the outcome or not. As he was pondering the situation, he suddenly remembered the pocketwatch Rachel had given him two months earlier.

Switching on the ceiling lamp, he strode to his room and removed the watch from the drawer of his bedside table and held it up to the light to examine it. The silver-plated case was slightly discolored, but the design etched on the front of it was still sharp and clear. Snapping open the case, he studied the handsome timepiece. The watch had belonged to Rachel's father, and she'd mentioned that her father had carried it with him every day in his vest pocket. He thought about what little he knew of Ethan Kade and wished he'd had the opportunity of meeting him. Not only would he have enjoyed the association, but it would have given him some further insight into his two daughters. Judson probably should have returned the pocketwatch to Rachel this evening, but he had promised himself that he would put the watch into Rebecca's hands, for she was the one who cared the most about it.

As he stared at the timepiece, he wondered when would be an appropriate time to visit Rebecca at the ranch and give her the watch. He closed the case and returned the watch to the drawer. Tomorrow, he would make a decision about when to see Rebecca again.

CHAPTER ELEVEN

On Saturday, Judson awoke before it was fully light. He lay in bed with his eyes open, staring at the curtained window that shut out the gray dawn of early morning. He was still upset about his conversation with Rachel from the night before and unsure if he'd made the right decision in ending their relationship.

Throwing off the blanket, he got out of bed, dressed, and shaved. As he sat down at the table for a bite of breakfast, he pondered the day before him. He could spend the day in his shop, for he had a lot of projects to finish, but he didn't feel like staying indoors working. And because it was Saturday, Daniel wouldn't be coming into the shop to assist him. He stared out the window above the table. The edges of the sky were beginning to turn pink, and the first rays of sunlight were breaking over the mountain peaks. The streets remained in shadows, silent and deserted. There was still plenty of time to catch the morning train to Draper.

As Judson traveled south on the train, he noticed the sky filling with gray clouds and the leaves on the trees shivering in the wind. He hoped the impending rainstorm would hold off until after he arrived at the ranch. He felt the solid weight of Ethan's pocketwatch resting in his vest pocket and rehearsed the words he would say when he handed the watch to Rebecca. He was nervous about seeing her again and reluctant to tell her about his breakup with Rachel. She might think badly of him for bringing an end to the courtship.

After a ride of more than an hour, he exited the train at the Draper depot and then walked to the nearby livery stable to rent a horse for the trip out to the Double K. The horse he was given was a sturdy buckskin with black legs, mane, and tail. The animal moved at a quick pace without much urging from Judson.

As he traveled the dirt road leading south to the Kades' ranch, he studied the low clouds nestled along the length of the mountains, obscuring their lofty peaks. When he'd started out on horseback, the sky was threatening rain, and now a light drizzle began to fall. He hadn't gone much farther before it changed into a downpour. The wind picked up, bringing with it the strong smell of sagebrush and wild grass. Judson didn't mind the cool rain. Summer storms seldom lasted long and afterward left the air feeling fresh and clean. He pulled his hat lower on his forehead to protect his face from the rain and pressed his horse forward.

Before long, he spotted the single-story, adobe ranch house situated on the brow of a hill and protected by a pair of tall, leafy trees. His breath came a little faster as he stared at the house, wondering what kind of reception he would receive—if Rebecca would be ill at ease because he had come without Rachel or if she would be annoyed by his unannounced visit. He hoped his presence would be welcome.

By the time he reached the house, the rain had slowed and the sky was clearing. He could see patches of blue overhead and a ray of sunlight piercing through the clouds. He eased down from the saddle and tied the buckskin to the hitching post. Drawing a deep breath to steady himself, he stepped onto the porch. As he stood there with his hat dripping rainwater and his coat hanging damp and limp against his chest, he hesitated before knocking. Just as he lifted his hand to the door, it opened and Rebecca stood framed inside the doorway. A smile sprang to his face. "Afternoon, Miss Kade," he greeted her. "Forgive me for dripping a stream of water onto your porch."

"Good day, Mr. Carter. I saw you ride up when I passed the window. Come inside and get out of the weather."

He removed his hat and shook the water from it and scraped the mud from his boots, then stepped into the hallway.

"Have you been riding in the rain all the way from Draper?" Rebecca asked as she took his coat.

"In my defense, it wasn't raining when I started out," he replied with a grin. "How are you?"

"I'm well, thank you." She led him to a chair in the small parlor and hung his coat on the back of it to dry. "Would you like something hot to drink to warm you?"

He shook his head and sat down on the chair she offered him. "No, I'm fine. It wasn't a cold rain. The wind was more bothersome than the rain." He couldn't help noticing the bloom of color on Rebecca's cheeks and the soft curve of her chin. Her hair was tied back with a red ribbon. She had on a plain blouse and skirt, but the simplicity of it was flattering. She seemed pleased to see him, and he hoped that it was not a pretense.

Rebecca seated herself across from him and folded her hands in her lap. "The wind blows almost constantly out here, rain or shine," she remarked.

"So I've noticed."

She shifted her position in the chair. "When Brigham Young first sent settlers south to Draper from Salt Lake City, he received a message from them after a few weeks."

"And what was the message?" Judson asked, running a hand through his damp hair.

"They wrote to say that they were stopping until the wind died down." Rebecca's mouth twitched with a smile. "They stayed and never left."

Judson laughed, amused by her story.

Rebecca glanced away. "I'm guessing that my sister was too busy to come here herself and so she sent you."

"Actually, I didn't tell Rachel I was coming." Now would be an appropriate moment to tell Rebecca about his breakup with Rachel, but he hesitated. He didn't know how to broach the delicate subject.

"Oh?"

"I wanted to know how you're faring—what kind of toll that disease took on your herd."

Rebecca told him about the cattle she'd lost to the outbreak of blackleg and of her plan to purchase more.

"Will you be able to replace the cattle and turn a profit after the sale of your stock?" Judson asked.

"I hope so. The market value for cattle depends on many things—the health of the herd, the price per head, the cost of feed—even the weather is a factor. If the grass on the range is poor due to lack of rainfall, the cattle will be thin and not fetch as good a price as they might have if they'd had better pasture."

"It sounds as if cattle ranchers are often at the mercy of circumstances beyond their control," Judson commented.

"That's true to a point. But a smart rancher plans ahead for such eventualities. He keeps a tight rein on his expenses and makes wise use of his land for grazing. My father kept this ranch running successfully for over twenty years."

"And you're still determined to do the same?"

"Yes, I am."

Their conversation turned from cattle ranching to other topics. Judson told her a little bit about his family—his parents and younger sister and brother—and his boyhood in Michigan.

"May I ask you a personal question, Mr. Carter?" she said when he'd finished.

"By all means."

"Rachel mentioned to me that you're a member of the Mormon Church. Is that correct?"

That particular query surprised him. "That's right. But I'm not what one would consider to be a practicing Mormon." He smiled. "Does that disappoint you?"

"I was only curious on my sister's account," she responded, her cheeks reddening.

"I wasn't under the impression that Rachel is particularly religious." One brow hitched up in a doubtful expression.

"Perhaps she could be influenced by someone who is strong in the faith."

"Do you mean me?" Both brows lurched up now. "I'm afraid you have the wrong fellow. The last time I exhibited any faith was the day I was baptized in the creek outside a member's home in Michigan."

"And how long ago was that?"

"I was seventeen when a friend of mine gave me a Book of Mormon to read. He'd gotten hold of it from a pair of missionaries, liked what it had to say, and wanted me to read it and tell him what I thought about it."

"And?"

"I was baptized two months later. He never joined," Judson added with a self-deprecatory smile.

"I see."

"I attended my meetings and tried to live the way I'd been taught for a while. But by the time I was twenty, I'd found other interests."

Rebecca remained silent, listening to what he had to say.

Judson glanced out the parlor window, surprised to find himself wanting to tell Rebecca how he'd felt when he'd first become acquainted with the gospel of Jesus Christ. He wanted to explain how his heart had swelled within him as he read the Book of Mormon and how the gospel message had brought peace and comfort to his soul. He hadn't shared those feelings with anyone in a long time or even thought much about them. He let the subject drop, however, more concerned about finding a way to inform her about the situation with Rachel, especially now that she had brought up the topic concerning the two of them. "Well, what do you know? It has stopped raining," he said, turning to her.

Rebecca's gaze moved to the window, too.

Judson got to his feet and held out a hand to her. "Come with me."

"Where are we going?" Rebecca asked as she stood and let Judson take her hand.

"To gallop our horses through a field of wildflowers after a spring rain."

From her shy smile and the flush that came upon her cheeks, Judson knew she was pleased that he'd remembered this detail from their conversation when he'd last visited the ranch, but she didn't comment.

He tugged gently on her hand. "Will a summer rain do just as well as a spring one?" he asked, smiling.

She chuckled. "I suppose it will."

Judson hoped once they were outside, away from the confines of the house, he would find a way to tell her about Rachel and himself and then return the pocketwatch to her.

While she went to the corral to saddle and bridle her horse, he mounted the buckskin he'd rented from the livery stable and met her behind the house. They started off together, riding southeasterly along the ridge of the hills. The wind blowing across their faces smelled of rain and wild sagebrush. Judson told her about the gray gelding he owned, corralled behind his workshop in Salt Lake City; then the conversation turned to Rebecca's quarter horse. She detailed the animal's many fine qualities—its smooth gait, its speed and endurance, its skill in herding cattle. They rode leisurely along a dirt trail that wound through clumps of sagebrush and greasewood. Droplets of water from the recent rain glistened like glass beads on the blades of tall grass. "You've been bragging about this horse of yours," Judson said, chuckling. "Now it's time to show me what he can do."

Rebecca flashed him a confident smile, then tapped Onyx with her heels. The gelding burst into a gallop. Judson lashed his horse with the reins, urging it into a run, and the buckskin picked up speed; but it couldn't keep pace with the black horse. Judson watched Rebecca's black pull steadily ahead, its gait powerful and even. He smiled to himself, impressed by the gelding's beauty and strength. Rebecca turned in her saddle, the wind rippling the red ribbon tied in her hair and her skirt billowing out behind her. After a few moments she reined in her horse, swiveled in the saddle, and waited for Judson to catch up.

"You weren't exaggerating, were you?" Judson said as he directed his horse alongside hers. The buckskin was winded; its sides heaved and its nostrils flared. Rebecca's black stood pawing the ground as if anxious to continue the run.

"Did you think I was?"

He laughed. "You'd have a good shot with that gelding at winning the half-mile race in Salt Lake next month."

Rebecca shook her head. "I'm not interested."

"Fifty dollars in winnings is nothing to take lightly. If you don't race Onyx, that will increase the odds for me taking home the money," he said with a wink.

"You're going to race your gray?"

"I'm planning on it." Judson watched her chew at her lip. He knew she was calculating how far fifty dollars would go in solving the financial problems plaguing the ranch. And after seeing Onyx run, Judson was convinced the horse had a good chance of winning. "But if you race that quarter horse of yours, I'll bet my money on him," Judson said.

Rebecca nudged Onyx forward at a walk as the two of them rode side by side through the grass.

"I know someone who might ride Onyx for you in the race, if you decide to enter," Judson said.

"Oh?"

"His name is Daniel Briggs. He's a young man I've hired at my shop. He's seventeen or eighteen years old, slim and lithe. He'd make a good jockey for your horse."

"What does he do at your shop?"

Judson smiled, realizing she was skirting the issue of the horse race. "I'm training him to become a cabinetmaker. He has a genuine talent for woodworking."

"Is he from Salt Lake City?"

He frowned, remembering Rachel's same question and her response upon meeting Daniel at the shop. He wondered if Rebecca's prejudices were the same. "No. Actually, he's half Ute Indian." He studied her face for an instant to see her reaction. If she was repelled by that fact, she didn't show it. He told her what little he knew of Daniel's past and how the government had forced his people to move onto the Ouray Reservation.

"Ouray? I've heard mention of that name before. Wasn't Ouray an important Indian chief?"

"That's right. Daniel has spoken often about him—how he was a respected chief of the Tabeguache Ute band, of his intelligence and wisdom, and his dexterity in dealing with the white man. He cooperated with government officials in order to spare his people from the kind of attacks made by the United States Army on the Sioux at Wounded Knee and the Cheyennes and Arapahos at Sand Creek." From the corner of his eye, Judson saw Rebecca shudder at his mention of those Indian massacres.

"But Daniel's not living on the reservation now?"

Judson shook his head. "I've gathered from what he's told me that his white father deserted his Indian mother before Daniel was even born. But when Daniel was ten, a benefactor made arrangements to send him to a boarding school for white children. It was there that Daniel learned to speak, read, and write in English."

"That must have been difficult for him, being away from his family and living in an unfamiliar environment. Children can often be cruel in their treatment of outsiders."

"Daniel hasn't said much about his experiences at school, but he seems adept at handling prejudice." Judson's mind went back to the occasion of his first encounter with the young man. He scowled, thinking about how Murdock and his two partners had mistreated Daniel in the saloon.

"It's kind of you to take Daniel under your wing," Rebecca remarked.

"It's not kindness that prompted me to hire Daniel. I recognized a gifted artist in that young man." Judson went on to describe the wolf ornament Daniel had carved and wore on a necklace around his neck. He was explaining about some of the projects he and Daniel were working on at the shop when he sighted in the distance an open meadow sparkling with wildflowers. A glittering display of pinks, reds, purples, and yellows gleamed like jewels strewn throughout the grassy meadow. "There are your wildflowers," he said to Rebecca, nodding toward the spot.

Rebecca turned in her saddle. He smiled, thinking she would be pleased with the blaze of color spread before them. But instead of a smile, Judson saw her face grow pale.

At first, he thought she might have missed seeing the meadow. "Look over there, just past that hollow." Judson pointed to a rocky low spot of ground several yards away.

Rebecca sat as stiff as a statue, her eyes unblinking as she stared at the hollow and the open meadow beyond.

"Let's ride down there and pick a bouquet for you to take home."

"No," she replied in a hoarse whisper.

Judson started, surprised by her reaction. "What?"

"Not here. I don't want any flowers from here." She started to rein Onyx into a turn.

"Wait a minute," Judson said, leaning forward in his saddle.

"I can't stay here," Rebecca said. She pulled hard on the reins, leading Onyx in the opposite direction, then spurred the gelding into a gallop. The horse bolted away.

"Rebecca! Wait!" Judson called. He rammed his heels into the buckskin, trying to catch up with her.

They had traveled a good distance back down the dirt trail before Rebecca abruptly wheeled her horse to a stop and waited for Judson to reach her side.

"What's this all about?" he asked in bewilderment, reining in his horse. When he saw her tear-stained face, his chest tightened. "What is it? What's wrong?" He could see her shoulders heaving as he swung down from his horse and approached her; she looked as if she were shivering with cold.

"I want to go somewhere else. Anywhere else," she said, her voice trembling.

"Give me your hand," Judson offered. "I'll help you down from the saddle. We can sit here and talk for a while."

Rebecca let him assist her off her horse. Leading her to a fallen limb beside a brook, he seated her on it and sat down beside her. He couldn't understand the reason for her behavior.

"I'm sorry," she began in a quivering voice. "I shouldn't have run off like that. It's just that . . ." She stopped, the words trapped in her throat.

"It's just what?" he urged gently. Her face was ashen, and her eyes were glistening with tears. He fought an urge to take her in his arms to comfort her.

Rebecca dabbed at the tears with the back of her hand. "I had to get away from that place . . . I couldn't go down there." She glanced with a fearful expression toward the ravine and the meadow beyond it, as though the place was haunted by demons.

"Will you tell me why?" Judson asked.

She didn't answer immediately, and the soft sighing of the trickling brook filled the silence between them. Finally, she looked over at him, as if gathering strength to finish the sentence. "Because it's the place where my mother died."

CHAPTER TWELVE

Judson felt the color drain from his face. "I'm sorry. I didn't know."

"It's my fault. We came upon the hollow before I realized it," Rebecca said, her voice filled with despair.

They sat in silence for a moment, then Judson took her hand into his. "How did it happen? Do you feel like talking about it?"

Rebecca glanced off into the distance, her thoughts etched plainly on her face. "Mother and I had been out riding that afternoon. We were on our way to the meadow to pick wildflowers for the supper table. She didn't want to go—she was busy cooking supper—but I insisted."

Judson heard a sob escape her throat. He tightened his hand around her fingers. "Go on."

"I persuaded her to race our horses to the meadow. She called for me to stop, but I didn't. I was laughing, thinking only about winning the race between us." Rebecca paused and Judson saw her eyes stray back to the hollow. "I galloped my horse down the draw and was starting up the other side when I heard her mare whinny. I turned and saw her horse stumble or trip. Perhaps the mare stepped into a hole or lost her footing on the rough, steep ground. I don't know . . ." Rebecca's voice trailed off into silence.

Judson said nothing, waiting for her to resume the story.

"Mama was thrown when her horse fell. When I got to her, she was already dead." Rebecca swallowed, making a gulping noise. "Her neck was broken."

Judson closed his eyes to blot out the grim picture painted by Rebecca's words. "How old were you?"

"Fourteen."

"Fourteen," Judson echoed. "Just a girl. I can't imagine the horror of that moment for you."

She turned to look at him, and her lips trembled. "I was old enough to know better. I should never have challenged Mother to a race. She wasn't used to riding much." Rebecca dropped her gaze. "It was my fault that she died."

Judson stared back at her as she removed her hand from his, her shoulders slumping. He didn't know what to say to comfort her.

"I've never been to that hollow since. Or the meadow beyond it," she whispered in an anguished voice.

"It wasn't your fault," Judson offered. "You didn't know that her horse would fall."

"No, it was because of me that she died." She shook her head slowly, and the tears spilled down her cheeks.

Sitting huddled on the fallen limb of the tree, Judson thought she looked as small and helpless as a child. He wiped away a tear from her chin. "Tell me about your mother. What was she like?"

Rebecca closed her eyes before answering. "She had the prettiest smile," she replied, eyes still closed as if she were viewing the memory. "People always complimented her on her smile. She was beautiful, too. Raven hair. Emerald green eyes. And that smile. Papa adored her."

Judson watched her face intently as she recounted the memory. The tender expressions flickering across her features were easy to read. When she opened her eyes, he was still looking at her.

"Mama was the kind of person who was always happy. No matter the circumstances, she found something to be joyful about. She liked being around people. I think it was hard for her to come out here to the ranch with Papa, away from town and the society of her friends and family, but she never said a word in complaint about it."

"Was she from Salt Lake City?" Judson asked.

"Yes. She grew up in the city. Her father owned a book shop, and she worked for him during the day. That's where she first met my father."

"Oh?"

"Papa saw her working behind the counter one day and fell in love with her at first sight."

Judson smiled, visualizing that moment as it must have been when Rebecca's parents first met one another. "Did your father live in the city as well?"

"Yes, while he was growing up. His father was a physician in Salt Lake. But Papa was working as a ranch hand in this part of the valley when he met Mother."

Judson was glad to see Rebecca's spirits lifting as she talked about her parents. "And then you and Rachel were born," he said, nudging her shoulder with his to encourage her to continue.

"Yes. My parents were married about six years before we were born. Mother had a couple of miscarriages before that, and after our birth she wasn't able to have any more children."

Judson's gaze focused on the tips of his boots as he listened to the story she was relating.

"Papa chose our middle names. Rachel's is Susa and mine is Ann. Two parts of the same name. Susannah."

"Rachel Susa and Rebecca Ann." He smiled at the sentimentality of Ethan's choice of names for his daughters. "I like the sound of them."

The pain that had seized Rebecca's heart on stumbling upon the hollow seemed to be easing as she recounted her memories. "Rachel was born three minutes before midnight, and I was born two minutes after the hour; so our birthdays are actually on different days. On every birthday, Mama would come into our room where we were sleeping and wake us with a kiss—Rachel at exactly three minutes before midnight and me at two minutes after." Rebecca smiled with the recollection. "Then the three of us would sit together and talk for a while. She was a wonderful mother."

Judson rose to his feet and extended a hand to Rebecca. She took it and together they began to walk alongside the stream. A soft breeze came up, cooling their faces; and the brook murmured at their feet. Judson noticed a ray of sunlight breaking through the clouds. It dappled Rebecca's cheeks with a golden glow. "And you've lived here on the ranch your whole life," he said, "amid the wildflowers, mountain streams, and wooded hills."

She smiled at his colorful description. "Yes. And the wind, insects, and rattlesnakes."

"Rattlesnakes?" He made a pretense of glancing down apprehensively at the area around his feet.

"Don't worry. You'll hear them before they strike."

"Thanks for that encouragement," he returned, grinning at her. "I prefer sunflowers to rattlesnakes, however." As he spoke, he bent down and snapped from its stalk a broad-faced, yellow sunflower. "For you," he said, presenting it to her with a bow.

She took the wild sunflower from his hand, and Judson could see a smile warming her face. "Thank you."

He picked several more as they walked, collecting a small bouquet for her. After he handed her the bouquet, he chose the biggest, brightest sunflower from the lot and tucked it into her hair. Then he stood back to admire his handiwork. He saw her blush under his gaze. "You ought to see yourself with sunflowers in your hair," he said. "You look like morning sunshine."

Rebecca smiled at his remark, thinking, Judson supposed, that he was still spinning poetic phrases.

Judson raked a hand through his hair and cleared his throat. "Rebecca, I want to speak to you about something that's been on my mind." He paused, unable to phrase the words he wanted to say to her. "It seems that I . . . that is, Rachel and I . . ." He left the sentence dangling when Rebecca lifted her eyes unexpectedly to meet his. They were the clearest blue he had ever seen, the color of the sky at midday. Why he had not noticed this fact before startled him.

"What is it you wanted to say?" she asked.

Judson's heart began banging in his chest, and his head started buzzing. He could hardly draw his eyes away from her. He stepped back abruptly. "Never mind. It wasn't important."

"Oh."

Judson lowered his eyes, afraid she could read his thoughts. Afraid that she might guess how much he wanted to kiss her.

"I should probably be getting back to the house," Rebecca said hesitantly, glancing away.

"Yes. I've kept you too long from your chores." He was stammering and tripping over his words.

Neither of them spoke as they walked back to their horses. He held the bouquet while she climbed into her saddle, then he handed it to her and mounted his buckskin. The ride back to the ranch seemed to go at a snail's pace. Judson's stomach was churning. He was sure that Rebecca must have sensed his attraction for her. If so, she'd think he was a base fellow who, while wooing one sister, made advances to the other. He cringed, picturing himself in that light. He wouldn't be able to tell her about his breakup with Rachel now; the topic would be too awkward. His hand traced the bulky outline of the timepiece he carried in his vest pocket. He had intended to return the pocketwatch to Rebecca, accompanied with an explanation. But now he'd have to wait until a more appropriate time arose.

He glanced at Rebecca from the corner of his eye as they rode toward the ranch house. She seemed composed, but he knew she was still suffering from the pain of revisiting the events surrounding her mother's death. What had started out as a pleasant ride under a fresh, clean sky had ended in betrayal and despair. For both of them.

On Monday morning, Judson was up and working in his shop before the sun rose. As he fitted the dovetail joint at the corner of the drawer, his thoughts were not completely on his work. He was still smarting from the whiplashing he'd given himself the day before on the subject of Rebecca Kade. As much as he was attracted to her, he could not in good conscience act on his feelings because of his previous relationship with Rachel. He had painstakingly come to that decision and was determined to abide by it. But often, in an unguarded moment, he found himself still thinking about her.

"Are you finished assembling that drawer?"

Judson's head jerked up. Daniel Briggs stood looking at him, a sander gripped in his hand.

"Yes, I'm through," Judson answered quickly. He studied for a moment the joint he'd just affixed, then handed the drawer to Daniel for sanding. Daniel took the drawer, sat down on a stool with it, and started gliding the hand sander back and forth at one end.

"This is a sturdy drawer. Mr. Addams should be pleased with the progress being made on the bureau."

"Yes, he should," Judson replied absently, his thoughts still on Rebecca.

"I'm sure Miss Addams will be happy with her piece of furniture."

Something in Daniel's tone caused Judson to glance over at him. As he watched the young man meticulously sand the wood, he had an uneasy feeling concerning him. And it wasn't the first time he'd experienced such a feeling. Once before, when Daniel had mentioned Louisa Addams' name, Judson had heard a peculiar quality in his voice—almost an eagerness—that was not usually apparent. Judson had shrugged off the impression, but now that almost imperceptible strain of brightness was present again in Daniel's comment.

"I bumped into Miss Addams on the street yesterday. She asked how the work was coming along on her bureau and side table," Daniel said, his head down and his eyes fixed on his work.

Judson felt a growing sense of apprehension. "Oh? Did you speak with her long?"

"No. Only long enough to remind her that the construction of her furniture was in the hands of a master craftsman." He looked up at Judson and smiled. "Yourself, of course."

Judson forced a smile in return. He wondered if he should caution Daniel about fraternizing with Henry Addams' daughter. Addams had made it clear that he had little regard for the mixed-race young man Judson had hired. He was sure Addams would not hesitate to speak his mind if he caught Daniel and his daughter socializing.

Judson sighed and returned to his work. The frame for the chest of drawers was well under way, and today he'd started on the drawers. Daniel had done an excellent job in assisting Judson with the work. Not only had they made good progress on Addams' order, but they had moved ahead quickly with several other contracts for furniture that Judson had received over the past few weeks. Judson hoped his new apprentice wasn't planning to move on; Daniel hadn't said anything more about wanting to continue the search for his father. Judson glanced over at the youth. Daniel was focused on his work, sliding the sander rhythmically along the grain of the wood. From his chest dangled the carved wolf ornament. Judson had never seen him without it around his neck. Even though he'd worked side by side with Daniel for the past five weeks, he still knew very little about him.

Judson picked up his tool and began making notches in the corner of the next drawer, preparing to assemble the corner joints. "When you're through with the sanding, you can start carving the rosette designs into the corners of the chest," he said to Daniel.

Daniel's head shot up, and his eyes widened. "Do you think I am prepared enough for that?"

"I wouldn't assign you the work if I didn't."

Daniel didn't reply, but Judson heard him take a deep breath.

Judson set down his tool and looked Daniel in the eye. "It's obvious that you're skilled with a carving knife. It's time to put that talent to use."

"Yes, sir, Mr. Carter."

Judson could see that the young man was uneasy about taking on this new responsibility. "Look at that carved wolf you wear around your neck. That's an excellent piece of workmanship, Daniel, and you carved it without any formal training in woodworking. Now that you've learned the basics of the trade and honed your skills, you're ready to put your talents to work."

"Yes, sir," Daniel repeated.

"You've practiced the motif Miss Addams wants carved on her bureau a dozen times already on wood scraps. You're capable of transferring that skill to the original."

"All right, Mr. Carter. I will try my best."

"Not try, Daniel. Do."

"Yes, sir. Do my best."

Judson turned back to the drawer he was working on, chuckling to himself. As Daniel sat motionless on the stool assimilating this new assignment, Judson said to him, "Tell me about that wolf carving, will you? Does it have some special significance?"

Daniel's hand moved to the wooden ornamental piece. "It represents the name my mother gave me at birth." Daniel pronounced a difficult sounding Ute word, which Judson couldn't replicate. "It means gray wolf."

"Your Indian name is Gray Wolf?" Judson asked.

"Yes. The day I was born, my mother saw a large, gray wolf near our tepee. It paused to look at her before trotting away. It is the custom of our people to give names that symbolize an event or the character of a person. She hoped her child would develop the wisdom, courage, and cunning of the wolf."

Judson rubbed a hand across his chin. "I think your mother's desires have been realized."

The light in Daniel's eyes blazed a little brighter with Judson's words.

"Do you know anything about your father?" Judson asked after a moment's silence.

Daniel shook his head. "My mother told me that he was a soldier who had come to the reservation with his battalion. After he left, my mother did not hear from him again. When I was five years old, our people were forced to move from the reservation in Colorado to Utah; it was here the Ouray Reservation was created as a place for the

Tabeguache Utes to live. Although this reservation carries the name of our great chief, Ouray, it is not our home."

Judson easily detected the ire in Daniel's voice.

"Then one day, when I was ten and living on the reservation in Utah with my mother, the Indian agent took me into his office and told me a benefactor had arranged to pay for my board and room at a white man's school. It was only a year ago that I learned who that benefactor was."

"Your father?"

"Yes."

Judson studied the young man's expression; written on his face was a multitude of conflicting emotions. Fiercely proud of his Indian heritage, he vacillated between rejecting and embracing his white ancestry. This dichotomy had shaped his character.

Daniel had spoken occasionally of the *Núu-ci*, or Ute people, who had always lived in harmony with the land, showing respect and reverence for its bounties—hunting, fishing, gathering roots, nuts, and wild plants. The land was central to the *Núu-ci*'s survival. He had told Judson how they moved from place to place with the seasons, gathering together at winter camps near rivers and creeks and traveling in the summer months to hunt bison, deer, elk, bighorn sheep, and antelope. He spoke of how Mother Earth provided them with food, shelter, and clothing. Their homes were hide tepees or brush shelters. They slept on mats of juniper bark, evergreen boughs, or woven willows covered with rabbit-skin blankets or buffalo robes. He'd described how Ute men wore buckskin shirts and long leggings;

women dressed in fringed deerskin dresses, knee-length leggings, and moccasins.

The Utes were skillful horsemen who owned sizable herds, Daniel had explained; their many horses were a source of pride and a symbol of their wealth. They prided themselves on their success in hunting, trading, and warring with other tribes. The *Núu-ci* had a reputation for courage and skill in warfare. Although they were generally recognized as a peaceful people, they frequently engaged in raiding and stealing, either to avenge a wrong or to secure goods, captives, or horses.

Daniel had told him about the *Núu-ci* ceremonial dance that takes place in the early spring. This is the season when the fearsome bear awakes from hibernation, and the *Núu-ci* gather together to celebrate the Bear Dance. The tradition of the Bear Dance began long ago, Daniel had recounted, when a hunter came upon a bear leaving its winter den. The bear told the young hunter that his people would remain strong if they would dance the Bear Dance. Every spring since that time, the Utes had come from their winter camps to gather for this important celebration. They believed the dance would ensure successful hunting and the birth of many children.

Daniel's attachment to his Ute heritage was obvious. He revered the customs and traditions from the past, but they often clashed with the realities of the present. His Indian ancestry was his anchor, yet his father's bloodline brought him many benefits and opportunities as well. Judson was curious to see how the young man would reconcile these two opposing forces in his nature.

He was about to inquire further concerning Daniel's father when the door of the shop opened and a young woman stepped inside. As Judson rose to his feet to greet the woman, it took him an instant to recognize that it was Louisa Addams standing inside the shop. "Good afternoon, Miss Addams," Judson said approaching her. He noticed that Louisa was dressed in an attractive frock with a matching hat, and she was carrying a fringed parasol.

"Good day, Mr. Carter." Louisa looked past Judson's shoulder. "Good day, Mr. Briggs."

Judson turned in time to see Daniel's cheeks flame as he sprang from his seat to join them. The young man mumbled a greeting, then dropped his gaze. Judson turned back to Louisa. "What can I do for you, Miss Addams?"

"Would you be so kind as to show me what's been accomplished on the bureau since my last visit?" She gave Judson a disarming, but genuine, smile. "I'm quite enchanted with what I've seen already."

Her request was nothing out of the ordinary. Judson's clients often stopped by the shop to see how a particular job was progressing. Judson had previously shown Louisa the sketches of the design on paper that he'd drawn up for her approval. She had picked out the particular details she wanted and chosen the rosette motif to be carved into the four corners of the bureau and a simple vine and leaf pattern across the front of each drawer. But on the occasion of that visit, Louisa had been accompanied by her father. This time she came alone. Judson had the uneasy feeling that her purpose in visiting the shop was not solely to see the progress being made on her furniture.

"Certainly. It's right over here. Daniel and I were just discussing the carved decorations for the piece." He led Louisa to the rear of the shop where the frame for the chest of drawers stood.

She studied the piece for a long moment without speaking, causing Judson to wonder if she was pleased with what she saw.

Finally, she turned to look at Judson. "It's beautiful, Mr. Carter. Such graceful lines."

"Thank you. I hope it meets your expectations."

"Oh, indeed, it does. The artistry is superb."

Judson shrugged modestly. "Your specifications for the piece were well thought out, an excellent foundation upon which to build."

She smiled again at him, then turned her gaze back to the boxed frame.

Judson glanced at Daniel, who was standing slightly behind him. The youth was staring, trance-like, at Louisa Addams, and his eyes easily betrayed his emotions. Judson was little surprised to see that Daniel was smitten with her. Louisa was as pretty and charming as a songbird and had a friendly manner. From her fashionable appearance, Judson had assumed that she would be as vain and prideful as her father, but he was beginning to think otherwise.

"Mr. Briggs," Louisa said, turning to Daniel. "Will you be the one carving the rosettes?"

Her smile brought another wave of color to Daniel's cheeks. "Yes, Miss Addams."

"I shall look forward to seeing the results."

"I hope my efforts will please you," Daniel said.

"I'm sure I will not be disappointed, Mr. Briggs."

Judson looked from Daniel to Louisa Addams and realized with a start that Daniel was not alone in his sympathies. The feelings seemed to be reciprocated on Louisa's part. Judson frowned, concerned about the ramifications of this new development.

"Mr. Carter, you have chosen a beautiful piece of wood for the bureau. It looks as smooth as silk," Louisa said, turning her attention back to Judson. "I can hardly wait to see the finished product."

Judson quickly reversed his frown so Louisa would not detect his concerns. "Your decision to select mahogany was an excellent choice. The pigment in mahogany is uniformly distributed throughout the wood, creating an even color and exposing the beauty of the grain."

"I have most certainly depended upon your expertise as to the selection of the wood, Mr. Carter, and your skillful craftsmanship."

"Thank you, Miss Addams," Judson replied, giving a slight bow of his head.

"Well, then," Louisa said, glancing from Judson to Daniel. "I will leave you two gentlemen to your work. Perhaps you wouldn't mind if I paid another visit to your shop in a week or so."

"We will look forward to it," Judson replied, accompanying his words with a smile he did not wholeheartedly feel.

"Good day." She nodded to them both and left the shop.

After she'd gone, Judson turned wordlessly to Daniel. The young man met his gaze, then lowered his eyes and walked back to his work bench without saying anything. But both men understood the unspoken communication that had passed between them.

CHAPTER THIRTEEN

The air had grown cooler with sporadic rain falling throughout the week. Rebecca noticed the brush on the hillsides beginning to turn from summer's green to orange. At night the air had a nip to it, and the angle of the sun during the day proclaimed that autumn had arrived and winter was not far behind. Rebecca dreaded seeing the winter come. The short, cold days of winter were often lonely for her on the isolated ranch. She'd always had her family around her before to share the long evenings, but this winter she would be all alone.

As she brushed Onyx's black coat, she thought about her cattle grazing on the mountain slopes. She'd been riding in the high pastures with Hernandez and Andrus all morning tending to them. In general, the herd looked to be in good shape. They had grown fatter and stronger due to the recent rains which had nourished the grass and bolstered the mountain streams. In another week she and the ranch hands would begin the fall roundup, gathering the cattle to count them, sort them, brand the calves, and make preparations for market. She was just waiting for Micah to arrive back at the ranch. He had left for Ogden the day before to attend the cattle auction there. Rebecca was still unsure about her plan to purchase more animals to replace the ones she'd lost. She'd decided to wait for Micah's report concerning the condition and availability of the steers for sale before making a final decision.

Onyx snorted and stamped his feet. "Easy, boy," Rebecca murmured, rubbing the strip of white on the horse's forehead. She gave his coat a few more firm strokes with the brush, then combed out his coarse mane and tail. The gelding had picked up a few burrs from the morning's ride in the hills, and she carefully removed them. As she groomed her horse, her thoughts moved to the letter she'd just received from Rachel. Micah had collected the ranch mail from the post office in Draper while he was there waiting for the train to take him north to Ogden and paid a boy a few cents to carry the letters by horseback out to the Double K.

Rachel had responded to her letter of two weeks ago with a short note, expressing dismay over the loss of the cattle as well as Rebecca's plan to buy more. Even though she sounded concerned about circumstances at the ranch, Rachel remained noncommittal as to when she would be coming out to the Double K again. Rebecca assumed that Judson Carter had given her a report of the affairs at the ranch after his visit; she hoped he had not included a recital of the emotional scene that had occurred near the meadow.

Rebecca's cheeks burned as she thought about that incident—both because of her reaction to the memories of her mother's death and because of Judson's tender response. She felt a tingle travel along her spine as she recalled the touch of his hand and the expression of concern in his eyes as they'd sat together on the fallen limb beside the stream. He'd wanted to talk to her about something that was on his mind, he'd said, but then he'd abruptly decided otherwise and fallen silent. Even though he'd mentioned Rachel's name in connection with his thoughts, she felt sure that whatever he'd intended to say concerned her as well. She'd sensed a subtle change in his attitude toward her from the moment he'd arrived at the house, and his disposition at the creek confirmed that feeling. Rebecca held her breath as she contemplated what he might have been about to say.

Onyx began pawing the ground, drawing Rebecca's attention back to the job at hand. She finished combing the horse's ebony mane, then untied his halter and turned him loose into the corral. After putting away the saddle, blanket, and bridle in the tack room of the barn, she left the corral and went out to the cornfield to finish gathering the ears of ripe corn. The crop had not done as well as usual because of the summer's scant rainfall. Many of the ears were stunted, and insects had taken their toll. Rebecca snapped the ears off the stalks and put them into baskets. She would be bottling the corn and the rest of the vegetables and fruits over the course of the next few weeks, preserving the food for winter.

The sound of fallen dry cornstalks rustling underfoot alerted her to the fact that someone was approaching. She looked up expectantly. Jake Baxter stepped through the row of cornstalks, parting the plants before him like a curtain.

"Afternoon, Miss Rebecca. Been lookin' for you. I figured you might be out her."

A frown sprang to Rebecca's brow. In addition to her general dislike for the cowhand, she didn't appreciate how he'd recently begun calling her by her given name. It sounded too familiar and brazen. "What is it, Jake?"

"I wanted to talk to you about the roundup. Micah's not here, you know, and it's already later in the season than usual when we should be startin' the roundup."

"Micah will be back in a couple of days. We'll begin then, when he's here to oversee it," she replied firmly.

"I can be gettin' a start on it in the meantime," Jake pressed.

"You and the other hands have plenty to do to keep you occupied until Micah returns," she said, reaching to pick another ear of corn from the top of the stalk. She was already irritated with Jake's sloppy work. The irrigation ditch she had asked him to dig earlier in the summer was totally inadequate. She wished her father had never hired the man.

Jake stood a few paces away, eyeing her with an inscrutable expression. "Can I carry those bushel baskets of corn to the house for you, Miss Rebecca?"

"All right. Thank you."

He picked up two of them, carrying one in each arm. "I'll empty them on the back porch and be right back."

She nodded without looking at him and continued plucking the corn, occasionally glancing up at the gray sky. Dark clouds scudded overhead, threatening more rain. She hoped to get several more rows of corn picked before it started raining.

Jake seemed to take an excessively long time before returning to the field with the empty baskets. "The corn's heaped on the porch," he said.

"Thanks."

"Want me to help with the picking?" he asked after a moment's pause.

"No. I can do it. You have chores of your own."

"I'd like to give you a hand. My chores can sit a spell." He moved closer to her, a false smile spreading on his face.

Rebecca felt a sudden rush of fear. Jake's toothy grin was reminiscent of his demeanor on the night of the dance in Draper. Her encounter with him was still sharp in her memory. She straightened and warily took a step backward. "I'm nearly through here. Thanks anyway."

He drew closer. "You don't much like havin' me around, do you, Rebby?"

"I'd appreciate it if you'd address me as Miss Kade," she said, hoping to divert his attention.

He laughed harshly, and the sound of it sent chills down Rebecca's spine. With alarming clarity, she remembered the warning her sister had given her—*You'll be the only woman for miles around, without Papa here to protect you.* A shiver ran through her. She kept thinking that she couldn't let Jake sense her fear.

She grasped the bushel basket she'd been filling, placing it in front of her like a shield. Holding her breath, she started past him, hoping he wouldn't try to stop her. He didn't. She walked quickly through the row of corn.

But just as she was about to leave the cornfield, she heard him growl, "Someday you might change your mind about me."

She flinched, as if his words had been blows, and nearly stumbled. Gripping the bushel basket tighter in her hands, she kept walking until she reached the safety of the house.

Once inside, she leaned against the closed door and drew a long breath. Then she went to the window and carefully moved aside a corner of the curtain. No one was in the yard; she couldn't see Jake anywhere in sight. She let the drapery fall back into place. As soon as Micah returned from Ogden, she decided, she'd talk to him about Jake Baxter.

Rebecca stayed in the house the rest of the day, not wanting another confrontation with Jake. She kept herself busy husking and bottling corn, then boiling the filled quart jars on the old black iron stove in the kitchen. By nightfall, she was exhausted from her labors. She read from a book by coal oil lamplight while lying in bed, and when the words began swimming before her eyes, she turned out the lamp.

The following morning she was up early, ready to start her chores for the day. The memory of Jake's threatening words seemed less menacing in the bright morning light. She worked outside in the yard until noon, and while she was preparing her noon meal a knock sounded at the door. When she opened the front door, a messenger boy from Western Union stood on the porch holding a yellow sheet of paper.

"I've a telegram for Miss Rebecca Kade," the boy said. "And I'm instructed to wait for a reply."

"I'm Rebecca Kade," she responded, taking the paper from his outstretched hand. She quickly read the short message from Micah. He'd looked over the cattle to be auctioned off at an Ogden stockyard. The cattle were thin and of poorer quality than those raised at the Double K, he'd wired, but under the circumstances, he felt the purchase would be advantageous. He wanted to know how many head Rebecca wished to bid on and how she wanted to carry out the transaction. "Wait right here for a moment," she said to the boy, "while I pen a reply."

She hurried into the house and sat down at her desk. Retrieving her key to the bottom desk drawer, she bent to fit it into the lock. The lock fell away as soon as she touched it. Surprised, she picked it up and looked at it. The metal lock had been battered open; one whole piece of it was bent and broken. Rebecca's breath wheezed in her chest as she jerked open the unlocked desk drawer. The few papers inside were lying in a jumbled heap, and on top of them was the quart jar that had held her money. But the jar was empty.

Rebecca snatched up the glass jar, staring at it in horror. Where was her money? She frantically searched through the mess of papers in the drawer, but the money was not there. The room seemed to start spinning around her. She put her hands to her head and groaned. Her money, all of it, gone. The shock of the loss nearly swept her from her seat.

Then she remembered the messenger waiting for her outside. With shaking hands, she drew a sheet of paper from the drawer and wrote out a quick note. Her legs were wobbling beneath her as she took the note to the messenger boy who was awaiting her reply and handed it to him. The boy touched his cap in response, then mounted his horse and rode off.

Rebecca stumbled back into the house and searched through the desk again. Who had taken her cash? Who would wish to rob her? Her mind raced through a list of possible suspects. Was it someone who worked at the ranch? One of the ranch hands? Her thoughts immediately centered on Jake Baxter. Jake knew where she kept the jar of money because he'd seen her take it from the desk. How could she have been so careless about keeping the money safe? She sucked in her breath remembering that not only Jake, but Micah, too, was aware of the cash in the quart jar. Surely,

Micah couldn't have been the thief; Micah had always been loyal and trustworthy.

She stood up and began pacing across the room. Who else had been to the ranch recently? A stranger who might have entered the house while she was away? With a start, she recalled Judson Carter's visit. *"I took the liberty of nosing around the grounds while you were gone."* His words echoed in her head. Had he also taken liberties with her possessions inside the house? Her stomach clenched as she realized that she hadn't looked to see if anything else in the house was missing.

She darted into her bedroom, going straight to the dresser drawer where she kept her cameo necklace secured in the velvet pouch. When she felt its familiar shape under her fingers, she blew out a breath of relief. Tucking the pouch safely into the drawer, she checked every corner of her room and then searched her father's room. She found nothing further out of order or any indication that her things had been tampered with. Apparently, the thief knew exactly what he was after and where it was to be found for he'd left everything else untouched.

She sank down onto her bed, the awful reality of her loss pressing all around her. Without more cattle to boost the numbers of her herd, she wasn't sure if she'd clear enough money to get through the winter. She felt sick inside and fearful of the future, and she had never in her life felt more alone.

Micah returned two days later without the cattle as Rebecca had instructed in her wire. When she told him about the theft of her money, he reacted with shock and anger and urged her to inform the authorities in Draper. She needed advice from someone she could trust, someone who was intimately acquainted with the problems besetting her, and so she wrote again to Rachel, asking her to come out to the ranch immediately.

While she waited for her sister's response, she joined the ranch hands in preparing for the roundup. All of the cattle wearing the Double K brand needed to be gathered and herded into a central location for sorting, branding, and counting. Then the heifers and steers selected for market, and any old bulls and cows to be sold, had to be culled from the herd and kept in holding pens. The roundup and sale would take about four weeks to complete, and the normal, daily chores had to be kept up as well during that time.

The weather remained constant with sunny days and cool nights. October began its parade across the mountain slopes in costumes of gold, rust, and crimson. This was normally Rebecca's favorite time of year, when the hills were dressed in radiant hues. She relished the brisk morning air and the exhilaration of working outdoors amid the changing colors. But this year, beset with so many problems and worries, she found little enjoyment in the season.

To Rebecca's surprise, Rachel acted promptly on her sister's request to come out to the ranch. She arrived a week after Rebecca mailed her the letter. Rachel was waiting for her when Rebecca returned to the ranch house after a full day of working with the cattle. She stepped out of the house as Rebecca reined her gelding into the yard. "What is so urgent that you needed me here at once?" were Rachel's first words.

"It's good to see you, too," Rebecca responded with a wry smile as she climbed down from the saddle. Holding the horse's reins, she went to Rachel and gave her a hug. She could smell the faint scent of rosewater that Rachel always dabbed into her hair. "I'm glad you're here. Thank you for coming so quickly."

Rebecca tied her gelding to the hitching post, and she and Rachel went inside.

"Tell me what the trouble is," Rachel said as she closed the door behind them.

"I need to talk over some matters with you," Rebecca replied. "But first let me fix you something to eat. You must be hungry and tired from your trip." She led the way into the kitchen.

"I am. It's a long ride in the buggy from Draper." Rachel carefully seated herself on a kitchen chair so as not to wrinkle her blue velveteen dress.

Rebecca set about preparing some supper for her sister. As she removed a plate of left-over chicken from the icebox, she glanced at Rachel. The blue frock her sister had on was slim-fitting with billowy sleeves and ornamental stitching on the collar and cuffs. The dress was stylish, but impracticable for wear on the ranch; Rebecca hoped her sister had brought along clothing suitable for riding and working.

"How many cattle did you lose to the blackleg?" Rachel asked as Rebecca set the chicken and a plate of biscuits on the table in front of her.

"About ten percent of the herd." Rebecca sat down opposite her sister. "Papa had an emergency fund saved, and I was planning to buy more cattle with it before market."

"Do you think that's wise? Perhaps we should hold on to that cash." Rachel bit into a biscuit she'd stuffed with chicken and cheese.

"Well, it's too late now," Rebecca said dispiritedly. "All the money is gone. It was stolen."

"What?" Rachel exclaimed. She set down the sandwich. "Stolen? What do you mean?"

"Just what I said. After I discovered it was missing, I sent you the letter."

"Maybe you just misplaced it, Rebecca. Have you searched the house?"

"Yes, and I didn't misplace it. It was in the quart jar where Papa always stored it in the bottom drawer of the desk. When I went to get it, the jar was there, but empty."

Rachel leaned back in her chair and briefly closed her eyes. "This is terrible. How did it happen?"

"Someone must have come into the house while I wasn't here and took it. It's just that simple," she answered glumly.

"Who do you think did it?"

"I don't know."

"One of the ranch hands?" Rachel suggested.

Rebecca shrugged her shoulders. "Possibly."

"What are you going to do now?" Rachel asked after a moment of silence.

"I was thinking of trying to get a loan."

"From a bank?"

"Yes. Or a personal loan. Do you have any savings you might lend me, Rachel? I'd return the amount immediately with interest after selling the cattle at market."

"Me?" Rachel almost laughed. "I barely have enough each month to keep my room in the city. The only savings I have is to buy my next meal."

Rebecca tried not to let her disappointment show. She had been hoping Rachel would help her secure the money she needed. "Do you know anyone who might lend us the money?"

Rachel bit her lip, pondering the question. "Maybe Judson."

"Judson?" A fractured image flashed through her mind of Judson entering the house and stealing her cash from the quart jar. "No," Rebecca replied hastily. "Don't mention it to Judson. Let me think about the matter for a while first."

"All right, but not too long. The ranch is half my inheritance, too. I'd prefer to simply sell it and split the money."

Rebecca put her chin in her hands, mulling over the problem. When she raised her gaze to look at Rachel, another thought came into her mind. "Rachel, did you give Papa's pocketwatch to Judson?"

Rachel's eyes narrowed as she stared at her sister. "It was mine to do with as I pleased, wasn't it?"

"Yes. But I hoped you'd want to save it as a keepsake."

Rachel didn't reply. Instead, she shifted in her chair and took another bite from her sandwich.

"So did you or not?"

"Yes, I gave it to him. And he was pleased with it."

Rebecca's heart sank. The watch, a precious family heirloom, was gone, resting in the pocket of someone who'd never even met her father. Someone who might even be a thief. She lapsed into silence.

Rachel finished her sandwich and wiped her fingers on a napkin. "You didn't eat anything. Aren't you hungry?" she said to Rebecca.

Rebecca shook her head. "No, I'm too tired to eat."

"You should let the men handle the roundup. I don't know why you think you have to be out there with them."

"We're shorthanded as it is. That's part of the reason why I asked you to come to the ranch. I hoped you could take care of chores around the house and yard while I'm helping with the cattle."

A frown wrinkled Rachel's nose. "I can't stay here for more than a few days. I have my job in town."

"I know," Rebecca replied. "But even a couple of days would be helpful."

Rachel folded her arms and looked closely at her sister. "Is there something else bothering you?"

Rebecca stared into her lap. "Yes, there is. I'm having trouble with one of the ranch hands and don't know quite how to handle it."

"What kind of trouble?" Rachel asked, leaning forward in her chair.

Rebecca told her about the incident with Jake Baxter at the dance in Draper four weeks earlier. "Ever since then, he's become more brazen."

"You should have let him go immediately," Rachel said, her voice filled with indignation and her green eyes flashing.

"I know I should have. But the roundup was nearing, and I needed every hand."

"You're going to have to deal with Jake sooner or later. There's no telling what a man like that might do next."

"I don't think he'll try anything with Micah here."

"Well, Micah isn't always on the premises, Rebby. If you don't get rid of Jake until after the roundup, you'd better take extra precautions when you're here alone."

Rebecca nodded, feeling the hair along her arms prickle.

Rachel pushed her empty plate away. "I wish you'd reconsider the idea of selling the ranch and moving to Salt Lake City with me."

Rebecca ignored her remark. Rising from her chair, she reached for Rachel's plate. "Are you finished with this?"

Rachel nodded. "Think about what I've said, Rebby. We could have a nice time together in the city without the strain of worrying about the ranch."

Rebecca took her sister's plate and walked to the sink with it. Selling the Double K and moving in with Rachel would be a last resort. She was grateful to have her sister here for a few days, but she wondered if Rachel would be much help in solving the problems facing her.

CHAPTER FOURTEEN

The next morning Rachel joined Rebecca and the ranch hands in riding up into the hills to gather and pen the cattle in the high pastures. As the sun peaked in the sky, Rachel began to complain about the heat, the dust, and the wind. "When are we going back to the house, Rebecca? I'm hot and dusty."

"When we're through here."

Rachel pulled her horse up short. "I am through. I'm going back down."

Rebecca sighed in defeat. "All right, I'll go with you. We can help with chores in the yard."

Rachel turned her horse around with Rebecca following suit. "How do you stand all this dust? It gets in your eyes and throat." Rachel started coughing and sputtering to make her point.

"Why don't you stop complaining and enjoy the scenery while we work?" Rebecca suggested. "Look at the colors draping the hills."

Rachel made a hasty glance around. "It looks the same as it does every fall."

"But you haven't been here for the last two autumns. Haven't you missed seeing the changing colors of the leaves?" Rebecca asked, trying to coax her sister into a lighter mood.

"I can see the mountains just fine from my room in the city. And I took a buggy ride into the canyon shortly before I came here."

Rebecca reined Onyx along a dirt trail leading back to the house with Rachel following beside her on one of the ranch horses. "Did you go with Judson on the buggy ride?"

"Judson? No, it was another fellow with whom I'm acquainted."

Rebecca was surprised to hear this detail. "I thought you and Judson were courting."

"We have been." With the reins in one hand, Rachel fussed with the angle of her straw hat with the other. "Don't you ever get tired of this work?" she grumbled.

Rebecca shot her sister a sideways glance. She'd noticed that Rachel hadn't said much about Judson during her visit. Whenever Rebecca had raised the subject, Rachel evaded any comment. Rebecca wondered why her sister didn't seem to want to talk about him. "Of course I get tired sometimes. And discouraged. But I just can't quit because I'm uncomfortable. I have responsibilities here."

Rachel grunted her disapproval and jabbed her heels into her horse's flanks. The animal lunged ahead into a trot. Dust swirled up from the horse's hooves as it moved across the bare ground.

Rebecca urged her own gelding to quicken its gait. As the two horses trotted down the hilly slope, Rebecca dismissed the topic of Judson and Rachel from her mind and focused instead on the splendor around her. The fall colors looked like a woven Indian rug spread out on the mountainsides. The leaves on the aspens were as yellow as lemons and the brush dotting the slopes looked like fat pumpkins. Rebecca thought the scene was prettier than a picture postcard. The sisters had no further conversation until they came within sight of the ranch house. "You can go inside while I unsaddle the horses," Rebecca said.

"All right. I'll start some lunch."

When they reached the yard, Rachel dismounted and handed the reins to Rebecca, then she headed toward the house. Rebecca led the two horses into the barn and removed their saddles and bridles. Filling the feedboxes with a few handfuls of grain, she brushed both of them with a soft-bristled brush while they munched on their oats; then giving Onyx a final pat on the rump, she left the barn. When she walked out into the corral, she found Jake Baxter there hefting a saddle onto his horse. He turned at the sound of her approaching footsteps. From his expression, Rebecca knew she'd startled him.

"Afternoon. Didn't see you ride in, Miss Kade. Are you finished up for the day?"

Rebecca paused beside Jake's horse. It was a lean, muscular gelding, its coat the color of nutmeg. "No, not yet. Micah and the others are still out gathering the strays."

"Sounds like things are goin' along all right. I just came in from the north pasture. Found a few steers there and drove them to the pen." Jake's eyes darted to his horse. He fumbled with the girth strap he was fastening.

Rebecca stroked the gelding's neck. "You've been keeping the horses in good condition."

Jake cinched the strap tight. "Just doin' my job."

His words and actions seemed more hurried than usual, Rebecca thought as she watched him tighten the saddle strap. Although she usually tried to avoid contact with him, she lingered this time, her suspicions aroused by his behavior. "We'll need to finish harvesting the grain soon. I think we'll have a good crop of hay," she said, deliberately detaining him.

Jake nodded. Finished with saddling his mount, he grasped the horse's reins in hand. "I'll be headin' out now. Got chores to do."

Rebecca noticed a nervous twitch at the corners of his mouth. Jake was uneasy about something and anxious to escape her.

"I'm gonna check on the stock," he said as he prepared to climb into the saddle.

It was then her eyes fell on the polished, gleaming leather saddle. She started in surprise. "Jake, is that a new saddle you have?" she asked brusquely.

He glanced at the shiny leather. "Naw. I've had it a while," he mumbled. He quickly stepped into the stirrup.

"Wait a minute," she commanded, putting a hand on the seat of the saddle before he could swing into it. "This isn't the saddle you've always had. This saddle is as shiny as a new penny. When did you get this, Jake? And how did you pay for it?" she demanded, her voice rising.

"That ain't none of your concern," he said. He stood across from her on the opposite side of the horse, his eyes threatening her.

Rebecca refused to be intimidated by him. "I know for a fact you could never afford a saddle like this one, especially before your wages have been paid. Where did you get the money for it?" Rebecca was seething with silent fury. She suspected the new saddle was purchased with *her* money, stolen from the quart jar.

"I won the saddle in a card game. Lucky streak," he snarled. "And I don't care a whole lot for your insinuation."

Rebecca grasped the horse's bridle. "There's no insinuation intended," she rasped, anger boiling inside her. "The fact is you bought this saddle with money you stole from us, didn't you?"

"You're way too mouthy for a lady," Jake spat. He leaned over the saddle, his breath hot on Rebecca's face. "Someone needs to take you down a notch or two."

Rebecca felt like a volcano ready to explode. "You're fired," she said through clenched teeth. "Take your gear and get off my land."

Jake's eyes blazed. "You're makin' a mistake you'll come to regret, missy," he hissed. He swung into the saddle, shot her a dark look, then dug his spurs into his horse's sides. If she hadn't jumped aside, his horse would have trampled her in response to the savage spurring Jake gave it.

Rebecca entered the house fuming. She stomped into the kitchen where Rachel was setting a bowl of soup on the table.

"What's wrong? You look as if you're ready to strangle someone," Rachel said, putting her hands on her hips.

"I am. And Jake Baxter's throat is just the right size."

"Jake's giving you more problems?"

"I'm almost positive it was Jake who stole Papa's savings."

Rachel's brows lifted in surprise. "What makes you think so?"

"Because he's just low enough and mean enough to do it. And he has a brand new, expensive saddle on his horse." Rebecca's shoulders were heaving with emotion. "I wish I could get my hands on him."

Rachel pulled a chair out from the table for her sister. "Sit down and we'll figure out what to do about him."

Rebecca huffed into the chair. "I already did something about him. I fired him."

"Good for you," Rachel proclaimed. "You did the right thing."

"I think so." She paused, considering the consequences. "We won't have a wrangler for the horses now."

"We'll make do with the ranch hands we have."

Rebecca frowned, hoping she hadn't been too hasty in letting Jake go. Perhaps she should have waited until after market to fire Jake. And she owed him money for his work on the ranch. Normally, a ranch hand would receive his wages after the sale of the cattle at market, but she suspected Jake would ask for his before moving on. And she had no money to pay him.

For the rest of the afternoon Rebecca worked alongside the ranch hands on the range, gathering the cattle. Jake didn't make an appearance all day, but after supper he rapped at the kitchen door. "I'm here to collect my pay," he growled when Rebecca answered his knock. The cowhand's eyes were red and bleary, and his breath smelled of whiskey.

"You know I don't have any money to pay you until after market," she said sharply. "I believe you already have all my money anyway." Jake's bulky form seemed to fill the whole doorway. Rebecca felt a shiver cut through her; she kept her eyes locked on the cowhand's face.

"I didn't take no money. I told you already, I won that saddle in a card game."

"As soon as I get the cattle sold, I'll give you your wages. You come back then. But until that time, you stay off my property," Rebecca said sternly.

"You ain't gonna have no extra money to pay wages after market, what with losin' a tenth of your herd," Jake snapped. "You let me stay on until then, and after we settle up, I'll be clearin' out."

"No. I want you out now." Rebecca saw his eyes narrow into an angry slit, and he took one step across the threshold toward her. Her heart quickened with fear.

"I believe my sister told you to get off our land," came a sudden voice from behind Rebecca's shoulder. She turned to find Rachel standing there, holding their father's loaded shotgun.

Jake's eyes slid to Rachel. A scornful smile parted his lips, revealing crooked teeth. "It don't make no difference what you two say. I'm entitled to my wages. And I want 'em right now."

"If you press the issue, Jake, I'll get the sheriff to step in. I believe I could convince him that you're a liar and a thief," Rebecca vowed.

Jake wiped his brow with his sleeve. "I come here askin' for a fair shake. You fire me for no good reason, then you refuse to pay what you owe me," he said, his voice almost a whine. "How am I supposed to get by with no job and no money?"

"I'm sure you'll find a way," Rachel responded in a scathing tone.

Jake ignored her and turned to Rebecca. "If you'd be agreeable, the two of us could put our heads together. Figure out some plan to make a profit. I got a lot of experience when it comes to ranchin'. You and me could—"

Rebecca cut him off with a wave of her hand. "I have no intention of ever associating with you again. But I won't cheat you out of your wages. You know that." Rebecca's distaste for him was overwhelming. "You get off my place now. I'll have Micah pay you as soon as we get our money from the sale of the cattle."

"You heard her," Rachel added. "Don't come around here any more."

Jake glared at them both, then cursing under his breath he turned and stalked off.

Rebecca watched until he was swallowed up in the darkness, then she closed the door and bolted it, chills tumbling down her spine. "He's the most odious man I've ever met," she said, turning to Rachel.

Rachel bit her lip. "I'm afraid you've made an enemy. A man doesn't take kindly to being spurned."

Rebecca shivered, feeling a cold sense of dread. She walked back to the table and sat down without speaking. Well acquainted with Jake's character, she knew he was capable of doing almost anything.

The exchange with Jake Baxter left Rebecca feeling jittery. She had a hard time falling asleep that night, and in the morning the gloom she felt still hovered over her like a black thundercloud. Jake had taken his things from the bunkhouse and left. Micah didn't say much when Rebecca told him about her conversation with Jake and the fact that she'd fired him from the ranch; he merely raised one eyebrow and nodded his head as if to confirm that she'd taken the right course of action.

Jake's departure, however, left them shorthanded. Rebecca tried to take up the slack and enlisted her sister's help as well. Rachel grumbled about being saddled with chores, but to Rebecca's relief, she carried them out. Rachel stayed for two days longer than she'd planned, then left the ranch on Thursday to return to Salt Lake City.

A few days afterward as Rebecca tumbled into bed exhausted and sore from a full day's work, she lay on her back staring at the ceiling. Unable to sleep, the problems associated with the ranch weighed on her mind. Finally, she threw back the quilt and got up. Putting a robe over her nightgown and slippers on her feet, she tread quietly out to the parlor. She needed something to take her mind off her worries.

Switching on the coal oil lamp, she went to the small bookcase in the corner of the room and let her fingers wander over the spines of the books on the shelf. Her father's cattle magazines and almanacs were mixed in with copies of *The Adventures of Huckleberry Finn* and *The Prince and the Pauper*. Mark Twain had been her father's favorite author ever since Susannah had given him a copy of *Roughing It* before the two of them were married. It had been the first book written by Twain he'd ever read, and Rebecca suspected that his affinity for that particular author stemmed from Susannah's gift.

Susannah's books were also on the shelf; novels by Charles Dickens, Henry James, and Louisa May Alcott, along with assorted magazines such as *Scribner's Monthly* and *Ladies Home Journal*. Susannah had been a woman of culture and refinement who loved reading and learning. She'd worked at her father's book shop on Main Street in Salt

Lake City until she'd married Ethan; Rebecca remembered visiting the shop when she was younger. Her Grandfather Hamilton was dead now, and the book shop sold, but she still carried a tender spot in her heart for the building in town where it had been housed. Susannah had often read to her young daughters. Even after Rebecca could read for herself, she loved listening to her mother read aloud. The soft, lyrical sound of her mother's voice caressing the words still shimmered in her memory.

Rebecca's fingers paused at a slim volume of poetry written by the reclusive poetess Emily Dickinson. Miss Dickinson's book, entitled *Poems*, had been published posthumously only a few years earlier. Rachel had given her a copy of the book of verse last Christmas as a gift, and it had quickly become one of Rebecca's favorites. She took the book from the shelf and thumbed through its well-worn pages, pausing to read a line here and a stanza there. Taking the book with her to the couch, she snuggled in and began to read some of her best liked poems.

Perhaps it was the filmy light given off by the lamp that caused Rebecca at first to ignore the hazy glare outside the window. Thinking it was a lantern's light causing the glowing, orange illumination, she dismissed it and continued to read. But when the orange light flared into a sudden tongue of flame, Rebecca leaped from the couch and rushed to the window. She gasped as she stared out at flames shooting from the roof of the barn. Crying out in horror, she bolted from the house still dressed in her robe and slippers, shouting to the sleeping ranch hands for help. As she sped toward the barn, she saw flames spurting from the roof and heard the horses trapped inside shrieking in terror. The whole sky above the barn was lit up with an orange glow, and embers were drifting through the air. When Rebecca reached the burning building, she threw open the door, ready to dash inside, but the billowing, black smoke was so thick that it drove her back. She coughed, the smoke burning her throat and eyes.

Inside the barn were four horses locked in their stalls, and Onyx was among them. She heard their frantic whinnying and their hooves clattering against the floor in their panicked efforts to break free. Tears surged to her eyes as she searched for something to hold over her mouth and nose so she could pierce the smoke and rescue the horses.

Tearing off her robe, she doused it in the water trough standing inside the corral, then hooded it over her head and darted inside the burning structure. The heat was intense, stifling her breath and searing her throat. She cried out in fear, stumbling forward through the smoke and heat. Flames shot up along the back wall of the barn and onto the roof. Feeling blindly, she inched her way along the stalls until she reached the one where Onyx was confined. She fumbled with the latch, unable to see anything in the suffocating smoke. The fire crackled around her, but over its noise she could hear the cries of the ranch hands outside the barn.

Finally, she managed to unlatch the bar and yank open the stall door. But instead of dashing out of the stall to safety, Onyx reared and clawed the smoke-filled air with his hooves. The horse was crazed with fright. He thrashed against the stall in a wild panic, and Rebecca heard the wood splintering. From the other stalls, the horses' terrified cries clanged in her ears. In an act of desperation, she used her robe to flail at Onyx, trying to drive him out of the fiery maelstrom.

"Rebecca! Rebecca! Get out of there!"

She couldn't be sure if it was Micah's voice she heard screaming out to her or the roaring fire thundering in her ears. In the sea of sound and heat and flames, she heard a creaking and cracking overhead. Instinctively, she shielded her head with her arms and ducked down just as a burning timber crashed to the floor amid a shower of sparks and flames, clipping her shoulder as it fell. The noise of the crashing timber drove Onyx into frenzied action. He leaped in one flying motion over Rebecca's crouching body, passing so closely that Rebecca felt the whoosh of air over her head and heard his hooves rumbling across the ground as he scrambled out of the barn.

Rebecca sat hunched on the floor of the stall, her head swimming and her lungs aching from drawing in the heat and smoke. As she began struggling to her feet, dazed, she felt strong hands lifting her.

"Come on. We're getting out of here," Micah yelled. He grasped her around the waist and practically carried her out of the stall.

"The other horses! We have to save the horses!" she cried as Micah propelled her toward the barn door.

"There's no time. This place is burning down around our heads."

The horrifying screams of the horses trapped in their stalls echoed in her ears as Micah steered her out of the barn. Tears coursed down her bruised cheeks.

"Are you all right?" Micah shouted as he and Rebecca emerged from the burning barn.

Coughing and wheezing in an effort to clear the smoke from her lungs, Rebecca clutched Micah's arm to steady herself. Her shoulder, where the flaming timber had struck her, throbbed with pain. Her throat hurt with every breath so that she could barely speak. With tears streaming down her cheeks, she nodded in answer to Micah's question. One of the ranch hands threw a blanket around her trembling shoulders, and she hugged it tightly against her. With Micah's arm supporting her, she stared in horrified disbelief at the orange flames spitting into the night sky.

The other cowhands stood together outside the corral watching the inferno. No one spoke. The only voices were the frightened bellowing of the cattle in their pens. The air was filled with choking smoke, the roar of flames, and the crashing of timbers as they collapsed in an eerie red glow of sparks and cinder. The agonizing sound of the dying horses trapped inside the barn reverberated through the darkness.

CHAPTER FIFTEEN

At first light Rebecca arose, dressed, and quickly left the house. Alone in the yard, she held her breath as she approached the carnage of the night before. Nothing was left of the barn but a skeleton of black, charred timbers. The smell of smoke still hung in the air, and its stench was strong in Rebecca's nostrils. Her gaze took in the scorched ground and the buckets that had been filled with water and left haphazardly when the cowhands ceased their fruitless efforts to put out the fire.

While Rebecca had rescued Onyx, the cowhands had managed to save only one of the other horses in the barn. A mare and her foal had perished in the blaze. The flames had shot 15 to 20 feet into the air, a frightening spectacle that must have been seen for miles around. Tears sprang to Rebecca's eyes as she recalled the scene, and she was nearly overcome with despair. This loss signaled the end of all her hopes and struggles to keep the ranch afloat. She knew she could not recover from it, either financially or emotionally. Tears slid down her cheeks unchecked as she began sifting through the debris to see if there was anything left to salvage. As she walked slowly through the charred remains, her spirits sunk even lower.

She hadn't been at the task long before Micah emerged from the bunkhouse and walked over to join her. He carried his hat in his hand, and his gray hair was rumpled from the few hours of sleep he'd gotten. "You should be in bed, nursing that shoulder," he said gruffly.

She dashed the tears from her eyes so Micah wouldn't see them. "I'm all right. My shoulder is sore and bruised, but I don't think there are any broken bones."

Micah squinted at her out of piercing blue eyes. "I'm going into town to fetch the doc. Let him be the judge of how badly that shoulder is injured."

"That's not necessary, Micah. I'm fine." She moved her arm at the shoulder, demonstrating its agility, but the movement made her wince with pain. The shoulder had hurt all night. Every time she'd turned over in bed onto it, she'd awakened with a jolt of pain shooting through her.

"It was downright foolish of you to go dashing inside that burning building. You could have been killed as likely as not," he scolded.

"I wasn't thinking of anything else but getting the horses out. I thought I could do it before the fire got too bad."

"I reckon we were lucky, losing only the one mare and her foal."

Rebecca nodded, not trusting her voice to speak.

"How is the black this morning?"

"I haven't been to check on him yet. The sorrel looked all right last night, some cuts and scratches, but I'm worried about Onyx. He has several deep gashes on his legs and a nasty cut on his withers."

Micah stuffed his hands in his pockets and surveyed the damage around him. "Got any ideas of how the fire started?" he asked, scratching his chin.

"No. Do you?"

"Nope. Not till I sniff around a bit."

"Maybe a lantern tipped over. Or perhaps a strike of lightning started it. Rain was threatening when I went to bed last night."

"Maybe." Micah kicked at a pile of ash with his boot.

"Rummage through what you can, Micah. I'll be in the corral tending to the two horses."

When Rebecca reached the corral where her gelding and the sorrel were secured, she found Onyx standing listlessly with his nose against the fence. The sorrel was browsing the sparse grass inside the enclosure. As Rebecca approached, the black gelding lifted his head and looked at her.

"Easy, boy," Rebecca crooned. She walked up to the horse and slipped her arm around his neck. She stroked the coarse mane, black as coal, and rubbed Onyx's velvety nose. "How are you feeling, boy?" she murmured.

She ran her hand over the gelding's back and down his haunches. The horse twitched when her hand came near the jagged, deep gash on his rump.

"You're going to be fine," she said to the animal. She studied the wound as Onyx switched his tail nervously. Last night, before she'd stumbled into bed after the fire, she'd washed the horse's wounds and applied medicating salve on the cuts and scrapes. But the long, jagged tear in Onyx's hide was crusted with dried blood, evidence that it had still bled even after her ministrations.

She felt along Onyx's right front foreleg, all the while talking soothingly to the animal. Cuts and patches of swollen flesh materialized under her probing fingers, and there were areas where the hair was singed or burned away. Although the gelding had suffered serious injuries in his desperate attempt to escape the stall when the fire erupted, Rebecca felt grateful that he hadn't perished along with the other two horses. She rested her cheek against Onyx's broad, muscular neck and stroked his head. With her nose pressed against the horse's skin, she could smell the lingering scent of smoke permeating his coat.

She spent the next hour attending to the gelding's wounds. The deep cut on the horse's foreleg had her worried. This morning, Onyx wasn't putting any weight on his front leg. She led him by his halter in a circle around the corral, studying the leg as he walked, but the horse was unmistakably limping. Rebecca was afraid that the gash along the front part of his foreleg might be more serious than she'd first thought. After tending to Onyx, she spent a few minutes with the sorrel, checking the severity of his wounds. The reddish-brown colored horse seemed to be recovering well.

When she was finished nursing both horses, she left the corral and went to the pens holding the cattle to check on them as well. While she was at the cattle pens, Micah joined her.

"Look what I found in the rubble," he said, a scowl planted between his brows.

Rebecca stared at the gallon can he held up for her to see. "What is it?"

"Take a whiff," Micah replied, moving the can under her nose.

Although the can was empty, pungent fumes from its previous contents caused Rebecca to jerk back and wrinkle her nose. "What is that smell? Some kind of paint?"

"Turpentine. I found the discarded can behind a bush a few yards from the barn."

Rebecca's gaze slid again to the battered can, then back to Micah's face. "What are you saying?"

"I think we've found who—or rather what—fueled the fire."

Rebecca's eyes bulged. "You think the fire was deliberately set? Who would do such a thing?"

"Someone who has a grudge against the Double K, I'd wager," Micah growled.

Jake Baxter's sneering face sprang to Rebecca's mind. Jake was the only person who had something to gain by trying to destroy Rebecca and the ranch. Revenge. She gritted her teeth. "I think we ought to get the sheriff, Micah."

"I doubt one turpentine can is going to be enough evidence for the sheriff to arrest anybody," Micah grumbled. "But it pinpoints the origin of that fire in my mind."

"Yes. Mine, too," Rebecca responded. She wanted to see Jake Baxter behind bars for setting the fire, as well as for stealing her money; she felt sure he was guilty of both crimes. Although her parents had taught her that it was wrong to harbor hatred and malice in her heart, she found it difficult to purge those emotions when it came to Jake Baxter.

The next day while Micah and the ranch hands began clearing away the debris from the fire, Rebecca prepared to drive into Draper to buy supplies for the ranch. The fire in the barn had destroyed the grain kept in the feed stall and the hay the cowhands had harvested and stored in the loft; but, thankfully, Andrus had pulled the saddles, blankets, and bridles from the tack room before it went up in flames. She made an inventory of the losses, then hitched a pair of the ranch horses to the buckboard and set out for town.

The day was warm and mild, and autumn was in the air with its particular smells of harvesting and reaping. As she drove, she passed fields thick with golden stalks of grain. She could smell the sweet scent of ripe apples, the fragrance of blooming flowers, and the earthy smell of the soil. She settled deeper into the wagon seat, breathing in the October air and trying to dispel the horrors of the night before last. Her shoulder ached with each bounce and lurch of the wagon, reminding her continually of the losses she'd just sustained.

When she reached Draper, she reined the team to the mercantile to purchase the supplies. After securing the reins to the hitching post, she stepped inside the two-story building housing the Rideout General Merchandise Store. The upper floor was where she had attended the dance a few weeks earlier. David O. Rideout had built his store and dance hall a dozen years ago, in 1883, an enterprise that proved so successful that he'd recently constructed a frame addition on the north end of the building.

The big, open room was crowded with merchandise. Customers milled around long tables laden with items of wearing apparel; shelves weighed down with dry goods; and fat-bodied barrels heaping with nails and hinges and bolts. Rebecca passed a display of ready-made shoes and ladies' hats. She stopped to glance at a woman's tailor-made suit priced at $12.95. The jacket was sewn with balloon sleeves from the shoulders to the elbows and then snuggly fitted to the wrist with six big black buttons sitting two abreast down the front. For an instant, she imagined herself dressed in the stylish outfit, then smiled wryly at her own vanity. On a nearby shelf she saw a collection of kid gloves marked for sale at 90 cents. On display were shawls and capes at a discounted price, selling from $1.50 for a plain, short cloak to $7.00 for a fashionable shawl. There were laces and embroideries, flannels and silks, and shiny buttons. Rebecca eyed them all, then reluctantly moved on.

She walked to the shelves filled with dry goods, coffee and spices in tins, boxes of tea, five-pound sacks of sugar and flour. She selected some of these items and put them in her shopping basket. She added a few cans of baked beans and canned fruit, then paused to scan the opposite shelf with its bottles of hair tonic for men and sweet-smelling rosewater for ladies. These rested alongside pills, powders, and syrups—remedies for coughs, indigestion, rheumatism, and other ailments. As she was about to make her way toward the hardware section at the rear of the store, she caught sight of a young woman with curly hair straightening the items on the shelves. The stock girl had her back to Rebecca, but Rebecca easily identified her. "Lettie. Hello, there."

The curly-haired young woman turned her head, her hands still shuffling the products lining the shelves. "Rebby! How nice to see you!" She hurried to Rebecca's side and gave her a hug. "How are you?"

"Getting along. And you?" Rebecca replied, pleased to see her friend.

"Same as always," Lettie answered, following her comment with a giddy, carefree laugh.

"Still working at the store, I see."

Lettie gestured to the shelves of goods behind her. "Yes. My job is to keep the shelves full for the customers."

Rebecca saw the shine of pride in her friend's lively, blue eyes. "How do you like it?" she asked.

"I enjoy it, actually. So many people come in, and I get a chance to visit with them." She squeezed Rebecca's arm. "How are you getting along since I saw you last at the dance?"

Rebecca told her briefly about the fire.

"Oh, that's terrible!" Lettie's brow wrinkled with a worried frown. "What are you going to do?"

"I don't know yet. I wish Papa was still alive to make that decision. Running the ranch without him has been difficult."

Lettie's expression was sympathetic. "Perhaps you should hire a man to come out and help you with it," she suggested.

"I have Micah, the foreman. He's my right hand."

"What about a young man of your own age?" Lettie asked. Her brown, slender brows lifted slightly. "A good-looking, young man with money in his pocket."

"What do you mean?" Rebecca asked.

Lettie giggled her little trilling laugh. "A husband, silly. A husband to help you with the ranch and comfort you in front of the fire in the evenings."

"Oh."

"I aim to find myself a husband. It may be that I'll meet him right here in the mercantile." Lettie glanced around the room, as if she were searching at that moment for a candidate. "But I'm picky. And you should be, too."

Rebecca couldn't keep a grin from surfacing. "Picky, huh? How do you mean?"

"Oh, you know," Lettie said with a wave of her hand. "He should be handsome of face and figure and charming in manner. And kind, of course. And well situated. I aim to marry a man of substance," she concluded.

Rebecca chuckled. "I wish you luck in that endeavor, Lettie. As for myself, I'm not interested in marrying. Not yet, anyway."

From far down the row of shelves came a woman's booming voice. "Miss Miller. I believe you have work to do, do you not?"

Both Lettie and Rebecca turned to look at the heavy-set woman with the scowling face standing at the end of the aisle. Her iron-gray hair was done up in a bun, the hair pulled back so tightly that the edges of her face puckered. She stood with her feet planted firmly apart, her hands on her hips, and an apron tied around her ample waist, staring sternly at Lettie.

"Yes, ma'am," Lettie answered meekly. Lettie returned to her work, but not before giving Rebecca a sly grin and whispering in her ear, "That's old Mrs. Snowden, the manager. She tattles to Mr. Rideout if I'm not working my fingers to the bone every moment."

Rebecca turned away, chuckling to herself. She had no doubt that Lettice Miller was a great source of trial to Mrs. Snowden. It was hard to keep an irrepressible spirit like Lettie's under control. And yet that was the thing Rebecca liked best about her friend—Lettie's vibrant personality and sunny nature.

Rebecca started again for the back of the store where the hardware and farm supplies were kept. She selected two coal oil lanterns to replace the ones lost in the barn fire and a new curry comb for the horses, then headed up front to pay for her groceries. She got in line at the counter behind a young mother with two small children clinging to her skirts. One of them, a little girl with curly, blonde hair who looked to be about four years old, gave Rebecca a shy smile. Rebecca smiled back at her. She almost envied the young woman who had hold of the little girl's hand. Although she had told Lettie only moments before that she wasn't interested in marrying, she wanted a husband and children one day. The small girl in front of her ducked behind her mother's skirt and peeped out at Rebecca from its folds. Rebecca could almost imagine being the one who bent down to gently take her little daughter's hand, place a soft kiss atop her blonde head, and press her close against her knee.

When at last it was Rebecca's turn at the cash register, she set down her basket of items onto the counter in front of the clerk. It was the same middle-aged man behind the counter as the last time when she'd come into the mercantile. She flushed remembering her conversation with him about her father's store account. This time, however, he said nothing to her about it, just rang up her purchases then reached under the counter for his ledger book and penciled in the amount owing. As she waited for him to finish, her eyes strayed to the array of hard candies nestled in glass-fronted drawers behind the counter. The candies sparkled like jewels in a crystal case. Although she couldn't afford the treat, she asked the clerk to get her a small bag full and paid for it with the few coins she had in her handbag.

When she stepped outside the store with her purchases, she spied the young mother with her two children waiting beside their buckboard while the stock boy loaded her groceries. The little girl turned to glance at her out of round, blue eyes just as Rebecca reached into her sack for a piece of candy. Rebecca paused and smiled at the girl, then she approached her mother. "May the children each have a piece of candy? I just purchased it from the store," she added. "I was standing in line at the counter behind you."

The woman's face broke into a friendly smile. "Certainly. And thank you."

Rebecca bent down in front of the girl and opened the sack. "Would you like a candy? You may choose whichever one you want."

The young girl's eyes widened as she looked from Rebecca to the sack of candy, then she thrust her little hand into the bag, fingered through the lot, and withdrew a shiny, red peppermint drop. She smiled at Rebecca and popped the morsel into her mouth. The girl's older brother edged closer for his treat. She held the sack open for him. Plunging his hand into the bag with gusto, he quickly drew it out again clutching a licorice-flavored sweet.

"Tell the lady thank you," their mother directed.

"Thank you," they chorused in unison.

"You're very welcome." Rebecca watched them clamor up into their wagon, sucking happily on their candies. The small act of kindness she'd extended warmed her heart as thoroughly as if she'd distributed gold coins to the poor. She'd been so wrapped up in her own problems and worries over the past few months, that she had neglected even thinking about the concerns of others. She made a decision to mend her ways and look for opportunities to be of service to those around her. That small thought lifted her heart and lightened her burden. Placing the groceries in the wagon bed, she drove to the feed store to purchase some grain for the horses. What hay she had stored in the barn had gone up in flames, but she was grateful there was still another crop in the fields yet to be harvested. When she finished with her shopping, she stopped at the cemetery to sit for a while at her parents' graves.

She arrived back at the ranch an hour and a half later. As she reined the team into the yard, she stared at the unfamiliar horse tied to the hitching post in front of the house. She climbed down the buckboard, and from the periphery of her vision caught sight of a figure on the porch as he rose from the porch chair to meet her.

CHAPTER SIXTEEN

"There you are, Rebby. I've been waiting for you all afternoon," a familiar voice called out.

Rebecca shaded her eyes against the glare of the late afternoon sun as she took a step forward. "Patrick?"

The lanky, young man on the porch started down the steps toward her, wearing a smile. "How are you, cousin?"

"Patrick McKellar! What are you doing here?" She hurried to his side and threw her arms around him in a tight hug.

"Mother sent me to see how you're getting along and to give you a hand with the roundup."

"Oh, it's so wonderful to see you again!" Rebecca exclaimed. "Let me get a good look at you." She stood back and eyed him from head to toe. "I believe you're even taller than when I saw you last. And definitely more handsome," she teased, grinning.

She laughed when she saw his cheeks burn. He shoved his hands into his pockets.

"When did you get here? How long have you been waiting for me to return home?"

"A couple of hours. What happened?" he asked, nodding toward the burned spot where the barn had stood.

Rebecca linked her arm through his as the two of them walked to the barren square of ground. They stood together staring at the charred space. Nothing remained of the barn. Micah and the other ranch hands had torn down the skeletal remnants of the building while Rebecca was in town, and all that was left was a scorched patch of earth. "Night before last the barn caught fire and was completely destroyed. We lost a mare and her foal."

Patrick let out a long, low whistle. "How'd it happen?"

"We're not sure yet," Rebecca answered, avoiding a full explanation for the present. "Are you hungry? Let's go inside, and I'll get you something to eat."

He helped her carry the sacks of groceries from the buckboard into the house, then unhitched the horses while she fixed them both some supper. While they sat together at the table over a sandwich and a bowl of soup, Rebecca asked about his family.

"Everyone is doing well. Busy with the ranch like always," he responded.

"And your brothers?"

"Ornery and lazy as ever."

Rebecca leaned back in her chair and smiled, thinking about Rory and Jessica's five sons. She and Rachel had grown up alongside them on the Double K and shared many pleasant hours.

"Father said that he'd send Wyatt out here, too, if you need more help with the roundup."

Rebecca pictured the McKellars' eldest son. Wyatt was two years older than she and the most handsome of the lot. Rebecca had always liked his wit and humor and had enjoyed being with him when the McKellars had lived on the ranch. She loved all of the boys, however, each for their individual qualities—Rourke with his quiet sensitivity, Bret for his rugged strength and persistence, Gideon because of his lightheartedness and easy-going nature. "I appreciate having you here, Patrick. You arrived at the perfect time. Truthfully, things here at the ranch are not running very smoothly and seeing you gives me such a boost."

Rebecca went on to tell him how difficult it had been to lose her father and then to have to shoulder the responsibility for operating the ranch. She explained about the outbreak of blackleg among the cattle, the theft of her money, and now the fire. She told him about her fears of losing the Double K entirely and the despair she was feeling over the heavy financial burdens. She had just come to the decision this afternoon while driving home from Draper, she related, to sell the ranch as Rachel had urged and salvage what money there was to be made.

Patrick leaned back in his seat, crossing one booted foot over the other. His lanky frame dwarfed the small, kitchen chair. "Father and Mother instructed me to tell you that they are ready to offer any assistance you need. They have a little cash saved that they would be willing to lend you, if necessary, and if you are short of cowhands, Wyatt's also prepared to come out to the ranch and stay as long as you need him."

Gratitude swelled Rebecca's heart. She knew both Wyatt and Patrick were skilled cowhands and cared about the Double K Ranch almost as much as she did. It was not surprising that Jessica and Rory had selected their second-born son to send to her aid. Although Patrick was quiet and unassuming, and more plain-faced than his brothers, he was the most competent, steady, and hard working of any of the McKellar boys. As they sat at the table, she and Patrick discussed various options that might save the ranch from sale or ruin. They talked until late into the evening and by the time Rebecca had gotten her cousin situated in the bunkhouse, she was exhausted from her worries and the constant, wearing pain in her shoulder.

"Don't think about your problems anymore tonight," Patrick suggested as they lingered at the door of the bunkhouse. "We can talk about it some more tomorrow. I'll be up at first light to help with the branding."

She stood on tiptoe to kiss his cheek. "Thank you, Patrick. I can't tell you how grateful I am to have you here. Sleep well."

As she turned to leave, he called to her. "Wait, Rebby. I almost forgot. Mother wanted me to give this to you." He bent down and opened the traveling bag resting at his feet, rummaged through it, and then withdrew an object wrapped in a soft, cotton cloth.

"What is it?" Rebecca asked as she took the parcel from his outstretched hand. She removed the cloth folded around it and then held the object up to the lantern's light to better see it.

"It's a pencil drawing of our Great-Grandmother Kade. I've forgotten her first name," he confessed with a smile.

"I know this picture," Rebecca said softly, holding the framed drawing to the light. Some of the penciled lines were faint and fading, but she could still easily see the lovely portrait drawn on the page. "Your mother showed this to me when I was younger."

"Since my parents have no daughters, only sons—whom Mother says are useless when it comes to appreciating family heirlooms—she wants you to have the drawing. She said she hopes it will remind you of your heritage."

Rebecca stared at the portrait. It showed a young woman with her hair long and loose about her head and a slight smile parting her lips. A feeling of tenderness filled her heart as she gazed at the picture. "Please tell your mother when you return home that I appreciate the gift and will treasure it."

"I will," he nodded. "I'll see you in the morning."

He turned and went inside the bunkhouse. Rebecca gripped the drawing carefully in her hands as she walked back toward the house. The moon was rising in the sky, illuminating her path to the porch. She stared at the pencil portrait as she walked, studying the lines sweeping the page and wondering who had drawn it. The young woman pictured there was pretty; Rebecca wished she knew more about her great-grandmother. Like Patrick, she couldn't recall the woman's given name.

When she got back inside the house, she set the drawing on the kitchen table while she poured herself a glass of milk. Sitting down at the table with her milk, she gazed at the picture as she drank from the glass, trying to remember what her father had told her about his Grandmother Kade. She recalled him saying that his grandmother had lived in Missouri and Nauvoo, Illinois, during the years the Latter-day Saints were so badly persecuted, and that her husband had worked for a newspaper. She turned the drawing toward the light of the coal oil lamp fixed to a bracket on the kitchen wall. The woman drawn on the page seemed to gaze out at her, and her parted lips looked as if she might speak. Rebecca wished she could speak—what stories she would be able to tell!

Rebecca took another sip from her glass, wishing again that she could remember the woman's first name. Was it preserved in any of the papers her father had kept? She stood up and went to her father's desk and searched through all the drawers. Nothing there but ledgers and records dealing with the ranch. She put her hands on her hips and glanced around the room, wondering if there might be a record of her ancestors kept someplace else.

Then her eyes lighted on her parents' copy of the Book of Mormon resting on the mantle above the fireplace. She walked over to the hearth and stared at the book without touching it. She hadn't opened that book ever since her mother had died. Her father had read from it regularly—nearly every evening after he came inside from working with the cattle—but she had made it a point to give the religious book a wide berth.

Now, as she stood there looking at it, she remembered that her father had written down the names of his forebears as far back as he had knowledge of them. She could picture the list in her mind's eye and knew her Great-Grandmother Kade's name would be among those recorded.

Hesitantly, she reached for the book. Memories flooded her mind as she closed her hand around the brown, hardbound cover. Running a fingertip across the printed letters on the spine, she whispered the title—the Book of Mormon. She distinctly remembered the feel of the smooth, stiff pages and the sight of line after line of crowded black print. She recalled hearing her father and mother read aloud from the book and then passing it to Rachel and Rebecca so each of the girls could have a turn reading, too. Then family prayer followed, and afterward the girls were tucked into bed with a kiss and a hug from each parent.

The memories warmed Rebecca's heart and brought solace to her troubled mind. She had forgotten about the feelings of peace that had always seemed to accompany the words of scripture. She had been so focused on blaming herself for her mother's death and so sure of God's displeasure with her, that she had abandoned every outward show of religious activity to punish herself for her heinous action. It felt almost sacrilegious to her now to be handling this sacred book. Even though she had discarded the old patterns of scripture reading, prayer, fasting, and church attendance, she had never been successful in extinguishing the last glimmer of testimony that burned like a flickering candle within her soul. In spite of all her attempts to abandon her religion, she knew that the teachings of the gospel of Jesus Christ, as embodied in this book of scripture she held in her hand, were true. And that knowledge tortured her.

Rebecca's desire to recover the name of her great-grandmother overrode her reluctance to open the book. She carried the volume of scripture to the table and sat down again. Her throat felt dry and her lips parched as she slowly opened the book. The front cover was scuffed and the pages worn from use. At the bottom of the title page, Rebecca read the words: "PALMYRA: PRINTED BY E. B. GRANDIN, FOR THE AUTHOR. 1830." She was surprised by the date of publication; she had not remembered that her family's copy of the book was so old. Perhaps it had belonged to her great-grandparents and passed down through the generations. That thought filled Rebecca with awe.

She slowly turned the first few pages, pausing to read a sentence here and there. The familiar words brought comfort to her heart. She skipped to the last page; opposite it was the page with the heading that read "THE TESTIMONY OF THREE WITNESSES." The next page was titled "AND ALSO THE TESTIMONY OF EIGHT WITNESSES." Turning over the flyleaf at the end of the book, Rebecca held her breath. There it was—the list of ancestral names written in her father's sprawling hand. Beside each name was a date of birth, and some had a date of death recorded as well. Rebecca's breath quickened as she stared at the names.

Beginning at the top of the list, she carefully started with the first name, reading it aloud and following across the page with her finger to the dates printed beside it.

Christian Kade	*born 1808*	*died 1866*
Lydia Ross Dawson Kade	*born 1809*	*died 1862*

Lydia Kade! The name jumped out at her. Yes, now Rebecca remembered her father telling her that his grandmother's given name was Lydia, that she had been baptized into the Church in Independence, Missouri, and married Christian Kade shortly thereafter. Both Lydia and Christian had sacrificed everything they had for the gospel's sake; stripped of their possessions by lawless mobs and driven first from Missouri and then from Illinois, they'd traveled by wagon train to the valley of the Great Salt Lake.

Rebecca's gaze moved to the pencil drawing lying beside the open Book of Mormon. In the twinkling light of the lamp, Lydia's eyes seemed to communicate with her, and her smile appeared to be one of encouragement. Rebecca's heart felt lighter just looking at the likeness of her great-grandmother's face. She turned back to the list of names.

Christian Kade and Lydia Ross Dawson married 1833,
  Jackson County, Missouri
Elizabeth Ann Dawson Kade born 1827   died 1890
James Dawson Kade   born 1829   died 1874
Roxana Jane Kade   born 1836
Millicent Kade   born 1838
Zachary Kade   born 1840   died 1848

Rebecca paused, recalling to mind the stories she'd
heard about her grandfather, James Kade. James had been
a respected doctor and a stalwart member of the Church.
He'd passed away before she was born, however, and she
knew him only through the stories and anecdotes passed
on to her by her father. Rebecca was acquainted with only a
smattering of information about her grandfather's siblings,
except for Elizabeth, who had remained in Nauvoo when
the rest of her family moved west. Elizabeth was Jessica
McKellar's mother, and Jessica had told her a bit about their
family life when she was a child growing up in Nauvoo.
Elizabeth's husband was not a member of the Church,
and Elizabeth had joined another denomination after her
marriage to him. Elizabeth had never reconciled herself to
the Church before her death.

Rebecca skipped down to the last name in the family
group. She paused, wondering about the circumstances of
Zachary's death. From the dates recorded on the page, he
would have been only seven or eight years old. She wished
the record contained details concerning his passing.

Her eyes moved down to the next group of names.

Elizabeth Ann Dawson Kade and Alexander Scott
    married 1846 in Nauvoo, Illinois
Emmaline Scott Wylie   *born 1850*
Jessica Scott McKellar   *born 1854*
Clarissa Scott Ferguson   *born 1856*

Rebecca smiled as she identified the name of her father's cousin, Jessica. She knew that Jessica's older sister, Emmaline, was a member of the Church, but her younger sister, Clarissa, had never joined. Clarissa and her husband still lived in Illinois.

James Kade and Inger Johanssen married 1850 in
    Salt Lake City, Utah
Ethan Niels Kade   *born 1853*
Samuel Anders Kade   *born 1855*
Birgithe Kade Warren   *born 1857*

Rebecca's eyes grew moist as she read her father's name and the names of his younger brother and sister. She recalled Samuel's visit to the ranch soon after Ethan's death, and Birgithe's heartfelt letters of sympathy.

Jessica Scott and Rory McKellar married 1872 in
    Salt Lake City, Utah
Wyatt McKellar   *born 1873*
Patrick McKellar   *born 1875*

Rourke McKellar   born 1878
Bret McKellar   born 1880
Gideon McKellar   born 1883

Rebecca nodded to herself, reading on.

Ethan Niels Kade and Susannah Hamilton married
    1872 in Salt Lake City, Utah
Rachel Susa Kade   born 20 December 1875
Rebecca Ann Kade   born 21 December 1875

Her gaze lingered on the names of her parents, and tears trickled down her cheeks. In her mind, she formed a picture of the two of them. She saw them sitting together at the kitchen table; riding together in the hills near the ranch house; relaxing beside the fire on a winter's night, hand in hand. The memories brought a flood of emotions. Beside her mother's name, Ethan had written the date of her death—23 June 1890. The entry was scribed in a different shade of ink from the rest, attesting to a later notation. Ethan must have added the death date soon after Susannah's passing.

With tears pooling in her eyes, Rebecca went to her father's desk for a pen and a pot of ink. Returning to her place at the table, she dipped the pen into the ink bottle, paused for a moment with the pen poised above the page, and then carefully wrote down beside her father's name the date of his death. When it was done, she laid aside the pen and stared at the entry she'd made. Somehow, that simple act of recording the information made her feel as if she had accomplished something important to preserve her father's memory.

She sat at the table staring at the list of family names for a long time. It had grown late into the evening, and the moon had already traveled high in the heavens. Its light bathed the window, casting a golden glow onto the articles spread on the table. Although it was late and Rebecca was tired, she knew she'd be unable to sleep just yet. She sat motionless for several moments more, pondering and considering. Then drawing a deep breath, Rebecca returned to the first page of the book lying open before her and began to read.

Over the next few days as Patrick McKellar helped Rebecca with the roundup, they discussed different options for keeping the ranch afloat and financially solvent. Together they poured over the financial records and ledger books to assess the losses, determine where they could cut back, and decide which purchases were most critical to the operation of the ranch. The outcome was bleak. Rebecca did not have enough money to get through the next several weeks. In addition to that, the market price for cattle was nearing an all-time low because of the effects of the economic recession of the last year or two, which would yield a poor return on her cattle investment. Rebecca knew that drastic measures needed to be taken if she hoped to hold on to the ranch.

Patrick was the one who suggested the idea at first, although Rebecca had been mulling over the same possibility. "How would you feel about taking a job in town for a few months to supplement your income?" he asked one afternoon as they sat at the kitchen table together. "Wyatt could come out to the Double K to help with the roundup and get the cattle to market. That way you wouldn't have to hire any extra hands for the roundup, and you could be earning money at the same time."

Rebecca chewed on her lip, pondering her cousin's proposal. "Actually, I've been thinking the same thing. But after paying for room and board in town, would I have enough money left to make a difference?"

Patrick rubbed a thumb across his chin. "I think you could earn enough to support yourself and still have a fair sum to use toward operating the ranch."

Rebecca's brow wrinkled with doubt. "What kind of job would I get? I don't have any skills except ranching."

"You take some time to think about it."

Rebecca nodded, considering the possibilities open to her.

Patrick stood up from the chair, ready to return to his chores outdoors. He patted Rebecca's hand. "Do some praying about it. The right answer will come to you." He clamped on his hat and started for the back door.

Rebecca sighed as she watched him go. His suggestion to pray about the problem had been simply and sincerely put forth. It was something Patrick would have done without having to think twice about it. But for Rebecca, finding the courage to offer a prayer after such a long period of deliberate abstinence was a daunting task.

She already suspected, however, that Patrick's unannounced arrival at the ranch at such a critical time was an answer to her heart's unspoken prayer. She sensed that God had been mindful of her needs all along, even though she had not sought Him out. Perhaps He had forgiven her for her part in her mother's death. Her heart had seemed to soften and reshape itself into something new since she'd been reading each night and morning from her parents' Book of Mormon. The faint flame of testimony that had been flickering in her heart seemed to be growing brighter. Whether that last thought was merely her own imagination at work or not, Rebecca drew strength from it.

CHAPTER SEVENTEEN

Judson strode down Fort Street, his eyes focused on the sheet of paper in his hand. He did a quick calculation of the amount of cut lumber he would need for this new order of furniture and the number of hours it would take to build and assemble the pieces. A wealthy sheep rancher in Draper had contacted him the week before to set up an appointment, and Judson had just called on the man at his home to discuss the terms of the agreement. The man was building a new, large, red brick home that would feature railed porches, gingerbread trim, and tall windows. He wanted several pieces of handmade furniture for his parlor and study. He'd requested a mahogany cabinet for his wife's fine china, a cupboard fitted with carved panels, and a matching writing table and bookcase ornamented with columns and carving. It would be the most costly project

Judson had ever undertaken. As he studied the dimensions and specifications, his step quickened with anticipation.

At last, he folded the paper and put it into his pocket, his mind buzzing with plans. He had already decided to stay overnight in Draper in order to compare the price and quality of lumber at a couple of the mills in town. He was always looking for new sources from which to obtain his raw materials in order to construct the best possible product for his customers.

It was only with effort that he forced his thoughts into a different channel. His purpose in coming to Draper had been twofold: to draw up the contract for the furniture and also to follow a lead on Daniel's father provided him by Lorin Stotts. When he'd visited the Blue Fly saloon last evening after work, Lorin had mentioned that he'd been asking his customers if they knew anyone by the name of Solomon Curtis, and finally someone had responded. Lorin had pumped the man for information. What he'd gotten was scarce—but enough to place Solomon Curtis in Draper as of six months ago.

Now as Judson turned his steps toward the town constable's house, his hopes were high. He hadn't mentioned anything to Daniel about the tip; he didn't want to disappoint the young man if the lead ran into a dead end. He'd gotten directions to the constable's home on Fort Street and found the place without difficulty—a small, adobe brick dwelling situated alongside an alfalfa field. In addition to his municipal duties, apparently the constable also farmed. He spotted a bearded man wearing brown denim trousers and a long-sleeved shirt in the field a few rods away, pitching cut hay into the bed of a wagon.

Judson made his way through the harvested furrows until he reached the hay wagon. The clean smell of newly cut hay saturated the air. "Afternoon," he called to the constable.

The man straightened and turned his gaze toward Judson, then waited in silence while Judson approached.

Judson introduced himself and stated his business. "I'm looking for a man by the name of Solomon Curtis who may have passed through here during the last few months. Would you have any way of knowing if he's still in town or where he might have gone?" Judson asked in conclusion.

The constable leaned on his pitchfork, considering. He was a stocky man with big hands and big feet. His cheeks were ruddy from working outdoors in the crisp October air. "Let me do some checking on it for you. Are you staying here in town?"

"I'll be here until tomorrow afternoon."

"Where can I get in touch with you?"

"I'm staying at the hotel up the block. If they have a telephone, you can reach me there. I'm sure someone at the desk could leave a message for me."

The burly constable shook his head. "There's no telephone at that establishment. In fact, there're only a handful of telephones in the whole community. But you'll find one you can use, if you need to, at the Rideout store."

"Where would that be located?"

"Just north of the hotel. It's a big, two-story, brick building. You can't miss it."

"All right, thanks. And I appreciate your looking into the matter for me."

"Glad to help." The constable grasped his pitchfork and returned to his work.

Judson crossed the dusty field and started north up the block toward the store the man had mentioned. He'd introduce himself there, find out if a telephone was available, then nose around town for a bit. An unwelcome thought skittered through his mind—so long as he was this far south, it would be an easy matter to ride out to the Double K to see Rebecca. He quickly squelched that notion. He was determined to forget about Rebecca and direct his attentions to some other girl. He had, in fact, called on a young woman in Salt Lake City a few nights before. But the evening had turned out disappointing for him. Although the girl was pleasant and attractive, he wasn't interested in fostering a relationship with her.

As he walked the few blocks up the road toward the mercantile, he studied the homes lining the streets, and the fields, orchards, and gardens bordering them. A canal carrying muddy, brown water flowed along the edge of the road from which hand-dug channels branched out to irrigate yards and farmlands. In many instances, homes and places of business coexisted along the narrow, straight street; to the east, craggy, wind-swept mountains kept a benign watch over the town. Judson drew in a deep breath, feeling the brisk air expand his lungs. Although it was the last day of

October and the temperature was cool, he was comfortable dressed in his suit without an overcoat. The weather had been mostly clear throughout the month with few storms for which he was glad. He felt a sense of contentment as he strode up the road.

It wasn't long before he reached the mercantile. The lettering on the picture window read *David O. Rideout, General Merchandise Store*. He glanced up at the second story of the building where five oblong windows stared out onto the street, the blinds drawn down part way like half-closed eyes. Pushing open the door, he went inside. He stood for a moment gazing at a host of tables and shelves laden with merchandise, then made his way to the counter. A young woman with light brown hair and blue eyes stood behind the long store counter.

"May I help you?" she asked cheerfully.

"Are you the manager?" Judson inquired.

The girl giggled and rolled her eyes. "Heavens, no. I'm just the stock girl, but Mr. Rideout should be back shortly."

Judson gave her a cordial smile. "Is there a telephone I might be able to use?"

"Yes, sir. It's right there on the wall behind the counter. Just turn the crank and the operator will come on." The young woman's hand fluttered like a butterfly's wings as she gestured toward the wall.

"I don't need to make a call at the moment, but I might be receiving one tomorrow. I'm staying at the hotel down the block," he nodded toward the door, "and wondered if it might not be too inconvenient, when the call came, you could send one of the errand boys down to the hotel to let me know." He spoke the words slowly so that there would be no mistaking his instructions.

"Of course," the girl replied. "You're staying at Mr. Green's hotel?"

"That's right. My name is Judson Carter. Do you want to write that down?"

As the girl began searching for a pencil, Judson's eyes were drawn to a flash of movement in the small office tucked behind the counter. The door was open, and the person he least expected to see appeared in the doorway. "Rebecca?" he stammered.

Rebecca Kade stood looking at him in astonishment. The afternoon sun flooding through the window behind her highlighted the soft curve of her cheek. Her hair was arranged into a bun at the crown of her head, and she held a sheaf of papers and a pencil in her hand. For an instant, both were too startled to speak as they stared at one another. "Mr. Carter," she finally said. "What a surprise to see you here."

Before Judson could reply, the stock girl turned to look over her shoulder. "Oh, Rebecca," she said in a relieved tone of voice. "Have you a pencil? I've misplaced mine."

Rebecca stepped out of the office and went to the girl's side. She handed her the pencil she'd been holding.

Judson couldn't control his stare. It had been weeks since he'd last seen her, and all his resolve concerning her vanished in an instant. "Miss Kade, what are you doing here?" he managed to say.

"I heard your name and got up from my desk to see if . . ." she flushed and stopped in mid-sentence.

The brown-haired girl behind the counter looked confused as she glanced at them. "Do you two know each other?" she asked.

"Lettie, this is Mr. Carter," Rebecca said. She turned to Judson and introduced Lettie to him.

Judson stretched his arm across the counter to shake the girl's hand. "How do you do, Miss Miller?"

She responded with a smile and a sturdy handshake.

"Mr. Carter is Rachel's friend," Rebecca added.

Lettie's brows shot up. "Oh, I see," she said, her eyes widening.

Judson felt a surge of annoyance. It had been over a month since he and Rachel had parted company, yet it seemed Rachel had neglected to mention that fact to her sister. Judson forced a smile. "Miss Rachel Kade and I have not been keeping company for quite some time now." He felt embarrassed airing his private affairs before the eager eyes of Miss Miller. He heard the stock girl utter a gasp.

"Really?" Rebecca blurted.

"If you have the time, would you care to take a stroll outside with me, Miss Kade? If it is convenient."

Rebecca's lips parted as if to answer, but no sound came out.

"Go on," Lettie encouraged, giving her a little push. "Mr. Rideout won't mind if you leave for a few minutes."

"All right. Perhaps just for a moment, Mr. Carter," she said. She stepped back inside the office to lay her papers on the desk. When she reappeared, she looked more composed.

Judson helped her on with her coat, then offered his arm. She placed her hand inside the crook of his elbow, and they left the store and started down the plank sidewalk. "Are you employed at the mercantile?" Judson asked as soon as they had gone a few steps.

"Yes. I've taken a temporary position at the store keeping the books for Mr. Rideout."

Judson had a dozen more questions he wanted to ask and didn't know which one to pose first. He was jolted by this chance encounter. "How long have you been in Draper? Are you living here instead of at the ranch?"

"I arrived only last Wednesday and was fortunate enough to obtain the position at the store. I'm staying with Lettie." She paused and glanced up at him. "Why are you in Draper?"

"Business," he answered. "I've a client here in town. I'll be here until tomorrow." He slowed his stride. "How is everything at the ranch?"

"There has been one difficulty after another, but I think we've begun to work out a solution."

"We?" Judson felt a shudder run through him. Had Rebecca found a suitor who was advising her with decisions at the ranch?

"My cousins—Patrick and Wade McKellar. They've been helping with the roundup while I work here to earn some extra money for expenses."

Judson let out his breath in a quick puff of air. "Oh."

"Did I understand you correctly? About you and Rachel, I mean." Rebecca's cheeks flamed with the question.

"Yes. I'm surprised she hasn't told you. It must have slipped her mind," he added cynically. "Rachel and I are no longer seeing one another. I ended the relationship more than a month ago."

"You did?"

"It happened before I came out to the ranch the last time. I intended to talk to you about it then, but we went riding in the hills and . . ." His sentence trailed off into silence.

"Yes, I remember."

"The opportunity to discuss it with you just didn't present itself," Judson went on awkwardly. "And so I left the ranch without mentioning it. I thought Rachel would have let you know by now."

"No, she hasn't." Rebecca bit her lip, as if thinking on the matter.

"Well, it's over and done with now," Judson said, anxious to leave the sensitive subject behind. "Tell me how you like your job at the store."

"Well enough. But I miss being at the ranch, especially with the roundup going on." Her face took on a wistful expression. "It's the first time I've been away from the Double K during a roundup."

They continued to talk as they walked. Rebecca explained about some of the recent events that had taken place at the ranch, including the barn catching on fire.

"Did you lose any livestock in the fire?" he asked.

"No cattle, but two horses died—a mare and her foal. And Onyx was injured. He's not yet able to bear the weight of a saddle. I don't know if he'll recover enough to take out on the range again."

Judson heard the ache in her voice. "I'm sorry. I know how much that animal means to you."

"The irony of it is, I was considering entering Onyx in that horse race of yours," she said with a wry smile. "I kept thinking how much I could use the $50 toward expenses at the ranch."

"My hopes turned out to be just as vain. My gray came in third, and unfortunately, there was no prize money awarded for third place." Judson spoke the words lightly, but he'd been disappointed with the outcome. He hadn't counted on the participation of the tall, lean thoroughbred one of the men in town had entered at the last minute. The black thoroughbred had taken the lead from the outset and easily outdistanced the other horses competing in the race.

"I'm sorry to hear that," Rebecca responded.

"At least I made a little better showing than my friend, Lorin, whose bay came in last." Judson's chuckle was at his own expense.

They continued down the street, Rebecca's hand still resting lightly on his arm. Judson was surprised by the emotions that had surfaced simply from her touch.

"Is Daniel still working with you at the shop?" she asked.

"Yes. And his skills are improving every day."

"Have you work enough to keep you both busy?"

"More than enough at the moment." Judson went on to tell her about the contract he'd just concluded with his client in Draper. "He showed me the blueprints for his house. Five rooms with closets, a separate pantry, and a summer kitchen. He plans to create a formal garden complete with fountains and winding paths." Judson smiled. "It's going to be quite a showpiece."

"Mr. Rideout has been talking about building a bigger house for his family, too. But right now he's too busy campaigning for a friend of his who is running for the state legislature at the general election next week."

"A commendable cause," Judson replied.

"He's had meetings nearly every day at the store since I've been here." She smiled ruefully. "I think that's why he gave me the bookkeeping job—he's been too busy to look after the books himself."

"I'm sure his trust and confidence in you are well placed," Judson said. "You've had as much experience as anyone from keeping the books for your father."

"He'll be sorry he hired me if I don't get back to my desk."

Judson nodded. "I'll walk you back."

They turned and began retracing their steps to the store. An afternoon breeze had sprung up carrying with it a preview of colder weather. Rebecca pulled her coat tighter around her. The wind lashed a spot of color to her cheeks.

As they approached the door of the mercantile, Judson's mind was swirling. He wanted to see Rebecca again before he left town, but he was confused about what to do. Although Rebecca was now fully aware of the situation between Rachel and himself, that did not change the fact that he was reluctant to acknowledge his affection for her in place of her sister.

He opened the door to the store and stepped aside so that she could enter. When she'd crossed the threshold, she looked back at him. "It was nice to see you," she said.

"And you." He knew now was the pivotal moment. Rebecca lingered just inside the room as if awaiting some signal from him. He hesitated.

Rebecca dropped her gaze and began removing her coat.

Judson's heart was pounding, but his mind was fixed. "Good day, Miss Kade," he said, lifting his hat. Then he turned and walked away.

Dragging his step, he went back to his hotel. He ate dinner by himself and then went up to his room for the remainder of the night even though it was still early. Sitting alone in his hotel room, he was tortured by the knowledge that Rebecca was only a few blocks away and that he could be sharing her company right now if circumstances had been different. He endured a lonely evening convincing himself that he would get over his feelings for Rebecca if he went long enough without seeing her.

Judson spent the next morning in town visiting a couple of lumber mills and seeing to some tasks he wanted to accomplish with regard to his business. He was closing up his traveling bag and preparing to leave his room to catch the afternoon train back to Salt Lake City when a knock sounded at his door. When he opened it, a boy stood just outside the doorway.

"Are you Mr. Carter?" the boy asked, whipping off his cap.

Judson nodded.

"Mr. Rideout sent me here to tell you that a telephone message came for you, sir."

Judson's pulse spiked. "What is the message?"

"The constable wants to see you at his office."

"Where is his office?"

"At the jail, sir."

Judson got directions to the town jail from the boy, then tipped the lad a dime. He lifted his bag from the bed and left the room, paid the hotel proprietor for the night's stay, and quickly walked the few blocks to the jail. He found the constable inside, working at his desk. The man looked up when Judson entered and extended a hand. Judson grasped it in a firm handshake, surprised by the strength of the man's grip.

"Sit down, Mr. Carter," the constable said.

Judson took a seat across the desk from him. "Do you have news for me?"

The constable didn't waste any time in idle talk. "I've located the whereabouts of the man you were inquiring after."

Judson's breath quickened. "Solomon Curtis?"

The other man nodded. He leaned back in his chair, remaining silent for a moment. "He's right here in town," he said finally.

Judson could hardly believe his good fortune. He pictured Daniel's expression when he told him the news that his father had been found. "Where can I find him?"

The constable motioned toward the window where the glass framed a view of the mountains to the east. "Over there. Through the block."

Judson sat forward expectantly.

The constable ran a hand across his bearded chin. "Buried in the Draper Cemetery," he said.

"What?" James exclaimed, stunned by the constable's words.

"The first thing I checked was the death records we keep on file, and his name popped up."

Judson sagged in his chair. This wasn't the outcome he'd been anticipating.

"Captain Solomon Curtis, a career soldier in the United States Cavalry assigned to Fort Laramie in Wyoming Territory," he said, as if reciting from a written page. "His company of horse soldiers was probably posted in Colorado on the Indian reservation in the 1870s; and he met the boy's mother then, I'm guessing. If word got out that he'd sired an

Indian child, it might have jeopardized his military career. So he likely kept the whole thing quiet."

Judson couldn't disguise his surprise on hearing this information. "That would explain why he chose to remain anonymous with regard to his son."

The constable shifted in his chair. "He probably kept tabs on your young Indian friend through the years. Did you say he paid for the boy's education?"

Judson nodded wordlessly.

"How'd the boy track his father to Salt Lake City?"

Judson sighed. "He told me that he'd gotten a look at his school records—surreptitiously, I'm sure—and found out that the money for his schooling was being wired from Salt Lake City by his father. So when he finished his education, he took what money was left of the funds his father had sent and headed to Utah to find him."

"That's an enterprising young man," the constable remarked.

"Yes, Daniel is both bright and resourceful." Judson bit his lip, trying to digest everything the constable had told him. "How did Curtis die, do you know?"

The constable thumped his fingers on the desk. "Pneumonia. That's what's listed on the death certificate."

"Well," Judson said, struggling to collect his thoughts. "I appreciate your finding all this out for me. I'll tell Daniel."

"Sorry I didn't have better news to report to you."

Judson nodded. "I suppose there are military records available that Daniel could arrange to see if he wants to."

"I'd think so," the other man replied. "Curtis retired from the horse cavalry in 1890, but I suspect you could still get a hold of his service record."

Judson nodded again. Solomon Curtis had probably drifted south, passing through Salt Lake City, after his retirement from the Cavalry, he surmised. What a shame he hadn't chosen to see his son. Judson stood up and extended his hand to the constable. "Thanks again," he said.

The constable walked with him to the door. "Pass along my regrets to your friend," the man said.

"Thanks, I will." Judson replaced his hat and stepped out of the office. The wind blew cold against his cheeks as he started up the road, carrying his traveling bag, toward the train depot.

CHAPTER EIGHTEEN

When Judson exited the train at the Salt Lake City depot, it was after four o'clock. The ride from Draper to Salt Lake had seemed to take longer than usual—or perhaps it just felt that way to Judson because his mood was somber. Not only was he upset about learning of Solomon Curtis's death and facing the prospect of having to tell Daniel the news, but he was also hopelessly entangled in his feelings concerning Rebecca. He wished now that he hadn't been so stubborn and had spent some time with her when he had the chance.

As he left the depot, he took out his pocketwatch and consulted it. Daniel would still be at the shop, and Judson knew he shouldn't put off until tomorrow informing Daniel about the passing of his father. When he arrived at the cabinet shop, it was nearly closing time. He let himself inside and was surprised to see Louisa Addams sitting opposite the work bench from Daniel. Both of them looked up when Judson closed the door behind him.

Daniel scrambled to his feet. "Afternoon, sir," he said. "Did everything go well in Draper?"

Judson's eyes slid from Daniel to Louisa. She rose from her chair, too, giving him a smile. "Yes," Judson said curtly, turning back to Daniel. He hadn't intended to be short with him, but Louisa's presence at the shop caught him off guard. "Afternoon, Miss Addams," he added.

"Good afternoon, Mr. Carter. It's nice to see you again," Louisa said. "Mr. Briggs tells me that the bureau and side table are nearly completed. May I express my admiration; the furniture is exceptionally beautiful."

Judson knew the young woman was sincere in her compliments, and he also knew that her purpose in being here at the shop was to see Daniel; but he sensed no guile on her part or on Daniel's. They were simply two people who were attracted to each other and trying to become better acquainted under difficult circumstances.

Judson nodded, then giving Daniel a guarded look, he retreated to the back of the shop. He set down his traveling bag and removed his coat. Then he withdrew from his vest pocket the paper written with the order he'd received from his client in Draper and began to look it over. From the corner of his eye, he saw Daniel and Louisa drift toward the door of the shop. They paused near the door, talking together. Judson forced his eyes back to the paper to give the couple some privacy. He could hear their low, murmuring voices as they conversed for a moment. He glanced up once and caught a glimpse of them, their heads close together and Louisa's hand in Daniel's. He frowned. Perhaps the relationship was more serious than he had at first believed. He heard the door open, then close an instant later, and then the sound of Daniel's footsteps coming toward him.

"Miss Addams had been here only a few minutes before you arrived, sir," Daniel said, anticipating Judson's reaction.

Judson set down his paper. "I know neither you nor Miss Addams would do anything that could be construed as inappropriate," Judson said slowly. "But you must remember that Miss Addams is the daughter of a very influential man who carries an enormous amount of political and personal power. And I don't think he'd be in favor of a relationship between the two of you," Judson said regrettably. "He could make trouble for you, Daniel."

Daniel's gaze didn't waver. "I know that, sir. Louisa knows it, too. But it is too late." He paused, drawing a breath. "Louisa and I are in love."

Judson rose to his feet in consternation. "You barely know one another," he exclaimed. "And you're both too young to be in love."

"Louisa is seventeen, and I am eighteen, sir. We may be young, but we know without a doubt that we want to be together."

Judson dropped back down onto the stool, the paper on the work desk forgotten. "This course will only bring disappointment to you both," he said sternly. "If not for your own sake, then for Louisa's, think carefully about the consequences."

"I have. Louisa's welfare is uppermost in my mind. But her feelings match mine, and we are prepared to accept whatever consequences may follow."

Judson saw the familiar glint of determination settle into the young man's eyes. He knew he would not be able to talk Daniel out of the course he'd set upon. "Then, at least, use discretion in your relationship for the time being, until Louisa's father has time to come to terms with it."

A spark of defiance flashed across Daniel's face, and his shoulders stiffened.

"Believe me, Daniel. I know what I'm talking about," Judson warned, alarmed by Daniel's expression. "Reason and restraint fall by the wayside when men are inflamed by prejudice and hatred."

"I will keep that in mind, sir," Daniel replied, his resolve scarcely tempered by Judson's words.

Judson sighed. "Your relationship with Miss Addams is not the only concern at the moment. I have news of your father."

Daniel's dark eyes widened slightly. "What news?"

"Sit down," Judson said wearily. He pulled over a chair so Daniel could be seated. He stared at the young man for an instant, then lowered his gaze. "I didn't mention this to you earlier because I didn't want to get your hopes raised, but a friend of mine who owns a saloon in town passed along some information to me."

"That would be Mr. Stotts?"

Judson glanced up. Daniel knew of his friendship with Lorin Stotts. And he was aware of Judson's evening habit of visiting the Blue Fly.

"Yes, Mr. Stotts," Judson confirmed. He went on to tell him how Lorin had received the information about Daniel's father and the inquiries Judson had made while in Draper. "The constable informed me that your father died five months ago, shortly after he arrived in Draper."

Daniel's face paled. The young man didn't speak, just stared stoically at Judson.

"I'm sorry. I was hoping for a different outcome, as you were," Judson said.

Daniel dropped his gaze. "Thank you for letting me know."

Judson related what the constable had said. "Your father is buried in the Draper cemetery," he concluded. "You're welcome to take some time to visit the grave, if you wish," Judson said quietly.

Daniel nodded his head.

"I wish I had better news for you," Judson offered.

"I appreciate the help you have given me."

Judson watched as the young man's hand strayed to the carved wolf lying against his chest. "I can go with you to Draper, if you like," Judson said, hoping to comfort Daniel in his disappointment and grief.

Daniel's response was another wordless nod of the head. Then he got up from the chair and walked to the bench where he'd been working. He grasped the length of wood lying there and began sanding it. Judson watched him move the sandpaper back and forth along the board, Daniel's posture as rigid as the wood he worked.

Sighing, Judson turned back to the paper on the desk. He had been excited to share the news of this large, lucrative order with his assistant, but now the glow of success had faded under the harsh glare of disappointment and sorrow. He drummed his fingers against the sheet of paper. Unbidden, an image of Rebecca Kade surfaced in his mind. He pictured her at her desk in the cramped office at the mercantile and wondered if she had given him any thought at all since he'd left the store. He frowned, wishing he could see her again and talk with her about the worries burdening him.

Judson hung back while Daniel walked across the barren cemetery to a place near the west fence. Daniel paused there and stared down at a spot on the ground. Stamping his feet against the cold settling in his toes, Judson looked away. He and Daniel had ridden the train into Draper that morning with little conversation between them, then walked the few blocks to the cemetery. From the records kept by the caretaker, they had been able to determine which grave was Solomon Curtis's; the caretaker had told them that there was a small stone marker indicating the site, but no inscription on the marker. Daniel had apparently found the grave. As Judson glanced over at him, he saw Daniel kneel on one knee and bow his head.

Judson turned his gaze to the tall mountains bordering the valley to the east. The slopes were steep and jagged, and Judson noticed the first patches of snow capping the rugged peaks. In the valley below, the fields lay brown and naked—the crops gathered in and the harvest stored for the winter.

He looked back at Daniel. The young man remained motionless, perhaps communicating in prayer, Judson surmised. As he watched, Daniel removed the wolf necklace from around his neck, stared at it an instant, then carefully laid it across his father's grave marker. That simple act brought a lump to Judson's throat.

Daniel remained at the grave for several more minutes. Finally, he rose to his feet and strode back to where Judson waited. The two men exchanged a wordless glance, then Judson put an arm around the young man's shoulder and they left the cemetery together.

It was late afternoon by the time they arrived back in Salt Lake City and Judson let them into the cabinet shop. They had spoken little on the train, and Daniel still maintained an attitude of silent contemplation. Judson went to his work bench and took up a block of wood he'd been shaping and started sculpting it with his drawknife. Daniel, too, returned to a panel on which he'd earlier been carving a design.

They worked for a while on their separate projects without any conversation between them, then finally Daniel laid aside the piece of paneling and looked over at Judson. "Although I never knew my father," he said slowly, "I hated him."

Judson stopped his work, gaping at him. "What?"

Daniel stood and began pacing the floor. "All the years I lived with my mother on the reservation, I hated him. Hated him for leaving my mother and me. Hated him for being a white man."

Judson stared at the young man, astonished by his candor. "Go on," he said, putting down the drawknife.

"My mother never spoke about him. Only once did she tell me his name. I tried to convince myself that Solomon Curtis was not my father. That I was not half white." He halted, staring at his hands as if his next words were imprinted there for him to read. "I learned the Ute legends, practiced the Indian traditions. With my people, I danced the Bear Dance every spring so that our hunters would be successful and our women fertile and our tribe powerful and strong."

Judson's attention was riveted on what Daniel was telling him.

"I believed that Father Sky created the sun, moon, stars, and earth; and that Mother Earth provided her people with all things necessary to live. For many generations, my people hunted the *kúcu*, the buffalo; and when the buffalo grew scarce, we hunted deer, elk, antelope, beaver, fox, and rabbit."

Judson watched as Daniel resumed his pacing.

"We pitched our hide tepees in the tall grass beside clear streams, and our women picked berries, nuts, and seeds. Mother Earth provided for our needs so long as our people respected the land."

Judson nodded, listening without commenting.

"My mother told me about Senawahv, the Creator," Daniel went on. "Before there were people, Senawahv cut up sticks and placed them in a bag. The sticks would be different peoples, and Senawahv would give each an equal share of the land. But then Coyote, the cunning trickster, seized the bag and opened it. Many peoples spilled forth, speaking different tongues. When Senawahv looked again inside the bag, he found only one people remaining, the Utes, and to them he gave great bravery and strength so that they would be able to defeat all their enemies. I believed this legend with all my heart."

"It is a good legend," Judson affirmed.

Daniel paused to glance at him. "But then the white missionaries came to my village, and my mother believed the words written in their book. My mother kept the book the missionaries gave her, but she could not read the white man's words." Daniel walked to his chair and stiffly sat down. "When I was sent to the white man's school, I learned their language and how to read their words. After that, whenever I returned to my village, I read to my mother from the book the missionaries had given her."

Judson knew which book Daniel spoke of—the same Book of Mormon he read from each noon hour at the shop.

"I, too, came to believe the words in this book," Daniel said quietly. "The God of this book is not so different from Senawahv and many of the traditions of the Utes. But one thing is different. The God of this book teaches his people to forgive their enemies."

Judson swallowed hard. He realized what Daniel was driving at.

"My heart has been dark with anger and hate. I read the book that belonged to my mother so that I can grow a new heart."

Judson hardly knew how to respond. Daniel's dark eyes gleamed as if burning with an inner fire. "And so you have been striving to forgive your father," Judson said. It was not a question.

Daniel nodded slightly.

"I see," Judson replied, stirring in his chair. "And as for the book? Are you thinking about baptism?"

Again, Daniel nodded. "When my heart is worthy, I will go and speak to the Mormon chief."

Judson looked down at the block of wood he had been shaping before his conversation with Daniel. It was still in its natural, rough shape, but with effort and the right tools, it could be turned into something useful and beautiful. The analogy between the wood and the Master Builder was not lost on him. He glanced up again at Daniel. "I believe you will be able to achieve your desire, my friend."

That evening, as Judson sat at the bar with his whiskey, his thoughts kept returning to Daniel and the things the young man had told him. He tried to picture Daniel's life as a young boy on the reservation. Daniel had mentioned some of the hardships his people had passed through—the restrictions placed on the Utes by the government; their loss of tribal lands and ancestral hunting grounds; their dependence upon the Indian agents who distributed supplies. Sometimes the rations given them were scanty, Daniel had said, the flour moldy and the meat spoiled.

Judson could only imagine Daniel's reaction, when at the age of ten he was taken from his family and sent to the boarding school where he was thrust into the midst of a strange culture, language, and society. The white school Daniel had attended assigned him his Christian name—Daniel Briggs. It wasn't a name he had chosen or one that held any meaning for him; it was just the name given him. Judson suspected that every effort had been made by the school superintendency to wipe out Daniel's Indian heritage, and the young boy had suffered prejudice and persecution. That experience left its imprint on him; from it he had learned courage and self-sufficiency, but he had also been taught bitter lessons about betrayal, disappointment, and loss.

Judson took a drink from his glass, then wiped his mouth with the back of his hand. He thought about the contrast between his own upbringing and Daniel's, and the opportunities that had been afforded him. Just yesterday, he'd cast his vote at the November 5 general election, where he'd had the occasion to join his voice with others in ratifying the new state constitution and electing state officials and legislators. He had voted the Republican ticket, although there were aspects of the Republican platform with which he did not agree, particularly the tariff issue and the question of silver coinage.

Concerning the silver controversy, Judson's views were more in harmony with the stance adopted by the Populist Party. They advocated the unlimited coinage of silver at the ratio of 16 to 1. This meant that a dollar of gold could be bought for under 60 cents of silver. Populist Party leaders maintained that an increase in the supply of silver coinage would bolster the economy and rescue the nation from the ravages of the ongoing economic depression. The party had nominated a partial slate of candidates for state office, including the governorship. But Judson knew that the Populist Party in Utah carried little clout in comparison with the two major national political parties, and so he had not wasted his vote on the Populist candidates.

The Republicans had swept the elections, propelling Heber M. Wells into the office of governor and electing Clarence E. Allen, a non-Mormon, to Congress and James T. Hammond as Secretary of State. The members of the state legislature would later select two United States senators to complete the roster.

Judson finished the whiskey in his glass in a single swallow. Then he stood up and walked to one of the gaming tables where three men, who were acquaintances of his, were playing a game of poker. "Mind if I join you?" Judson asked them.

One of the men pulled out a chair from the table for him. "Evening, Judson. You look dapper; been out with a gal tonight?" the man grinned.

"Wish I'd been that lucky," Judson returned as he seated himself on the chair.

"The ante is two bits," the other man said, turning his attention to the dealer who was shuffling the cards.

Judson tossed the coins into the center of the table as the dealer distributed the cards. The five cards Judson was dealt included a pair of sevens. He discarded the rest and received three more from the dealer, but the hand contained nothing he could use. Nevertheless, he played the hand for a round or two before folding.

Judson and the others at the table had been playing for about a half hour when a man entered the saloon, ordered a drink, and then wandered over to their table. Judson glanced up at the stranger as he stood nearby, drinking his whiskey. The man was dressed in cowboy gear, wearing a pair of scuffed boots, a rumpled, wide brimmed hat, and a soiled neckerchief. His face was sunburned and his stringy hair came to the collar of his coarse, cotton shirt.

"Got room for another player?" the man asked. His voice was deep and rough.

One of the men at the table looked up at him. "Have a seat."

The man pulled a chair over to the table and sat down to watch them finish their hand of poker. He grinned when Judson won the hand and scooped up the small pile of cash and coins. "Nice playin'," he said to Judson.

Judson nodded briefly.

"Deal me in," the stranger said as the next round began. He snatched up the cards with thick, stubby fingers as quickly as they were dealt to him, coughed once, and then studied his hand.

Judson stared at his own cards and then laid them face down on the table. His hand was a good one, possibly good enough to win a second round. He studied the faces of the men surrounding the table while he waited for the fellow on his left to start the betting. Most of the men's faces were impassive, revealing little about their intentions for the play at hand. But when his eyes lighted on the newcomer at the table, it was a different scene. The stranger was frowning, almost glaring, at his cards and mumbling under his breath. Sweat glistened on his brow below the broad-brimmed, high-crowned hat he wore. A dark feather jutted from the fancy, rawhide hatband. Judson's eyes strayed to the telltale bulge in the man's shirt pocket where a large folding knife rested. Judson could see the tip of it poking above the top of the man's pocket, revealing an unusual, bone handle. The handle was yellowed and cold looking, with dark grooves in it. A chill shimmied down Judson's spine as he stared at it.

There was little talk as the men concentrated on their cards and their bets. Judson won the hand as he'd anticipated, and the stranger slammed down his cards in exasperation. "Bartender!" he shouted. "More whiskey."

Lorin's assistant, who was tending the bar that evening, carried over a bottle of rye whiskey. The stranger was leaning back in his chair as Judson shuffled the deck of cards. "Leave it," he said gruffly to the bartender as he reached for the bottle. He took a long, steady swig from it as he watched Judson deal the cards.

Judson didn't care for the man's bold stare. And he could tell that the other men at the table were beginning to resent the stranger's intrusion into their game. With each round, he became more agitated, twitching in his chair and muttering obscenities when he lost a hand.

"What'd you say your name was, partner?" one of the men at the table asked him.

"I didn't," he answered, squinting at the man across the table who had asked the question. "It's Baxter."

"You a cowhand?" the man continued.

"That's right." Baxter took another gulp from the bottle.

"Maybe you want to be taking it easy with that whiskey, Mr. Baxter," the man suggested pointedly.

Judson lifted his head to gauge Baxter's reaction to the other man's words. He knew a man like Baxter wouldn't take the suggestion kindly.

Sure enough, Baxter's eyes narrowed and his face turned a burnished red. "Maybe you want to keep your advice to yourself, mister," he replied in a threatening tone.

Judson tried to give his friend a warning glance. There was no sense provoking this stranger, who already seemed aggressive and volatile.

It was Judson's turn to deal again. He began passing out the cards, hoping to distract Baxter and defuse the situation. "Deuces wild," Judson announced as he distributed the cards.

Baxter grudgingly changed his focus to the cards in his hand. He swore under his breath after he studied them. He threw down four of the cards. Judson swept them up and dealt him four new ones. These, apparently, didn't satisfy him either. He slumped in his chair, mumbling under his breath and eyeing the others at the table menacingly.

Judson finished dealing the cards and the round began. He was surprised to see that he held the best hand he'd had all evening. The betting started, and when it was his turn, he raised the stakes slightly so that the others at the table wouldn't suspect what was in his hand. By the time the bet came back to him, the stakes on the table were high. "I'll see your five and raise it another five," he said, laying down the cash.

There was a chorus of groans from the others. His three friends tossed down their cards in disgust, but Baxter stayed in the game, matching Judson's bet and raising it even more. Judson hesitated. He knew Baxter didn't hold a winning hand, and he also knew the man was drunk and in a foul mood. He considered laying down his cards and letting the other man take the winnings to avoid a confrontation.

"What are you stalling for?" Baxter growled. He eyed Judson with a glare. "Play your hand."

The man's belligerence and ill temper irked Judson. Judson matched the bet and called. Then he displayed his cards so Baxter could see his hand.

A wild gasp of anger and disbelief erupted from Baxter's throat. He bolted up from his chair, throwing his cards onto the table. "You been takin' that prize money a little oftener than you should," he snarled at Judson.

"It was a fair play," Judson said calmly as he slid the large pile of cash toward him.

"Ain't nothin' fair about it," Baxter said, his voice rising. "I say you been cheatin'. Cheatin' all night, in fact."

Judson felt his face flush with anger. "No one has been cheating here tonight. Take what's left of your money and clear out before you lose it all," he snapped.

"Take your hands off that cash."

Judson looked up and was stunned to see Baxter on his feet with the blade of his folding knife pointed directly at Judson's chest.

"I said move away from that money," Baxter said slowly and emphatically. He waved the knife at Judson, and his wild-eyed gaze took in the other three men at the table as well.

"We don't want no trouble," one of the men said in a conciliatory voice.

"Ain't gonna be none. Just hand over that cash," Baxter said, motioning to the money heaped in front of Judson.

Judson glanced at the others at the table. One of them had backed his chair away from the table, as if trying to distance himself from the man with the knife. The other two sat motionless, saying nothing, but watching warily. Neither Judson nor the others were armed. It was a simple deduction—antagonize Baxter further and he wouldn't hesitate to use his weapon. Glowering, Judson shoved the cash across the table.

"That's a smart move, mister," Baxter snarled. He began scooping up the money with one hand and stuffing it into his pockets while still threatening Judson with the sharp-tipped knife. The four-inch blade glinted under the glare of the ceiling lamps. Judson watched him, his animosity for the man nearly choking him. No one else in the saloon interfered with the drama playing out at the table, including the bartender, although many must have seen or heard what was happening. Baxter collected all of the cash, then began backing toward the door of the saloon. When he reached it, he bolted and disappeared outside.

Judson let out an angry exclamation, then rose from his chair. The other three at the table, too, got to their feet.

"Sorry about your losses, Carter," one of them said.

The other two men shuffled away without speaking, unwilling to get involved. All of them knew that gambling was technically illegal in the city. In order to control and regulate the vice, the city council maintained the right to license gaming halls and require saloon owners to pay liquor license fees or fines. Lorin Stotts kept his establishment within those bounds, paying the fees and seeing that his patrons who engaged in card playing and alcohol consumption did not attract undue attention.

"Thanks," Judson mumbled. He shoved his hands in his pockets and started for the door of the saloon. As he passed the bartender, who was standing behind the counter drying a glass with his apron, the man lowered his gaze. If Lorin had been the barkeep that night, he would have refused Baxter service after seeing the man was drunk and belligerent. Judson frowned and shouldered his way out the door.

CHAPTER NINETEEN

On Monday of the following week, Judson sent Daniel to Draper to pick up a load of lumber he'd ordered from one of the mills there. While he was gone, Judson turned his attention to the two articles of furniture Addams had contracted for his daughter. The work on the bureau and matching side table was nearing completion; all that remained was applying the coats of varnish and polishing the wood. The pieces had turned out well. Daniel's workmanship on the carved rosettes and curling vines was outstanding down to the smallest detail. Both Addams and his daughter should be pleased with the job, Judson thought.

As Judson applied a layer of polish to the side table, he thought about the large order he'd received from his customer in Draper. He'd already begun the preliminary drawings and selected the wood, and he was anxious to get started on the actual construction. However, he had a few jobs to complete for other customers, including the matching set for Addams, before he could concentrate his efforts on this new assignment.

As he was rubbing the first coat of linseed oil into the wood of the side table, he heard the shop door open. Looking up, he was surprised to see Louisa Addams cross the threshold. He put aside his cloth and walked to the front of the shop to greet her. "Afternoon, Miss Addams," he said.

She returned his greeting with a friendly smile and pleasant word. As usual, she was smartly dressed—from the feathered hat perched stylishly on her head down to the patent-tipped shoes that hugged her small feet. She possessed a natural grace and beauty that reminded Judson of a gentle dove.

"I was just doing some work on the pieces you ordered. Why don't you come back here and take a look at them," Judson invited.

"Thank you, Mr. Carter." Louisa followed him to the rear of the room. She smiled and nodded as Judson showed her the furniture and explained the remaining work that still needed to be done.

As Judson conversed with her, he realized that her attention was not fixed on the set of furniture and what he was telling her about it. Her eyes kept wandering elsewhere, and her fingers fidgeted with the pink silk parasol she carried. He guessed that her real intent in visiting the shop was to see Daniel. That thought annoyed him just a bit.

As he was preparing to give her a date to expect the finished product, she cleared her throat and said, "I am pleased with all you've done, Mr. Carter. But, actually, I didn't come here today to talk with you about the set."

Judson frowned. "I'm afraid Daniel isn't here, Miss Addams, if that's why you stopped by."

Louisa's cheeks colored. "I know that. He told me that he would be in Draper. That's why I chose today to come and speak with you." She lowered her eyes.

Judson could see that she was nervous and ill at ease. "How can I help you, Miss Addams?" he asked, gesturing for her to take a chair.

Louisa sat down on the proffered chair and folded her gloved hands in her lap, and Judson seated himself across from her. "Daniel has mentioned something to you concerning our feelings for one another," Louisa began, staring down at her hands.

"Yes."

"I want you to know that my affections for Daniel are genuine." She lifted her gaze to look intently into Judson's face. "Even though you may believe I am too young to know my own mind, I assure you that I do."

"Miss Addams," Judson began, leaning forward in his chair, "there's no need for you to explain your personal feelings to me—"

Louisa cut him off with a shake of her head. "No, Mr. Carter, there is a great need for an explanation. Daniel and I have decided to elope."

Judson stared at her, not immediately comprehending her words. "Elope?"

She nodded. "Daniel wants to keep our plans a secret until after we are married, but I encouraged him to tell you. He didn't think it was a good idea because he felt you would disapprove, and he respects your opinion highly."

Judson tried to breathe normally, but his breath seemed trapped in his throat. When he was at last able to speak, his voice came out sounding hoarse. "Have you mentioned this to your father?"

Louisa shook her head, averting her gaze. "My father would be irate if he knew and forbid me to marry Daniel. It would be better to tell my father afterward," she added.

Judson swallowed hard. "Miss Addams, may I be plainspoken with you? I would strongly encourage you to abandon this course of action, especially without informing your parents."

Louisa's eyes shifted to Judson's face, and he saw the pain reflected in them. "Your candor is appreciated, Mr. Carter. But if I, too, may speak frankly in saying that my father has a deep dislike for peoples of the native race and would never allow me, under any circumstances, to marry a man of Indian ancestry."

Judson frowned, considering her words.

"You can see the dilemma Daniel and I face," Louisa said quietly.

Judson passed a hand across his chin. "Nevertheless, it would only cause further antagonism on your father's part if you and Daniel go forward with your plan. Perhaps your father's feelings will soften over time. Perhaps if you speak with him . . . give the relationship with Daniel some time to develop . . ."

"I know my father. His position will never soften."

Judson hardly knew what to say next to convince Louisa from taking this ruinous step. "I fear both you and Daniel would forever regret this action if you follow through with it."

Louisa clasped her hands together in her lap. "I appreciate your words of caution, and I'll discuss with Daniel what you have said. I realize you have taken on the role of Daniel's mentor, and I know he appreciates all you do for him—offering him employment, helping and supporting him with regard to the death of his father . . ." She paused, her voice trembling with emotion. "Both Daniel and I appreciate your kindness. And we will earnestly consider your words of advice."

"Daniel is a fine, young man. I'm sure everything will work out for the best." Judson gave her a reassuring smile. He could see by her expression, however, that she did not feel as confident about the outcome as he did.

"Thank you for your time, Mr. Carter, and for the beautiful furniture. I'll look forward to having it."

"You're welcome, Miss Addams." Judson walked with her to the door of the shop and saw her out. Afterward, he returned to his work bench. Hoping that he had convinced Louisa to abandon her idea of elopement, he picked up the cloth he'd been using and prepared to continue his polishing. After a moment, however, he paused, troubled by a new thought. If Louisa and Daniel disregarded his advice, how soon were they planning their elopement? Louisa had not mentioned a time frame. Suddenly, he felt uneasy about the couple. He remembered the unyielding look in Daniel's eye when the young man had first told Judson about his relationship with Louisa. A chill passed through Judson's frame. No matter which course the young couple pursued, problems were sure to result.

On Friday evening Daniel accompanied Judson to the home of Lorin and Catherine Stotts, where they enjoyed dinner with the couple. Lorin and his wife had invited Judson to bring his young assistant along so that they could extend a hand of friendship to him. Lorin's wife, whom Judson had met only once before, was a gracious, friendly woman who made both of her guests feel welcome. Five months pregnant, she was eagerly anticipating the birth of her first child. She spoke excitedly about the impending birth of the baby, but she also was interested in affairs outside the confines of her home. The four of them discussed several topics as the evening wore on—the results of the general election, the ramifications of impending statehood, and the monetary issue of silver versus gold.

"This whole controversy over silver has caused the nationwide depression," Lorin was saying. "It has shaken the confidence of businessmen across the country. If the government returns to a single gold standard, the economy can get back on its feet."

Judson sucked on his lip, thinking about Lorin's assessment. "I'm not sure the remedy is that simple. It's true that the government's fiscal policies directly influence economic development. Yet the lawmakers in Washington often disregard the one economic group that is the real backbone of America—the farmers."

Lorin nodded, listening carefully to what Judson had to say.

"Agriculture's role in the national economy has been largely ignored," Judson went on. "Agricultural production has increased significantly over the past thirty or so years, yet farmers are poorer than they were a few decades ago and suffering from a steady decline of prices for their goods."

"That's true," Lorin said. "And a return to the gold standard will benefit farm laborers as well as businessmen."

Judson smiled tolerantly. "An increased coinage of silver might stimulate the economy because it would put more money into circulation. That would raise farm prices and wages, which in turn would help halt the recession."

"Are you in sympathy with the silverites?" Lorin's wife asked, smiling.

"I think I can answer that for Judson," Lorin injected, a twinkle springing to his eye. "He has part ownership in the Lady Slipper, a silver mine in Park City."

"Aha," Catherine said.

"It's not as lucrative as it sounds," Judson replied with a chuckle. "I own a very small percentage of the mine, and it's producing poorly."

"Perhaps you should have bought into the Silver King Mine," Lorin suggested with a wink. "Someone told me that a fellow he knows who has an interest in the Silver King makes $1,000 a day."

Judson laughed. "I put my money in the wrong pocket, that's for certain. But even the Silver King, like most mining companies, is having difficulty because of the drop in silver prices. Mining, commerce, and transportation are all feeling the effects of the recession."

"And unemployment is widespread," Lorin added, his voice taking on a more somber note.

"With regard to your question concerning the silverites," Judson said, directing his comment to Catherine, "let me answer by saying that I think the pro-silver members of the Democratic Party have a sound leader in William Jennings Bryan. Bryan and his Populist supporters have forced the Democratic and Republican parties to address the money question in next year's presidential election."

Throughout the discussion, Daniel had sat quietly listening without offering an opinion. Lorin's wife turned to him with a smile and asked, "What are your thoughts on the political scene, Mr. Briggs?"

Daniel folded his arms across his chest. His black hair was neatly trimmed and combed for the evening's occasion, and his starched collar fit snugly beneath his chin. "I only know what I have read in the newspapers. Perhaps a change in the direction of the presidency would be beneficial."

Judson chuckled. "A reply certain to offend no one." He grinned at Daniel. "I agree with Daniel. President

Cleveland's administration has been riddled with problems, and his popularity is shrinking. Perhaps it is time for a change."

"And you wouldn't be averse to seeing a candidate from the Populist Party win the presidential election next year," Lorin said in a bantering tone.

"Maybe. The party was organized to address the plight of the farmer as well as to advocate unlimited silver coinage," Judson replied. "I liked Congressman Bryan's comment when he compared the president to the trainman who has opened a switch and precipitated a wreck. He was referring to President Cleveland's preference for gold over silver as the way out of the depression, but I think the analogy covers a broader spectrum than that." Judson smiled at his companions. "Some new blood might be better able to address the problems plaguing the nation."

They continued to discuss politics and economics while Lorin's wife made coffee for them. Their conversation lasted until late into the evening; and when Judson and Daniel left the Stotts' home, a quarter moon glimmered high overhead. It was cold outdoors, and a light snow was falling. Judson turned up the collar of his coat against a chilly blast of wind and pulled the brim of his hat lower onto his forehead. With just a sliver of a moon in view, the sky was black except for the falling flurries of snow.

They strode down the side of the road talking together and hadn't gone far when Judson noticed three men approaching from the opposite direction. The men seemed to suddenly loom out of the darkness like apparitions.

He overheard their loud, crude conversation before he recognized their faces. When the three stepped into the circle of pale light cast by a street lamp, Judson's chest tightened. Two of them were the same men he'd had the altercation with at Lorin's saloon—Murdock and his coarse companion—and the third was the cowboy named Baxter who had stolen his winnings at the poker table the week before. He was not surprised to see Baxter in the company of Murdock and his crony. Judson frowned, trying to smother the spark of anger that flared on seeing the three of them.

It was too late to escape the men's notice. When the group was only a few paces away, Murdock stopped abruptly. Baxter and the other man paused, too. "Well, if it ain't our friends the carpenter and his Injun helper," Murdock said sarcastically.

Judson felt Daniel stiffen at his side. The young man undoubtedly recognized Murdock, too, and disliked him. Judson gestured for him to remain silent, and he and Daniel kept walking without responding to Murdock's comment.

Murdock blocked their advance by stepping in front of them. "You ain't bein' very sociable, carpenter," he said, putting a rough hand on Judson's arm to prevent him for going further.

Judson felt his blood rising. "Take your hand off me," he snapped, glaring at Murdock.

"I think you and me got some unfinished business, don't we?" Murdock said with a sneer.

Judson met the other man's stare without flinching, but from the corner of his eye he saw Murdock's companion slowly begin to circle toward Daniel. Baxter remained standing where he was; Judson didn't think that the cowhand had recognized him in the darkness.

Murdock's hand tightened on his arm. Judson could feel the man's fingers digging into the sleeve of his coat. Before he could react, Murdock nodded at his companion. In a flash, the man cut between Judson and Daniel, separating them. Then Baxter moved to intercept Daniel. Judson could see the outline of the feather Baxter wore in his hatband silhouetted against the pale glare of the street lamp.

"Are you acquainted with our friend, the carpenter?" Murdock jeered, glancing at Baxter. "If not, let me introduce you."

Before Judson saw it coming, Murdock's fist rammed into his midsection. Judson grunted and doubled over in pain. He heard Murdock's harsh laughter rumbling like thunder in his ears.

With the breath knocked out of him, Judson could only watch as Murdock's companion drew back his fist to deal Daniel a blow; but Daniel sprang to one side, as quick and surefooted as a deer, and the man's fist swung harmlessly through the air. Without hesitating, Daniel darted forward and delivered a surprise punch to the man's jaw. The man yelped in pain. His knees buckled beneath him, and he went down face first, his legs sprawling onto the road.

Quick as lightning, Baxter's hand flew to his shirt pocket.

"Daniel, watch out!" Judson shouted. "He has a knife in his pocket!"

Simultaneous with Judson's warning, Baxter snatched out his folding knife and whipped it open, pointing the blade at Daniel. "Stay where you are, Indian," he snarled, jabbing the knife toward him.

Daniel crouched into a position to defend himself. Baxter was slashing the air with the knife, but Daniel managed to stay clear of the flashing blade.

Judson was burning with rage. He dodged Murdock's grasping hands, then lunged forward and caught Murdock by one arm, pinning it behind his back. He yanked hard, prepared to break the arm if necessary. "Tell Baxter to drop the knife and back off," he demanded between clenched teeth. When Murdock didn't immediately comply, he gave his arm a sharp twist.

Murdock cried out in agony. "Do what he says, Baxter," he shouted.

Baxter glanced toward Murdock while still threatening Daniel with the knife. Judson could see the hatred on his face. He gave Murdock's arm another jerk.

"Do it!" Murdock called, writhing to free the pressure on his arm.

Still Baxter hesitated. Judson knew instinctively that he was capable of using the weapon on Daniel. The bone handle of the knife in his hand glimmered menacingly in the lamplight.

The third man, whom Daniel had sent spinning onto the ground, was struggling to his feet. Once up, he swayed and stumbled; it was obvious that he was going to be of no help to his comrades.

Baxter swore, then snapped the blade of his knife closed. He shoved Daniel aside. "Stay out of my way, Indian. Next time we meet, I might not be feelin' so charitable."

Daniel took a swift step toward him, his face molded into a mask of fury. "If you ever come at me again, I will cut your heart out," Daniel hissed, his eyes blazing like hot coals.

"Daniel!" Judson barked. "Back off. We're through here." He released Murdock's arm and pushed him out of his way, then strode quickly to Daniel's side. He wasn't completely sure that Daniel wouldn't yet try to attack Baxter or one of the others. Daniel was breathing hard and seething with resentment. His anger made him unpredictable and fearless.

Judson picked up the third man's hat from the road and tossed it to him. "We're through here," he repeated coldly to the three of them. He took Daniel by the elbow and steered him forward, away from the three men who stood in a huddle muttering between themselves. He hoped Baxter and the others wouldn't try to attack them again; if they did, Judson was sure someone would end up hurt—or dead.

Neither Judson nor Daniel spoke until they were well up the block and certain they were not being followed. At the corner of the street, Judson stopped and looked sternly into Daniel's face. "That was foolhardy to antagonize Baxter further when you knew he had a weapon." He tried to keep his voice from rising, but he was brimming with anger, not only at the men who had assaulted them, but also at Daniel's reckless behavior. "Murdock is a bully. But the other one,

Baxter, has a hardness in his eyes. He's dangerous, Daniel. Don't push him."

Daniel lowered his gaze, but his expression remained intractable. Judson sighed inwardly. He hoped the streak of stubbornness and pride in Daniel's character wouldn't one day propel him into a dangerous situation from which he could not escape. He let out his breath slowly and arched his back. His stomach ached from the blow Murdock had delivered and his head hurt. He started up the roadside again in silence with Daniel striding beside him. When they reached the next corner where they would part company, Judson to return to his home and Daniel to his room at the boarding house, Judson paused and turned to him. "I'll see you in the shop on Monday," he said in a flat voice.

"Yes, sir. I will be there."

"Take care of yourself," Judson added as he walked off.

The following day was Saturday, and Judson spent the morning working in his shop. In the afternoon he attended to some personal errands and later in the evening he visited the Blue Fly for a drink. On Sunday, he slept in late. When he arose, he felt groggy from sleeping too long and from the alcohol he'd consumed the night before. As he washed his face, shaved, and dressed, he resolved to spend less time at the saloon in the future. The whiskey he was in the habit of drinking was having more of an adverse effect on his senses, perhaps because he was drinking more and enjoying the experience less. He muttered to himself as he pulled aside the curtain on his bedroom window. Looking outside, he was surprised to see that it had snowed heavily during the night—the roads were clogged and the mountains shrouded in white. The sky was overcast, threatening more snow. He stayed close to home all day, but he was restless and bored.

Monday morning he opened the shop for Daniel, then left to meet with a customer. When he returned around noon, he found Daniel bent over the lathe shaping a table leg for a new order. Judson removed his coat and hat, hung them on a hook beside the door, and stood for a moment watching Daniel work. It wasn't until then that he realized Daniel was upset about something. The young man's face was pale and his hands trembled as he worked the wood. Judson walked over to him. "What's wrong?" he asked.

Daniel looked up, then set aside the piece of wood he'd been shaping and ran a shaky hand across his chin. "Louisa's father just left here. He's forbidden Louisa to see me again and threatened to have me arrested if I try to contact her."

Judson groaned and sank down onto a stool. "Louisa told him about the two of you?"

"Yes."

Judson almost wished he'd advised Louisa otherwise when she'd come into the shop seeking his counsel. "Do you want me to try talking some sense into him?"

Daniel shook his head adamantly. "No. Louisa and I will handle this."

"The two of you are still determined to carry on this relationship?"

"Yes. Nothing her father can do or say will persuade us to part."

Judson's shoulders slumped. "What can I say to talk you out of this?"

"With all due respect, sir, nothing you can say will deter us. Louisa and I are in love and want to be together."

Judson glanced morosely out the window of the shop. More snow was falling, and the sky was the color of lead. He shivered. "Then I'll respect yours and Louisa's decision. If you intend to disregard her father's wishes, I'll turn a blind eye if Louisa meets you here at the shop."

The relief on Daniel's face was palpable. "Thank you, sir. I was hoping for as much."

"You and Louisa must be discreet, however," Judson warned. "If the two of you use the shop as a meeting place, Louisa must be safely home before dark."

"Yes, sir. I will see to it."

"And you'll conduct yourself as a gentleman at all times while she is here," Judson added with a frown.

Daniel looked insulted by the insinuation behind Judson's words. "I love Louisa. I would never do anything to bring shame upon her."

"Then you have my permission and my cooperation, although I don't like sneaking behind Addams' back."

"Nor do I," Daniel said.

"This arrangement is only temporary until you can persuade Louisa's father otherwise."

"I understand."

Judson scowled as he turned away. He wasn't at all comfortable with facilitating this deceit, but he knew if he didn't lend his assistance, Daniel and Louisa would seek out some other place to meet—one that might not offer as safe a haven as they'd find here at the shop. He felt trapped, almost powerless, as if being swept along in a raging torrent and not knowing what obstacles he might encounter downstream. He didn't like that feeling—didn't like feeling responsible for circumstances out of his control. He cursed under his breath, not fully aware whether his frustration was aimed at Daniel and Louisa for their lack of judgment in getting involved with one another in the first place, or at a world where people were led by bigotry and prejudice, blindly discriminating against those who were different than themselves.

That night while lying in bed, Judson was unable to sleep. He was worried about Daniel and Louisa and what measures they might decide to take next. Although he was concerned about them, and on a certain level angry with them too, he realized that he also envied them. The kind of love they shared for one another was a rare gift. He found himself hungering for a similar kind of commitment and passion. His thoughts wandered to Rebecca Kade and the feelings he still carried for her. Perhaps he should venture a chance and tell Rebecca how he felt; find out if she might possess a glimmer of those same emotions for him. Maybe the two of them could cultivate a relationship that might grow into something worthwhile and lasting.

He groaned aloud and turned onto his side, his eyes staring into the darkness of his room. Was he willing to set aside his pride if it meant finding love and companionship? He swallowed the fear of rejection that rose like a bilious lump in his throat. Perhaps he ought to approach Rachel and tell her of his feelings for her sister. That confession might clear his conscience and pave the way for a new, fresh start with Rebecca. As he pondered that possibility in the silence and stillness of the darkened room, his heart quickened.

CHAPTER TWENTY

The next morning, Judson awoke before dawn. Unable to go back to sleep, he finally rose from bed just as the first rays of sunlight streamed over the mountain peaks. He quickly dressed, ate a bite of breakfast, and then let himself into the shop to begin work for the day. Daniel arrived a couple of hours later, and the two of them spent the day fashioning a wooden chest for a customer. Just before closing, Louisa Addams came to the shop; Daniel let her in through the side door and furtively shut it behind her. Judson conversed with the couple for a few minutes, then he pulled the blinds facing the street and busied himself at the rear of the shop while the two of them sat close together talking and holding hands. He was uncomfortable with the subterfuge he was perpetuating, but didn't know of any other way to protect the couple. He considered making a call on Louisa's father, despite Daniel's resistance to the idea, but put off making a decision about it.

After staying for about thirty minutes, Louisa left the shop before dark, as Daniel had promised she would. Afterward, the two men exchanged little conversation as Daniel prepared to leave for his own quarters at the boarding house. Judson fixed himself some dinner after Daniel left, and then sat down alone to eat. Again he mulled over the idea of paying a visit to Rachel Kade and explored the possibility of going to Draper on the weekend to see Rebecca. He was both nervous and hesitant to take action on either front, but he finally decided that calling on Rachel might prove beneficial in any case.

After finishing his supper, Judson changed into a clean shirt and left the house. He saddled his gray and started for the boarding house where Rachel lived. His stomach felt tied in knots, and his hands were sweating even though the night air was cold. It was mid-November, and the ground was covered with frost. The trees along the street had lost their leaves, looking stark and barren, and snow blanketed the mountains. A harsh winter had been forecast, and Judson shivered as he contemplated how soon the snows would glut the roads, fields, and yards of the city.

A short time later, Judson tied his horse to the hitching post in front of the two-story house where Rachel lived as a boarder. As he dismounted, the wind whipped his coat and threatened to tear the hat from his head. He steadied his hat with one hand as he walked up to the house. The front door opened into a common parlor; when he entered, he found seated on a couch in the room a young couple engaged in conversation. Opposite them, an elderly woman sat near the hearth knitting with bright red yarn. Judson was beginning to lose his nerve; he hesitated, not knowing what he was going to say once he was in Rachel's company.

Just then the front door opened, letting in a gust of cold air. He turned and was startled to see Rachel step into the parlor. Her cloak and hat were dusted with a sprinkling of snow. As she started to remove her wrap, she caught sight of him. At first glimpse she seemed pleased to see him, but then a hardness settled over her face.

Judson waited for her near the staircase where he was standing. "Hello, Rachel."

"Good evening," she returned in a stiff voice.

"Are you free for a few minutes?"

"I suppose I have a moment."

Judson glanced at the couple seated on the couch and the older woman across the room. "Is there a private place where we can talk?" he asked Rachel.

"Perhaps the dining room. There's no one there at this hour."

Judson followed her into the adjoining room. He helped her remove her cloak. She set the cloak and her fancy bonnet on a chair, then took a seat. "What did you want to speak to me about?" she asked with a steely gaze.

He didn't know how to introduce the topic he wished to discuss. He cleared his throat. "How is the hat-making business?"

"Fine, thank you." She paused, staring into his face. "I'm sure you didn't come here to discuss fashion. What do you want, Judson?"

He cringed under her acrimonious glare. "All right, I'll get straight to the point. A couple of weeks ago, I ran into Rebecca at the mercantile in Draper."

"Rebecca?"

Judson could see from Rachel's expression that this was not what she was expecting to hear from him. He flushed, realizing that she thought he'd come to make amends. "Yes. We talked for a few moments."

"Is Rebecca doing all right?"

Judson nodded. "So far as I know. She said that she likes her work as a bookkeeper for Mr. Rideout."

"Yes, she wrote me about that," Rachel said impatiently. It was as if she wanted to rush past the topic of her sister and get on to the real reason for Judson's visit.

"I'd like to see her again," Judson finally blurted.

"What?"

Judson shoved his hands into his pockets. His palms were itching, and perspiration was breaking out along his brow. "That's what I wanted to tell you—that I plan on seeing Rebecca again, if she's agreeable to it."

It took a moment for his words to sink into Rachel's head. "Oh," she said, finally comprehending his meaning.

"I wanted you to know," Judson said, clenching his fists in his pockets.

"You want permission to court my sister?" Her eyes sparked with fury.

"I'm not seeking your permission. I'm telling you as a matter of courtesy," Judson replied brusquely.

"You're a fool, Judson Carter, if you think my sister would ever entertain thoughts of you as a suitor."

"That will be her choice."

Rachel let out a scornful laugh. "Do you really think Rebecca has any affection for you?"

Judson glared at her, but didn't reply.

Rachel got to her feet and snatched up her cloak and hat. "I'm glad you came to me with this. It convinces me how truly despicable you are."

Although Judson had anticipated her reaction, he was unprepared for this attack. He watched as she turned her back to him and stalked out of the room. Her stinging words had wounded him more than he had expected. He jammed on his hat and headed for the front door. He caught a glimpse of Rachel marching up the stairs and was aware of three pairs of eyes on him as he strode across the parlor and yanked open the front door. He breathed in a gulp of cold air, relieved to be out of the rooming house and away from Rachel's wrath.

Over the next week, the clandestine meetings between Daniel and Louisa Addams began to take on a familiar routine. Louisa came to the shop after working hours whenever she could break away for a few minutes from her parents' supervision. As Judson became better acquainted with her, he grew to appreciate and admire her character.

He liked her candor and directness and her guileless charm. And he saw how smitten she was with Daniel, as was he with her. Judson hoped the relationship would work out for the young couple and that eventually her father would give his permission for them to marry.

Late one Friday afternoon about two weeks after Louisa and Daniel had been secretly seeing one another, the couple approached Judson while he was sawing a length of wood at the back of the shop. "May we speak with you for a moment?" Daniel asked, his arm around Louisa's waist.

Judson set down his hand saw. "Of course. What is it?" He looked from Daniel's earnest face to Louisa's.

Daniel cleared his throat. "Louisa and I have decided to marry."

Judson was not surprised by this declaration. He smiled at the couple. "Your father has given his permission at last?" he asked Louisa.

She shook her head, and her eyes lost some of their sheen.

"Then I don't understand," Judson said.

"We do not want to wait any longer," Daniel explained, hugging Louisa closer, "hoping that someday Louisa's father might give his consent. We are planning to be married tomorrow evening at the home of Judge Ryland."

"We'd be honored if you would consent to be there," Louisa said with a timid smile.

"And to act as a witness to our marriage," Daniel added.

Judson was stunned. He thought the couple had given up the idea of an elopement. Hadn't he provided a safe refuge for them while they awaited her father's permission? He was almost angry with them for this decision to go ahead with a marriage expressly forbidden by her father and drawing him further into this conflict. Sharp words sprang to his lips, but he managed to hold them in check. "I can't agree with this course of action you're proposing," he said in a controlled tone.

Both Daniel and Louisa looked disappointed. "Whether you agree to attend the ceremony or not is up to you," Daniel said in a determined voice. "But we are going forward with it either way."

"And we hope we can continue to count on your discretion," Louisa added solemnly.

Judson knew there was nothing he could say to dissuade them from taking this action. He could see their minds were set. "You know my feelings on the matter, but I'll respect your decision."

"Then you will be in attendance at the marriage?" Daniel asked, his eyes hopeful.

Judson remained silent for an instant, then gave a short nod.

"Thank you, Mr. Carter," Louisa burst out, gripping his hand. "I can't tell you how much this means to us."

Her face was beaming. Daniel, too, grinned in relief and pleasure. Judson didn't feel any joy in giving his consent, but he tried to smile for their sakes.

Louisa eagerly told him the time and location for the marriage. Judge Ryland's home was only a few blocks away, and the ceremony was to take place at six the next evening. Daniel would leave the shop early and meet her there.

Judson was uneasy with the whole plan, but he resolved not to tarnish their happiness with his reservations. "You'll make a beautiful bride," he said with sincerity to Louisa.

"She will, indeed," Daniel echoed before she could respond, planting a kiss on her cheek.

The three of them made further plans for the next evening's event, and Judson succeeded in convincing them to tell Louisa's father about the marriage as soon after the ceremony as possible. The couple left the shop arm in arm, happily whispering together.

The next afternoon, Daniel left the cabinet shop at three to prepare for his wedding. Soon afterward, Judson pulled the blinds on the shop window and locked the front door. As he strode into the living quarters of his house to change into his best suit of clothing, he felt light-hearted. Daniel's enthusiasm and excitement over his upcoming nuptials had finally infected Judson as well. Judson hummed a tune to himself as he buttoned the stiff, detachable collar around his neck. He looked at his reflection in the mirror as he combed his hair into place. He was pleased that Daniel and Louisa had taken him into their confidence and invited him to witness their marriage. The misgivings he'd had earlier about the match had faded in the exhilaration of the moment. He slicked down a straying strand of hair, glanced a last time at his appearance, then turned away from the mirror and slipped on his top coat. His boots were polished to a high sheen, and his stylishly cut trousers and tailcoat were crisp and fresh. He was just ready to step out of the house when he heard an urgent knocking at the shop door.

He paused, his hand on the latch, ready to let himself out. The rapping sounded again, this time more insistent. He frowned, annoyed by the interruption. Whoever was at the door, couldn't he see the pulled shade indicating that the shop was closed for the day? The knocking came a third time, so hard that it rattled the pane of glass mounted in the carved wood door.

Scowling, Judson hurried through the entrance leading from his living quarters into the shop and approached the front door. He could see the silhouette of a person standing in front of the square of glass in the door. As he reached to raise the shade over the glass, prepared to turn away whoever was standing outside, a desperate rapping sounded on the window pane. He jerked up the shade and was stunned to see Louisa Addams standing there with her fist to the glass. He quickly unlocked the door and opened it.

"Oh, I'm so grateful you haven't left yet," Louisa burst out. "Is Daniel here?"

Judson saw at a glance the look of concern on her face. He motioned for her to come inside, then shut the door behind her. "I thought Daniel was with you. I was just about to leave for the judge's home," he said.

"We decided this afternoon to meet earlier and go to Judge Ryland's home together. I waited for Daniel at the appointed place, but he never came." Her voice was strained.

Judson frowned. "He left here two hours ago. Are you sure he wasn't planning to meet you at Judge Ryland's house?"

Louisa shook her head. "He was to have met me at five," she replied in a hoarse whisper.

Judson pulled over a chair for her to sit on. She took the seat without speaking. "Let's not get alarmed yet. There must be some explanation. Perhaps Daniel got detained and is on his way to the judge's house right now."

"He would have let me know if he was going to be late." She began wringing her hands in her lap.

She hadn't removed her cloak since entering the shop, and it hung open at the front. Judson could see a glimpse of her pale pink dress trimmed with satin rosettes and ribbons. She looked like a little girl dressed in her best frock to attend a tea party, he thought fleetingly. His heart went out to her in her distress.

"I'm sure everything is fine, Louisa. Why don't you wait for Daniel at the judge's home while I go to his room at the boarding house to see if he's still there. Then I'll come to Judge Ryland's house. Probably both of you will be there waiting for me by that time." He smiled, trying to set her mind at ease.

She stood up quickly from the chair. "If he's not there, will you search for him?" she asked. Her eyes were wide and anxious and seemed to reflect the color of the pale pink dress she wore. "I'm afraid something terrible has happened to him."

Judson walked with her to the door of the shop. "Nothing's happened to him," he reassured her. "Something unexpected has come up, that's all; and Daniel will take care of it and meet you like he said he would."

Louisa gazed at him with eyes yearning to believe his words.

Judson patted her hand. "Everything will be fine. You can give Daniel a good scolding afterward," he added, smiling.

She didn't return his smile. Her whole countenance was clouded with doubt and fear. Something in her look made Judson shiver, and he felt a cold dread begin to grip him. He knew as plainly as Louisa did that nothing would prevent Daniel from meeting her on time for their marriage—if he was able.

Judson opened the shop door for her. Dusk was settling in and a light snow had started to fall. Louisa slipped out into the night, her slight figure a shadow in the thickening gloom.

After she left, Judson stood beside the door for a moment contemplating the situation. A knot of worry was tightening inside him. He locked the shop door, pulled down the blind on the window, then left the house. The air was bitter cold, and a sharp wind pierced through his coat, chilling him. He blew on his hands to warm them, then thrust them into the pockets of his overcoat. He walked the several blocks to the boarding house where Daniel lived, climbed the stairs to the attic room, and knocked on the door. No one answered. "Daniel," he called. Still no response. "Daniel, it's me. Judson."

When everything remained silent behind the closed door, Judson turned away and began retracing his steps toward the shop. A feeling of doom was pressing upon him. He decided to saddle his horse and ride over to Judge Ryland's home to see if Daniel had arrived there yet. If he wasn't there, Judson didn't know where to look for him next. An image of Louisa's stricken face passed through his mind, and he hastened his steps. By this time it was nearing six, and darkness cloaked the streets and fields. A few electric street lamps provided a dim glow, but the patches of light were faint and far apart. Judson had to strain to see in the murky blackness.

As Judson neared the shop, he came abreast of an alleyway between two buildings. The alley was long and narrow, a black hole in the darkness; Judson shivered as he walked past it. Before he had taken very many more steps, his skin prickled with a sudden premonition. He paused and glanced over his shoulder at the entrance to the alleyway. The prickling made his hands tingle and the blood rush from his cheeks. Slowly, he turned around and started back toward the alley. The snow was falling thicker now, making it more difficult to see. It was building up into drifts, and Judson's shoes were soggy from slogging through it.

When he reached the entrance to the alley, he halted. It was dark in the space between the buildings, but a glimmer of light at the other end, where the alley opened onto the street across the block, cast an eerie glow. Cautiously, Judson started forward into the passageway between the two brick buildings. He stared straight ahead, pausing only once to swipe the snow away from his eyes. He'd gone about halfway through the block when he spied a shadow on the ground a few feet ahead of him. He squinted, trying to make sense of the shape. Then he heard a faint groan. His heart lurched in his chest and he sprinted forward, his eyes bulging as he fought to see through the darkness that filled the alley like a black vapor.

With the blood pounding in his head, he reached the spot in two or three running strides. The illumination coming from the street lamp at the opposite end of the block threw a wan circle of light on the figure of a young man crumpled on the cold, snowy ground. Judson's brow broke out into a sweat. "Daniel!" he cried out, his voice raw with shock and disbelief. He dropped to his knees beside the still form of his friend.

Kneeling beside him, Judson couched the young man's head in his lap. Daniel moaned again as Judson brushed the hair from his brow. "Oh, Lord, have mercy," Judson prayed urgently as he leaned over Daniel's limp body. Daniel was still dressed in his work clothes, and his coat hung open revealing his rumpled shirt bunched up at the waist. As Judson started to straighten the shirt, reacting in a haze of panic, he felt something warm and wet on his hand. He shuddered in horror when he saw the dark stain of blood seeping in an ever-widening circle on the front of Daniel's shirt. "Daniel!"

The young man didn't move, but Judson could hear his faint, shallow breathing. Judson's own breath roared in his ears. "You're going to be all right, Daniel. Hold on. I'll get help." Judson closed his eyes, squeezing them tightly to shut out the sight and sound and smell of death stealthily closing in around him. "Oh, Lord, please be merciful," he whimpered, rocking Daniel in his arms.

Late that evening, Judson sat alone in the darkness on the floor of his shop, his back slumped against the wall and his legs pressed against his chest. His hands hung limp over his knees, and his head sagged. He knew he would never be able to erase from his mind the sight of Daniel lying in that alleyway, his shirt oozing scarlet from the knife wound in his stomach. He had cradled Daniel in his arms, smoothing his black hair from his pale brow and knowing it was too late to save him. Daniel had died before Judson could even summon help.

Judson passed a shaking hand across his forehead. Having to tell Louisa had been excruciating; she had given an anguished scream upon receiving the news of Daniel's death, and nothing Judson said would console her. He had been the one to summon her parents to Judge Ryland's house, and they could scarcely calm their distraught daughter.

A sob welled up in Judson's throat. He laid his head on his arms and moaned, trying to block out the horrifying images. The grief he felt was as painful as if he'd been pierced through with the point of a sword. Groaning, he staggered to his feet and began pacing the room. He thought again about Louisa and the suffering she was experiencing. He was bitterly sorry now that he had discouraged her and Daniel from marrying; he regretted having counseled them to wait. They should have wed when they first decided upon it, he reasoned. At least, they could have had a few weeks of happiness together. But now . . . he couldn't even complete the thought, it was too terrible to bear.

He cast his eyes around the darkened room, seeking relief from his pain. Stumbling over to the lamp mounted on the wall, he switched it on. The light flickered, then flared into life, illuminating a portion of the room with a dull glow. He dropped onto a chair, exhausted and brokenhearted. As he leaned back in his seat, his glance fell on an object resting on the work bench. He reached over to the bench and retrieved it, realizing it was Daniel's book from which the young man had read nearly every day while eating his lunch at the shop. He gazed morosely at the volume. In his excitement and eagerness to leave the shop early and meet Louisa in preparation for their marriage, Daniel must have forgotten to take the book with him.

Judson's eyes itched with tears as he turned the volume over in his hands, recalling the many times he'd seen Daniel hunched over his book reading silently and attentively. With numbed fingers, he opened the book to the first page of text. The words on the page swam before his eyes. He blinked and harnessed his attention. Then he began to read the words aloud in a broken whisper as a tribute to the friend he had lost:

"I, Nephi, having been born of goodly parents, therefore I was taught somewhat in all the learning of my father; and having seen many afflictions in the course of my days, nevertheless, having been highly favored of the Lord in all my days; yea, having had a great knowledge of the goodness and the mysteries of God, therefore I make a record of my proceedings in my days."

During the few days between Daniel's passing and his burial, Judson read all of his friend's copy of the Book of Mormon. He considered placing the book in Daniel's coffin, so that it would be with him always. But then he decided that the book was for the benefit of the living, not the dead.

He made arrangements to purchase a burial plot in the Draper cemetery; it lay next to the grave of Solomon Curtis, Daniel's father. The only mourners to attend the service besides himself were Lorin Stotts and his wife. Louisa's parents would not allow her to come to the graveside service. The bishop of the Draper ward joined them at the cemetery and said a few words on Daniel's behalf and then dedicated the grave. Judson had carved a wooden marker with Daniel's Ute and English names on it, his age, and date of death. At the base of the marker, he had carved in bas relief the image of a wolf.

A week later, Judson completed the bureau and the side table he and Daniel had been constructing for Louisa Addams. He put the last coat of glossy finish on the wood and polished it to a gleaming shine. The carving Daniel had done on the two pieces was exceptional—perfect in form and detail. When Judson was finished polishing the table top, he sat back and took a moment to admire the finished product. He stared at the set of furniture, thinking about Daniel and Louisa.

For the past week, the couple had seldom left his thoughts. He kept remembering their love and devotion for one another and their joy in simply being together. From their example, he'd gained a new perspective on what it meant to give one's heart completely. He'd seen firsthand that love was something worth fighting for, nourishing, and protecting. His last visit with Rachel Kade before Daniel's death had been unnerving. Her vitriolic response had discouraged him and deterred him from approaching Rebecca openly and honestly about his feelings. For his young friends, love's bloom had been cut short; he resolved not to let a chance at love be too late for Rebecca and himself. That possibility gave him renewed hope, and with that hope, determination.

He ran his hand over the surface of the bureau, feeling its smooth finish. Tomorrow morning he would personally deliver the furniture to the Addams' home; that would give him an opportunity to talk with Louisa as well and see how she was faring. He blew a speck of dust off the top of the bureau, gazed at the handsome set one last time, then turned his attention to a rough square of walnut resting on his work bench. Last night, after closing the shop for the evening, he had cut the piece of handsome, dark wood into the desired size and begun to shape it. The exposed wood grain was distinctive in texture, pattern, and color; a beautiful sample, well suited for the design Judson had in mind. He spent an hour under the light of the electric lamp molding and shaping the wood, concentrating only on his work.

The next morning, Judson prepared to load the two items of furniture into the bed of his wagon for delivery to the Addams' home. Before carrying the chest of drawers out to the wagon, however, he took from the work bench a package he'd wrapped in brown paper and string. Across the front of the package he had written the name *Miss Louisa Addams*. He opened the bottom drawer of the bureau and carefully set the package inside. He stared at it for an instant, remembering Daniel's habit of reading from the book of scripture. Even though Louisa was not a member of the Mormon faith, she undoubtedly knew of Daniel's attachment for the book and what it represented, both in a spiritual sense and as a token of respect and remembrance for his mother. It was the right decision to give the book to Louisa, Judson resolved. Daniel would have wanted her to have it.

CHAPTER TWENTY-ONE

Rebecca turned aside from the adding machine and stretched her back. She had been at her desk all afternoon without a break, and her back was beginning to cramp. She massaged one shoulder with her hand. It was the same shoulder that had been injured two months ago in the barn fire when the falling timber had struck her, and at times when she stayed bent over the desk for long periods it began to ache.

She raised her head to look out the single window of the tiny, closet-like office. It was snowing, and people scurried along the streets bundled to their noses in coats and hats. No sound came from the window; it was as if the snow had muffled any outside noise. There was much more activity outside her office door, which led directly into the store. Customers came and went, chatting with one another as they shopped. As she glanced out the doorway, she spied Lettie straightening the goods lining a nearby shelf. She could hear Lettie humming to herself as she worked. Rebecca smiled as she watched her friend. Lettie's sunny nature was one of the things that had made it bearable for Rebecca to be away from the ranch for such an extended time. She had been living with Lettie in the small, rented room of a private home ever since coming to Draper to find employment.

The dual occupancy was turning out well. Most days, including Saturdays, both of them worked at the Rideout store, and on Sundays she had been accompanying Lettie to church meetings in the Draper Ward. Their relationship, living in such close quarters, had been a smooth one so far, free from disagreement or ill feelings. Rebecca attributed that to her friend's cheery disposition. Their rented room sat across the block from a molasses mill, and the sweet smell of molasses syrup seemed to seep into the walls and permeate the house. Rebecca's clothing, and even her hair, smelled of molasses. Perhaps it was this sweetness they breathed every day that also contributed to their feelings of cordiality, she thought with a smile.

Shutting her ears against the noise coming from the large, open room outside her door, Rebecca turned back to the store ledger lying open in front of her on the desk. Today was Saturday, and Mr. Rideout would be sitting down with her at the first of next week, as he did each week, to go over the account books. He kept a close eye on the store's financial records, studying the fluctuating numbers between the accounts receivable and the accounts payable. Rebecca admired Mr. Rideout; not only was he a successful businessman, but he played an integral part in community affairs as well. His store, and particularly the hall above the store, was home to all kinds of public meetings and gatherings as well as social and cultural events. In spite of her longing to be back at the ranch, she liked working for Mr. Rideout and enjoyed her job of balancing the books for his store. The work was time-consuming, but not difficult. Her experience in keeping the financial records of the ranch for her father had lent some familiarity to this new task. And she was earning enough of a salary to pay for her expenses as well as send some money home to help with the operation of the ranch.

Rebecca glanced at the clock on the desk. It was nearing four p.m. and her shift at the store ended earlier in the afternoon on Saturdays than on weekdays. She hurried with her work, focusing on the list of numbers she was entering into the adding machine. She had never used an adding machine before she began her job at the store, never even seen one, in fact; but she had quickly mastered the technique, and the machine proved to be a valuable and reliable time-saver in helping her with the accounting. Mr. Rideout also owned a fine, new Remington typewriter that he used to type correspondence for his business. Rebecca hadn't yet learned how to operate it, but she hoped Mr. Rideout would teach her in connection with her duties.

Absorbed with her work, she screened out the clamor coming from the main room of the store, and so she didn't hear Lettie approaching her. She jerked in surprise when Lettie tapped her shoulder. "Rebecca," Lettie whispered fervently. "You have a visitor."

Rebecca looked up from her ledger book. "What?" she blinked, staring at Lettie's twinkling blue eyes and eager smile.

"A gentleman caller. It's Mr. Carter. He asked if you're available to speak with him for a moment."

"Mr. Carter?" Rebecca repeated, still trying to collect her thoughts. "He's here? Now?"

"Yes, now. He's standing right outside at the counter."

Rebecca leaned in her chair to peek outside the room, but all she could see was the end of the long counter. "What did you tell him?" she asked Lettie, feeling her face flush with a sudden rush of self-consciousness.

"I told him I'd inquire. And he looks quite handsome, I might add."

Rebecca's cheeks flamed an even deeper shade of red. She stood up from her chair and smoothed the skirt of her dress. "Do you know what he wants?"

Lettie shook her head, and her brown curls jiggled. "But I wouldn't stand here keeping him waiting if I were you." There was no mistaking the gleam of excitement in her voice.

"All right. Please tell him I'll be out shortly."

Lettie squeezed Rebecca's arm in anticipation, then hurried back out to the counter. Rebecca heard her repeat the words and then Judson's deep voice answering in reply. She pressed her hands together nervously. Ever since

Judson's visit to the store nearly six weeks earlier, thoughts of him had been darting through the back of her mind like fireflies in the night sky. After he'd left the store on that occasion, she'd hoped he'd return to say goodbye before leaving for Salt Lake City. But he hadn't. She didn't realize until this moment, standing shakily beside her desk, how much she wanted to see him again. She drew a deep breath, ran a hand over her hair to smooth it, and stepped across the threshold into the main section of the mercantile.

Judson's head was turned when she entered, which gave her a chance to study him unobserved for an instant. He was dressed in a gray suit with matching vest and carried his hat in his hand. His dark hair was combed meticulously into place, and the sun coming in through the window cast a ray of light across his cheek. Lettie had been accurate in her assessment—he did look very handsome. He turned suddenly, and his face broke into a smile when he spotted her. She moved forward to greet him.

"Good afternoon, Miss Kade," he said, bowing slightly. "I wasn't sure you'd be here on a Saturday."

"I generally work until four o'clock on Saturdays," she answered. His presence started her heart pounding, and she blushed knowing her voice was too eager. She glanced at Lettie who hovered close by. "Both Lettie and I work on Saturdays."

Judson's glance flicked to Lettie. "Miss Miller was kind enough to mention that and relay my request to you."

Lettie nodded until her curls bounced. She stood all aflutter, eager, Rebecca supposed, to hear the purpose of

Judson's visit. Rebecca's eyes returned to Judson. "Have you business in Draper today, Mr. Carter?"

Judson transferred his hat to the other hand. "Not in the strictest sense of the word," he answered.

Rebecca tilted her head, not sure of his meaning.

"I didn't come to conduct business for the shop. I was hoping I might have the opportunity to see you."

"Oh." Rebecca was surprised by this response and by his lack of hesitancy in expressing it, even with Lettie standing near hanging on his every word.

Judson rested a hand on the counter. "It's nearly four now, Miss Kade. May I have the privilege of walking you home?"

Rebecca blinked, taken back by his unexpected request. "Well, I . . ." She didn't know what to say in reply. She paused, frowning with indecision.

A look of disappointment passed across Judson's face, and he began fumbling with his hat.

"What a splendid idea, Mr. Carter," Lettie suddenly sang out. "I have work to do here for another hour or so and can't leave yet. If you accompany Rebby home, she won't have to walk alone."

Rebecca turned to stare at her friend. Lettie knew perfectly well that they were planning to leave the store at the same time. Lettie sent her a swift, meaningful look. Swallowing, Rebecca shifted her gaze to Judson. "Thank you, Mr. Carter," she said. "I would enjoy your company."

Judson's face brightened. "When you're ready, I'll help you with your coat. The snowfall has begun to lighten, but it's still quite cold outside."

"Give me a moment to put away my things in the office, and I'll be ready to go."

"Certainly. Perhaps Miss Miller will be so kind as to keep me company while I wait."

"I would be delighted to do so, Mr. Carter," Lettie gushed.

Rebecca could hear the two of them talking while she closed her ledger book and straightened the items on the desk. Her heart was racing and her hands shaking as she reached for her coat. She paused to draw several deep breaths to steady herself and then exited the office. Judson was waiting for her in the same spot, but Lettie was away from the counter helping a customer.

Judson smiled as she approached. "May I?" he asked, holding out a hand to take her coat.

She handed the coat to him and he helped her on with it, then he opened the store door and they stepped outside. Hugging her coat tighter around her, she glanced up at the sky. Snow was still falling, but the sky was beginning to clear and Rebecca could see patches of blue overhead.

"How are you liking your work as a bookkeeper?" Judson asked as they started up the sidewalk together.

"I'm enjoying it. Mr. Rideout is a kind employer."

"And Miss Miller? Are you and she still sharing living quarters?"

"Yes. Lettie has been very generous."

"I imagine she can also be very talkative," Judson said with a wink.

Rebecca began to feel more at ease as they walked. The sidewalk was slushy and snow spilled over the top of her shoes, but the sun peeping out from the clouds warmed her shoulders. "Lettie is a dear. She always has some activity or other she's involved in and tries to get me to share in it with her."

"Such as?" Judson asked.

"For instance, she's a member of the Draper Dramatic Club. The club just finished putting on the play *Robin Hood*, and Lettie had a small part. She induced me to see the play three separate times."

Judson laughed at this last remark. "Enthusiasm can be as contagious as a case of the measles."

"Lettie has plenty of that." As Rebecca made the comment, her feet slid on the snowy walk, and she nearly lost her balance.

"You'd better hang onto my arm," Judson said hastily, extending his elbow toward her. "The snow is starting to turn to ice."

Rebecca slipped her hand through the crook of Judson's arm. His top coat provided a cozy, warm nest for her fingers. They had reached the corner of the street by this time. "We turn here," Rebecca said. "Our apartment is a couple of blocks down the road."

They continued talking as they walked. Judson asked her about conditions at the ranch, and she explained how her cousin Wyatt had gone back home after the roundup and sale of the cattle, but Patrick had remained to help at the ranch while she stayed in Draper to earn some extra money.

"Have you been home to visit at all since coming to Draper to work?" Judson asked.

"Only once for the weekend. Patrick is planning to ride into Draper next week to give me a report on things at the ranch. I'll be glad to see him."

"What about your gelding? Has he recovered from the injuries he suffered in the fire?"

Rebecca shook her head, and when she spoke sorrow tinged her voice. "The wounds to his leg have left him lame. He's pastured in a large corral on the hillside; with rest and care, I'm hoping he'll improve, but I may never be able to use him again to work cattle."

"I'm genuinely sorry to hear that." Judson drew her arm closer.

"I've been riding my father's horse when I'm home. He's a tall, strong chestnut who has a natural instinct for cow cutting. But I miss saddling Onyx for a ride into the hills."

"And the calf you nearly lost to the mountain lion? Is it doing well?"

Rebecca brightened. "Yes, fully recovered and growing healthy and strong. Micah told me when I was home last that he'd spotted cougar tracks in the snow around the cattle pens. He tried to hunt down the animal but wasn't successful. I'm guessing it was the same cougar that attacked my calf last summer."

Judson's eyes clouded and he looked away, as if he were viewing something in the distance that saddened him. "Life can be beset with cougars when we least expect it, can't it?" he said in a bleak tone.

His words were melancholy, and Rebecca wondered what thoughts prompted them. "How is your business doing?" she asked, hoping he might divulge whatever was troubling him.

"Business is good. I've been busy."

There was an uncharacteristic lack of enthusiasm in his voice, Rebecca noticed. "New customers?" she asked.

"Some." He glanced over at her and smiled again. Then lifting his head, he asked, "What's that pleasant smell in the air?"

"Oh, it's probably the molasses you smell."

"Molasses?" He sniffed the air.

"Yes," Rebecca said, chuckling. "Lettie and I live near a molasses mill. You can smell the molasses syrup from blocks away."

"Is that right? Have you ever been there to see how it's made?"

"Lettie and I visited the mill once. We saw how the stalks of cane are ground and the juice collected."

"I'd like to hear about that," Judson said.

"Well, the stalks are brought to the mill and stacked in large piles. Then a mill worker puts each stalk through a heavy iron roller that squeezes out the juice." Rebecca demonstrated the process with her hands as she talked. "The juice drips into a trough that empties into a barrel.

The barrels are emptied into a machine that boils the juice into molasses syrup. It's more complicated than how I've explained it," she smiled, "but that's basically the process."

"Interesting," Judson commented with a grin.

"The best part is if the mill operator gives you a taste of the syrup," Rebecca added, chuckling. "Lettie and I purchased a small bottle of the molasses syrup when we visited the mill, and it was the sweetest, smoothest syrup I'd ever tasted."

"All this talk about molasses syrup has whet my appetite," Judson said, tucking her hand more snugly into the crook of his arm. "Will you have supper with me this evening?"

Rebecca sucked in her breath, surprised by his invitation. "Yes, I guess I could," she stammered.

"I'm staying at the Green Hotel, and the proprietor's wife is a good cook. She serves supper at six."

"All right," Rebecca said.

"Let me pick you up at your place a few minutes before then. I'll bring a horse and buggy so we won't have to walk in the cold and the snow."

Rebecca had practically forgotten all about the snow. His words warmed her so that even the winter air was no longer chilly. "That will be fine," she replied.

"I'll look forward to it."

It was only a few steps further to Rebecca's door. "Here it is," she said. "This is where Lettie and I have a room."

Judson paused in front of the small adobe home. Two front windows, framed by yellow curtains, looked out onto a small porch. "This is nice," he remarked.

"The family who owns the home are hospitable people. They didn't mind when Lettie asked them if she could share her room with a friend." She removed her hand from Judson's arm and started toward the porch steps.

"I'll see you in a couple of hours," Judson said, lifting his hat.

His broad smile revealed the dimple in his cheek, and Rebecca suddenly found it difficult to catch her breath. "Thank you for accompanying me home."

"It was my pleasure."

As she started up the steps, Rebecca's heart was hammering with anticipation at the thought of the evening ahead.

Judson pulled out the chair for Rebecca to be seated at the linen-covered table. He hung her coat over the back of a chair and seated himself across from her. "I hope you trust my judgment on this place," he teased.

"I'm sure I won't be disappointed."

The proprietor's wife appeared at their table a few moments later; roasted chicken and dumplings were on the menu this evening, she explained, and Judson requested a plate for Rebecca and for himself.

As he ordered their meal, Rebecca forced herself to relax. She eased back into her chair and folded her hands in her lap. She had only dined out with a gentleman twice before and felt inexperienced and nervous. She was grateful to her mother for teaching her proper dining etiquette, and she relied on that training now. She picked up her napkin and laid it across her lap, then studied the silverware resting on either side of the empty space reserved for her plate. The hotel and dining room were not fancy by any stretch of the imagination, but the place was clean and crowded with customers.

Judson cleared his throat. "Thank you for joining me for supper."

"Thank you for asking me," she returned, smiling. She couldn't disguise the happiness she felt just being with him.

He leaned forward in his chair and placed his hands on the table. His fingers drummed the table top. "I was being truthful this afternoon when I told you that I had come to Draper to see you," he began slowly. He glanced up at her, and his eyes were solemn. "Part of the reason why I wanted to see you was to give you this."

Rebecca watched him reach into his trousers pocket and draw out an article wrapped in a bit of soft cloth. He removed the cloth and placed the object on the table. "Oh!" Rebecca's hand flew to her mouth when she saw what lay on the table. "Papa's pocketwatch!"

"Yes." Judson picked up the watch and cradled it in the palm of his hand. The silver case shimmered brightly through his fingers, and the chain made a glittering trail on the table in front of him, like a silvery stream of water.

"Rachel gave this to me when I came out to the ranch with her after your father's death. I always felt uncomfortable about taking it."

Rebecca stared at the timepiece, her emotions close to the surface.

"It doesn't belong to me." He held out the watch to her. "You're the rightful owner."

Gazing at the timepiece, Rebecca was unable to speak. The silver case was buffed to a gleaming shine, and the chain sparkled. Judson nudged his hand closer, and the chain made a tinkling sound as it traveled across the table. She lifted her eyes to meet his, then reaching out she took the pocketwatch from his hand. She studied the familiar etching on the front of the case and felt its weight in her hand. "Thank you, Judson," she said in a whisper.

"I shined it up a bit. I hope you don't mind."

The smile in her eyes answered his question. She opened the case and gazed at the front piece. The glass cover gleamed and glimmered under the lamp light. She put the watch to her ear to hear its soft, gentle ticking; it seemed to match the beating of her own heart. She looked up at Judson. "I didn't expect this, but I'm very grateful."

"I'm glad," he replied simply.

She stared at the timepiece again, then lovingly set it on the table in front of her where she could keep it within sight.

Judson stirred in his chair. "There's a second reason why I wished to see you," he said.

His voice sounded husky and drew Rebecca's attention. "Yes?" she asked.

"I want to know if you'll allow me to call on you in the future."

Rebecca's first response was confusion. "Call on me?"

"Yes. Call on you. Invite you out for an evening or visit you on an afternoon." He stuffed a finger between his shirt collar and his neck as if to loosen his collar so he could breathe easier.

"Oh. I see." She hid a smile behind her hand, enchanted by his request.

"I don't want you to say yes out of gratitude for the watch," he said quickly, as if the thought had just occurred to him.

"No, I wouldn't," she replied.

"And I only want you to agree if you really want to."

"I understand."

"You don't have to respond right now with your answer if you need time to think about it. I certainly would understand your hesitation, considering the past circumstances."

Rebecca could suppress her smile no longer. "Are you going to allow me a chance to answer or not?"

"Yes, of course. I'm sorry," he said, his face reddening.

She leaned forward in her chair. "Then the answer is yes. I would very much enjoy your calling on me."

He let out his breath in a quick puff. "That's good. That's very good."

As Rebecca sat at her desk in the small office of the Rideout store, she had a hard time keeping her mind on her work. She had to keep forcing her attention back to the figures on the page and focus on their meaning rather than let her thoughts wander to Judson and the evening they had spent together on Saturday.

She rested her chin in the palm of her hand and gazed out the window above her desk. The ground was sheeted with snow, and the sky was bleak. Gray, low-lying clouds stretched along the base of the mountains, concealing them from sight. She stared out the window, thinking about what Judson had told her of Daniel and Louisa's romance, and Daniel's tragic murder. The news of Daniel's death had brought tears to her eyes as she'd sat across the table from Judson listening to his account of it. She saw how much the event distressed him and how difficult it was for him to talk about it. He was anxious for the authorities to find Daniel's murderer and frustrated with the lack of progress they had made in the case. The subject had dampened their mood for the remainder of the evening, and Judson had apologized for that; but Rebecca felt relieved that he had discussed it with her.

As they drove home after supper in the buggy Judson had rented, he had told her about his visit with Rachel four weeks earlier, before Daniel's death, and their conversation together. Under a canopy of softly falling snow, he had shared his thoughts about his and Rachel's previous relationship.

He had cared for Rachel and at one time entertained thoughts of marriage, he'd confessed; but now he was glad they were not together. It would have been a tremendous mistake for both of them. Rebecca appreciated his candor and honesty; it cleared the air between them and allowed them to establish a foundation for their own relationship to blossom. Rebecca was unsure of what her sister's feelings would be in all of this. Rachel had not confided in Rebecca when she'd first begun her relationship with Judson, nor had she said anything after the courtship ended. But of one thing Rebecca was certain—the evening she had spent in Judson's company filled her with joy, and she longed to see him again.

Now as she struggled to concentrate on her work, she kept glancing at the clock on her desk. The minutes seemed to creep by. She stayed at her task throughout the morning, and after lunch she wrote up the weekly financial report for Mr. Rideout's review. She hurried through the process, completing it in less time than usual. Patrick was scheduled to meet her at the store sometime that afternoon to give her an accounting of what was happening on the ranch, and she wanted to be finished with her work before he arrived.

She glanced at the clock again, then arose from her chair. Arching her back, she walked out of the office and into the main section of the store. Several people were shopping in the mercantile; she stood just outside the door of her office watching them for a moment. She spotted Lettie down one of the far aisles helping a customer find an article on the store shelf.

Just as she was about to return to her office, she saw the door to the mercantile swing open and a tall, lanky fellow step inside. She smiled and hurried over to him. "Patrick, hello. It's so good to see you." She gave him a quick hug and then led the way to her office. Pulling over a chair, she invited him to sit down.

"How are you getting along, Rebby?" he asked, removing his hat and placing it on his knee. The hat was as rumpled and worn as an old shoelace.

"I'm doing all right. What about you? How is everything going at the Double K?"

He gave her a report of activities at the ranch. Micah had paid the wages to the cowhands after receiving the cash from the sale of the cattle at market, and there was a little more money than they'd hoped left for expenses. Jake Baxter had come to the ranch house for his pay and asked Micah to hire him back on as a cowhand, to which Micah refused. Patrick had bought some winter feed for the cattle and horses, and the stock seemed to be doing well. And the ranch hands had completed building the new barn with help from neighboring ranchers and friends.

Rebecca breathed a sigh of relief as she listened to his explanation. Although she missed being at the ranch, the extra money she'd earned in Draper had helped to tip the scales. Losing the Double K was less of a danger now. She and Patrick discussed other matters pertaining to the operation of the ranch and her work at the mercantile.

"I'll be coming home for Christmas, but then I'll return to Draper. I'd like to keep working for a few months more until we feel like we're on stable ground with regard to the ranch. How much longer can you stay at the Double K, Patrick?"

"As long as you need me," he replied.

"I can't thank you enough," she said, reaching over to squeeze his hand, "you and your parents. I know it's a sacrifice for them to have you away."

"Don't worry about that, Rebby. My brothers pull together in a pinch like a team of draft horses. I can say that much for them." His blue eyes crinkled with a smile.

"Nevertheless, I want you to know how much I appreciate it."

Patrick shrugged off her compliment. "I'd better be getting back," he said, replacing his hat. "I told Andrus I'd check on the stock in the north pasture this afternoon."

He rose to his feet, and Rebecca followed suit. She walked with him out of the office and toward the door of the mercantile. "Wait a minute, Patrick. There's the girl who's been sharing her room with me. I'd like you to meet her. Lettie," she called.

Lettie, who was standing only a few feet away stocking a shelf with goods, turned when Rebecca called her name.

Rebecca motioned her over. "Lettie, I want to introduce you to my cousin, Patrick McKellar. He's helping at the ranch while I'm away. Patrick, meet my good friend, Miss Lettice Miller."

Patrick swept off his hat. "Nice to make your acquaintance, Miss Miller," he said, accompanying his words with an awkward bow.

"And yours, Mr. McKellar. Rebby has told me how much she appreciates your help at the ranch." Lettie favored him with a friendly smile.

"It isn't all that much," he mumbled, twisting his hat in his hands.

"You're from Arizona, aren't you?" Lettie pursued.

"That's right. My family runs a cattle ranch there."

"And I miss the McKellars terribly," Rebecca interjected. "It's been wonderful having Patrick here for the last two months."

"She only says that because she doesn't have to stay at the ranch with me," Patrick said with dry humor.

Lettie giggled, and the blush on her cheeks brought her tawny freckles prominently to the surface.

"Well, I'd better be on my way," Patrick said. "Pleasure to meet you," he added, nodding at Lettie. He kissed Rebecca's cheek, then jammed on his hat and strode out the door.

Rebecca watched him until he was out of sight, smiling wistfully. She wished she were going to the ranch with him. She turned when she felt Lettie's hand grip her arm.

"Rebby, for heaven's sake, why didn't you tell me how charming your cousin is!" Lettie exclaimed.

"What?"

"Mr. McKellar. He seems so kind and considerate; and nice-looking, too. I've never seen eyes as blue as his."

Rebecca struggled to hold back a giggle. "Why, Lettie Miller, are you attracted to my cousin?"

A frown sprang to Lettie's face. "What would be wrong with that?"

"It never occurred to me to look at him in that light. He's just Patrick—plain, dependable Patrick."

"I imagine he's much more than that, Rebby." Lettie cast a longing look at the door Patrick had just exited. "Will he be coming into the store to see you again?"

"Yes, but I'm not sure when. We didn't talk about that."

Lettie plucked at a strand of curly hair. "When he does come back, will you tell me? I'd like to talk with him again."

Rebecca grinned. Lettie wasn't the least bit bashful about sharing her feelings. "I'll be sure to let you know."

Lettie returned to the shelf she was stocking, and Rebecca went back to her office. She sat down at the desk, smiling to herself. She wouldn't have imagined Patrick to be someone her friend would find interesting. Patrick was a wonderful person, but in her opinion was not especially handsome or charming. Of all the McKellar boys, Patrick was probably the least socially-minded and the most plain looking. She loved him like a brother, and picturing him in the role of a suitor was an unfamiliar thought. As she went back to work, she felt comforted after seeing Patrick and hearing his report concerning the Double K.

CHAPTER TWENTY-TWO

Rebecca climbed down from the buckboard, clutching her traveling case and purse. "Thank you for coming to Draper to get me and bringing me home," she said to Micah, who was collecting her suitcase from the bed of the wagon.

"You're welcome. Glad to see you back at the ranch, even if it's only for a few days," Micah said.

Rebecca stood beside the wagon trying to take in the view around her all at once. She couldn't wait to saddle Star and take a long ride across the ranch lands. She grasped a tighter hold of her satchel and followed Micah to the porch. He opened the door of the house for her and set her bag inside. "Thanks again, Micah."

He tipped his hat. "After you get settled, we'll talk some more," he said.

She nodded. Micah left the porch to return to his chores, and Rebecca spent several minutes just walking through the rooms of the house. Everything was as she left it last. She ran her fingers across her father's desk as she walked by it and straightened a book on the bookshelf. Drawing in a deep breath, she smiled, thrilled to be home.

After she'd unpacked her things, she went to the kitchen to prepare supper. Patrick would be joining her for the evening meal as soon as he returned from checking on the cattle. She glanced out the kitchen window. The sun shone brightly on the melting snow. Even though it was only two days before Christmas, the weather was as clear and sunny as a spring day. If the temperatures kept up as they had over the last week, she doubted there would be any snow left on the ground by the time Christmas arrived. She didn't mind, though. The warm weather would allow her the opportunity for a long horseback ride into the hills.

While she waited for Patrick, she removed her parents' Book of Mormon from her satchel. She had taken it with her to Draper and while there had read from it nearly every night. She opened the book near the center where she'd tucked a handwritten note; carefully, she removed the envelope from between the pages and lifted out the note. Written on an ivory-colored sheet of linen paper was a birthday greeting from Judson Carter. She read it over, her smile widening as her eyes moved across the words. Judson had visited her in Draper on her birthday and taken her out to dinner after work. At the restaurant, he'd presented her with a greeting card with the note tucked inside.

It expressed his pleasure of sharing with her the occasion of her 20th birthday and declared his affection for her. "With fondest wishes," he had written as a closing line.

Rebecca replaced the note inside the card and put the card and the Book of Mormon on her nightstand. Thoughts of Judson filled her mind. She had never been in love before, but if her feelings for Judson were any indication, then she was surely falling in love now.

The next morning, Rebecca started on her chores in preparation for the Christmas holiday and Judson's visit to the ranch. On her birthday, she and Judson had made arrangements for him to spend Christmas Day with her at the Double K; the trains would not be running on Christmas, so he was arriving the day before and would return the day after. Patrick had gone into the canyon two days ago to chop down a pine tree for the parlor, and he and Rebecca had decorated it together last evening. Rebecca had strung kernels of popped corn and shiny, red cranberries onto a long string and wound it around the branches of the tree. Then she'd hung her mother's colored glass ornaments and Christmas candles. She paused now from her work to admire it. The sun streaming through the window made the glass ornaments shine, and the popcorn filled the house with a savory scent. The only thing missing from her Christmas celebration, she concluded, was Rachel.

Rachel had telephoned the store several days earlier to tell Rebecca that she couldn't come to Draper as they'd planned to celebrate their birthday together; her employer needed her help at the millinery because of the many Christmas orders they had received. Rebecca had been disappointed. She'd been looking forward to spending some time with her sister for they hadn't seen one another in over two months, and she'd especially wanted to talk with her about her feelings for Judson. Because they hadn't been able to meet on their birthday, Rebecca had written her a letter explaining about her relationship with Judson. She'd mentioned that he was planning to spend Christmas Day at the ranch and hoped Rachel would join them there. Rachel had sent an angry note in reply—if Judson was going to be at the Double K on Christmas, she'd written, then she most definitely would not be. As Rebecca swept a speck of dirt from the hearth where she'd just kindled a fire, she tried to sweep thoughts of Rachel aside, too. She didn't want Rachel's bitterness to spoil her Christmas holiday.

A few minutes before noon, she heard the sound of a horse and buggy pull into the yard. Her heart leapt as she hurried to the door and opened it in time to see Judson climbing down from the buggy. He looked over at her and smiled. "The picture of you standing framed in that doorway looks like a scene on a Christmas card," he said in greeting.

She laughed. "That's hard to imagine, especially with no snow on the ground."

He tied the reins to the hitching post and hefted his valise from the floor of the buggy, then walked over to join her on the porch.

"Come inside and get warm. I have a fire going in the hearth," she invited.

He set his bag in the hallway and walked with Rebecca into the small parlor. "Look at that," he said, letting out a whistle. "That's a good-looking Christmas tree. Did you decorate it?"

"Patrick and I did."

"The two of you did an excellent job." He walked around the tree from one side to the other, admiring it.

"I'm anxious for you to meet Patrick. He'll be coming back to the house in a few hours when he's through with the cattle."

"I look forward to getting acquainted with him."

They sat down together in front of the fire. This was the first Christmas Rebecca had spent without her sister or either of her parents, and Judson's presence lifted her spirits. Concealed underneath the branches of the tree was a small gift she had purchased for him—a bottle of molasses syrup from the mill in Draper—and Rebecca was looking forward to giving it to him. The afternoon passed quickly, and when Patrick came in from the pasture, Rebecca introduced him to Judson. After supper, the two men played a game of checkers while Rebecca watched; and when Patrick was ready to turn in for the night, Judson went with him to the bunkhouse to sleep.

Rebecca hardly closed her eyes all night because she was so excited to spend Christmas with Judson. At first light she arose and prepared a big breakfast of steak and eggs, fried potatoes, and biscuits. Judson and Patrick entered the house just as it was ready for the table and teased her about being able to smell the tantalizing aroma all the way from the bunkhouse. They each ate two platefuls of food. Afterward, Patrick went to check on the stock, and Rebecca recruited Judson's help in making a mince pie for their Christmas dinner. As she stirred the ingredients and he rolled the dough for the pie crust, they laughed and joked together.

After the pie had baked and Rebecca had set it on the table to cool, she suggested a ride into the east pasture to take Onyx an apple for a Christmas treat. She hadn't yet had an opportunity to see the gelding and wanted to make sure he was well. She saddled her father's horse and Judson rode the roan he'd rented from the livery stable in Draper, and they set out. Nearly all the snow was gone from the valley floor, but the mountains were coated in white, like icing on a cake. She reined her horse along the familiar trails with Judson at her side.

In a short time they reached the high pasture where Onyx and some of the other horses were corralled. Onyx came to her when she and Judson slipped under the rail of the fence. "How's my boy?" she said affectionately, rubbing the horse's neck. Pulling the apple from her pocket, she held it in the palm of her hand for the horse to eat. She stroked the blaze of white running down the animal's forehead and threaded her fingers through his dark mane.

"This is where Onyx was injured in the fire," she said to Judson, sliding her hand along the horse's right foreleg. The leg was swollen at the knee, and there were patches of pink skin exposed where the hair had been burned away and had not grown back. She ran her hand along the horse's back and hips, checking his general condition. Then she caressed his neck and rubbed his nose. Afterward, she and Judson sat on the top rail of the fence to talk.

"How long have you owned Onyx?" Judson asked her, gazing out at the black horse.

"Since I was fifteen. My Aunt Jessica gave him to me about a year after Mama's death."

Judson was silent for a moment. "Have you been back to the meadow since then?"

Rebecca's eyes strayed past the snowy pasture to the ridge of the hill. Down from the hill was the ravine where her mother had died and beyond that lay the meadow. She shook her head. "I can't bear to go there. The memory is too painful."

"Maybe you should."

"What?" Rebecca froze at the mere thought of his suggestion.

"Perhaps you could come to grips with your feelings if you managed to ride into that ravine again."

"No," Rebecca said, shaking her head. "It's impossible."

Judson reached for her hand. "You're not responsible for your mother's death. Just because you were the one who suggested the ride to the meadow doesn't mean you bear the responsibility for what happened."

"If I hadn't urged her to go, or to race her horse against mine, she'd still be alive today."

"You don't know that, Rebecca." He heaved a troubled sigh. "But I understand a little bit how you feel. It's the same for me in a way with Daniel's death."

Rebecca turned her gaze to him. His face was pinched, and pain shadowed his eyes.

"It was wrong of me to allow Daniel and Louisa to meet secretly in the shop, and I should have put a stop to it."

"Even if you had forbidden them to meet in your shop, they would have found some place else to be together," Rebecca responded, shaken by his dark mood. "You couldn't have stopped that."

"I could have been more emphatic with Daniel about the need to curtail his relationship."

"What difference would that have made, unless you believe Louisa's father was involved in Daniel's death. Do you?"

Judson shrugged his shoulders. "I don't know. It's difficult to believe that he could have been, but he was adamant about Daniel staying away from his daughter. It's possible he could have hired someone to commit the murder."

A cloud drifted across the sun, and Rebecca shivered from the sudden chill in the air.

"The authorities haven't had any leads in his murder. If Daniel had been a white man, I expect they would have found something by now," he added bitterly. Judson climbed down from the fence and draped his arms over the top rail, staring at the horses in the corral. "But it's hard not to place some of the blame on myself."

Rebecca stepped down and joined him. "Guilt and blame are heavy burdens to bear. They weigh down one's heart until there's nothing left but sadness," she said more to herself than to Judson. "I've been reading from the scriptures the last little while—something I haven't done in over five years."

"Has it brought you any peace?"

"I think so. A little."

Judson stirred a patch of snow with the toe of his foot. "Daniel brought his copy of the Book of Mormon each day with him to the shop. He read from that book every noon hour while he ate. He and I had several conversations about it," Judson said wryly, smiling at the memory. "He believed what he had read and was preparing to be baptized into the Church."

Rebecca remained silent, listening to him.

"Daniel left the book behind on the day he was to be married. In his excitement, I guess, he forgot to take it with him. He never had the chance to come back for it."

"Oh, Judson," she murmured, bowing her head.

Judson shifted his weight and gazed toward the mountains. "I found his book on the work bench after I got home that night after Daniel's death. I was distraught and nothing I could do seemed to calm my turmoil. Then I saw his Book of Mormon lying there. I picked it up and opened it to the first page."

Rebecca held her breath. "And then?"

"I started to read it. I read most of the night and again the next evening. I finished it two days later."

Rebecca moved nearer, and their shoulders touched. "And what was the result?"

Judson cleared his throat, plainly struggling with his emotions. "It caused me to think about some important questions. I remembered how I'd felt the first time I'd ever read that book, and the feelings I'd experienced at the time of my baptism. I considered some of the choices I'd made since then and how they'd led me away from the peace and happiness associated with living the gospel."

He paused, and Rebecca held her breath, hoping he would continue.

"Daniel's death made me realize how tenuous life is and how precious. I needed a clear vision of the direction I should take in my life while I have the opportunity to change course." He turned to her and smiled faintly. "I haven't sorted it all out completely, but I'm working on it."

"I'm glad to hear you say that." She slipped her hand into his.

"I'm still trying to confront my own demons. Maybe it's time for you to face yours, too." He squeezed her hand and drew her closer to him. "I'll go with you if you want to ride down into the hollow."

She shuddered, even with his hand clasped in hers, comforting her. "I can't, Judson."

"Maybe it wouldn't hurt either one of us to pray for a little courage," he said.

She glanced through the fence at Onyx. His head was lifted and his ears pointed forward, alert to the sound of the wind sweeping across the high pastures. He snorted and pawed the ground, then began to trot around the perimeter of the large corral. Even though one leg was weak, causing him to stumble, he picked up speed. Rebecca watched as the horse broke into a canter, his black mane flying and his nose flaring in the crisp winter air.

She turned her eyes toward the gorge and the meadow beyond it. "If we went into the ravine," she said, her voice trembling, "could we ride double so I can hold onto you for support?"

"An excellent idea," Judson returned, smiling at her. "We can hold on to each other."

"Then I'll try. But you must promise to turn back if I ask you to."

He brushed his lips against her forehead. "I promise."

Judson hitched his roan to the fence, then he mounted Star and reached for Rebecca's hand to help her up behind him. When she'd settled on the horse, she hesitantly put her arms around his waist; as soon as she did, he patted her hands reassuringly. The feel of his strong hands on hers, and his sturdy back upon which to lean, calmed her and lent her confidence. They set off at a slow walk, saying little as they rode. Star's gait was smooth and easy, but Rebecca's heart was thudding as the horse crossed the high, windy pasture toward the ridge of the hill. Patches of snow lay on the ground where the sun hadn't yet penetrated, and rocks littered the trail.

When they had crested the hill and the steep gully lay before them, Judson reined the horse to a stop. "Are you ready?" he asked, twisting in the saddle to look at her.

She drew a quick breath. "I think so."

He closed his hand over hers, then directed the horse down the rocky incline. Rebecca's throat began to tighten and beads of perspiration broke out along her brow. She felt as though she couldn't catch her breath. Taking a gulp, she concentrated on just breathing in and out. She tightened her hold around Judson's waist as he urged the horse down the snow-packed slope. As the horse proceeded toward the base of the hollow, Rebecca clenched her eyes shut. It was here she had turned in the saddle to call to her mother to hurry on. The memory of her mother on the gray mare swam behind her closed lids; she remembered a flash of red calico and her mother's laughing voice floating in the air. She tried to hold back the wave of emotion threatening to overwhelm her. She clung to Judson, fearing she would burst into tears and beg him to turn back. Nearly giving way to her panic, she began to tremble and shake uncontrollably.

Just as she was about to cry out, she felt Judson's hand pressing on hers. "You're halfway there, Rebecca. We're climbing up the other side."

She willed herself to open her eyes. They were, indeed, starting the climb up the opposite slope. But this was the spot where she had been when she heard her mother's mare whinny and saw the horse stumble and fall. Her heart felt swollen and ready to burst inside her. She forced her eyes straight ahead, focusing on Judson's broad back rather than the terrifying images in her memory. But just as she was gaining control over her fears, she felt the horse beneath them start to slide on a frozen patch of snow. The gelding struggled to gain a foothold on the steep, slippery terrain. The image of her mother's mare losing its footing and plunging to the ground, sending up a wall of dust, played starkly across her mind's eye. *Was the same thing about to happen to her?* Rebecca's hands began to tingle and grow limp, and her head was suddenly dizzy. She felt herself starting to black out.

In that instant, she caught a glimpse of red calico at the top of the ravine in front of them, just where the meadow began. She blinked, then stared again at the spot. It seemed to her that her mother stood there, her dark hair blowing across her face in the wind and her skirt billowing. She appeared to raise a hand and draw aside the long, gusting strands of hair from her face; and when she did, Rebecca saw that she was smiling. In her mind's view, Susannah turned to glance at someone standing beside her. The blonde-headed man had on typical cowboy garb, including a hat and boots; and his arm was wrapped around her waist. Even though Rebecca caught only a glimpse of his face, she knew who he was.

Rebecca blinked a second time, and when she looked again, the image was gone and she was unsure if she had actually seen it or only imagined it. On the far side of the gorge, the wind skimmed through the barren brush and rattled the leafless branches of the trees. Rebecca became suddenly aware of Star taking a quick, jolting leap to regain his balance, and then scrambling the rest of the way up the slope. With a lunge, the horse plunged to the top and they were out of the ravine and facing the snow-laced meadow beyond.

When the horse had traveled a few more yards, they reached the meadow and Judson dismounted, then helped her down from the saddle. Her body was trembling so much she could barely stand. He took both of her hands in his. "You did it," he said. "I knew you could."

Rebecca closed her eyes and leaned against him for support, and he encircled her in his arms. She could feel his warm breath on her cheek. They stood together without speaking.

Finally, Judson took a step back. "I'm proud of you, Rebecca," he said, brushing a strand of hair away from her forehead.

She let him take her hand and they started to walk through the snowy meadow. Her thoughts returned to the brief scene she'd envisioned, but she didn't say anything about it to Judson because she didn't know if it had been real. She guessed that it had likely been a product of her nervousness and fear; but still the image was strangely comforting, as she reflected back on it. Her nerves began to calm as they strolled the broad meadow. Mounds of snow lay scattered about their feet and where the ground was bare Rebecca could see the tangled, dead stems of summer wildflowers. They paused while Judson cleared away a clump of snow from a ragged vine.

"I thought I saw a blossom that survived the snow," he said. "Perhaps we can come back here in the spring and pick a bouquet for you."

Rebecca lifted her gaze to him. "Thank you, Judson."

"For what?"

"For rescuing me."

He smiled slightly. "I think it is you who has rescued me."

"That was the best mince pie I've ever tasted," Judson declared as he helped Rebecca clear the remains of their Christmas supper from the table.

"That's because you did an excellent job with the pie crust," she returned, laughing.

"That's true."

"I hope you've saved me a big slice to eat tomorrow," Patrick said. "I could have easily tucked away two pieces tonight, but I wanted to show some restraint."

Judson chuckled at his remark, and Rebecca planted a kiss on her cousin's cheek. "You can have all the pie you want, Patrick."

Evening shadows were beginning to draw across the room, and Rebecca lighted the coal oil lamps in the kitchen and in the parlor. While Patrick went to check on the stock in the yard, Rebecca and Judson settled in the parlor to enjoy the lighted candles and shiny ornaments decorating the Christmas tree.

They sat on the floor beside the tree savoring the fresh, piney scent of its branches. Judson opened his satchel that he'd brought in from the bunkhouse and pulled out a wrapped gift. "Merry Christmas, Rebecca. This is for you."

She took the present and set it on her lap, intrigued by the sight of the beautifully wrapped package. "Do you want me to open it now?"

He nodded.

"I have a present for you, too." She reached under the tree and retrieved the jar of molasses syrup she'd bought for him. She'd tied a green ribbon bow around the neck of the bottle. "I thought you might enjoy this on your oatmeal in the mornings for breakfast," she said, handing him the bottle filled with thick, brown syrup.

"Is this from the molasses mill near your place in Draper?" he asked, examining the jar.

"Yes. I hope you'll like it."

"Like it? It will be a treat," he replied, grinning. "I can smell its rich flavor without even opening the bottle. Thank you very much."

She smiled, pleased by his show of enthusiasm.

"Now it's your turn." He nodded at the package resting in her lap.

She picked it up, testing its weight. The box was wrapped in silver paper with a wide, red ribbon tied around it. Smiling, she carefully removed the ribbon and then the shiny, silver paper. Glancing up at him, she lifted the lid from the box. "What could this be?" she asked with anticipation.

Without saying a word, he raised his eyebrows, heightening the suspense.

Inside the box was a nest of soft paper. She reached in and her fingers came in contact with a smooth, flat, wood object. As she took it from the box, candlelight glinted off its mirrored surface like streaks of silver light. "Oh!" she exclaimed, holding up the hand mirror by its handle. "This is beautiful." She gazed, spellbound, at it. "Did you make this?"

"I did."

Rebecca studied the frame of the mirror. The wood was a dark, rich walnut with the oval-shaped piece of sparkling glass set in the center of it. In each of the four corners of the square frame Judson had carved a sunflower, complete with an undulating stalk and leaves that trailed down and along the sides so that the whole border was decorated with carving. "I've never seen anything so exquisite," she said.

"I'm glad you like it."

She tilted the carved handle and caught a glimpse of her reflection in the glass. Her cheeks were as red as Christmas berries, and her eyes were shining as brightly as the gleaming glass ornaments on the tree. "Oh, Judson. It's lovely."

"I wanted you to be able to see how beautiful you look with sunflowers in your hair."

She glanced up quickly at him, blushing as she remembered the day last summer when they'd ridden their horses near the meadow, and he had picked a bouquet of sunflowers for her. She returned her gaze to the mirror and stroked the carved flowers on the frame with the tips of her fingers.

Judson moved closer until she could see both their reflections in the glass, like two halves of the same picture. The green flecks in his dark eyes shimmered in the glow of the lighted candles. She turned her face toward his, the racing of her heart making it nearly impossible to breathe.

"Rebecca," he whispered, cradling her cheek in his hand, "you are my heart's desire. I love you, and I will continue to love you for the rest of my life." Leaning forward, he softly kissed her.

CHAPTER TWENTY–THREE

Rebecca grasped the siderail of the buckboard as the wagon rolled over a lump of frozen, hard-packed snow on the road. The wheels lurched in the deep ruts, and the wind blew cold against Rebecca's cheeks. She pulled her hooded cloak tighter around her. "Thank you for driving me back to Draper, Patrick," she said, shivering in the chilly air.

"I'm happy to do it," he responded. "When I get back, I'll check on the steers in the north pasture like we talked about."

"Good. I'm worried that the next big snowstorm will pile up drifts along the fence line and cover the water trough and salt lick."

"I'll set out another piece of rock salt further up the fence."

Rebecca huddled in her cloak. The few days surrounding Christmas had been warm and sunny, but this morning the sky looked as gray as an old man's beard, and the temperature had plummeted. Snow was expected not only in the high pastures, but in the lower valleys as well.

As Patrick drove the wagon, he and Rebecca continued to discuss matters pertaining to the ranch. Rebecca felt pulled in opposite directions—she wanted to stay on the ranch and care for the cattle like she had always done, but at the same time she was anxious to return to Draper where she would be closer to Judson. She could hardly wait to see him again. His stay on the ranch at Christmas had cemented their feelings for one another. She felt a tremble pass through her as she recalled their kiss under the decorated tree in the parlor. He had kissed her again the next morning before leaving the ranch and expressed his desire to be with her soon. His words had been tender and gentle, and even now with the cold wind buffeting her face, her cheeks grew warm remembering them.

"Do you recall the winter a few years back when the snow fell nearly every day for weeks?" Patrick asked. "The drifts were piled six feet high against the fences."

Rebecca focused her thoughts on what Patrick was saying. "I remember it clearly. One blizzard followed another, and the high winds drove the snow into drifts. The ranch was buried in snow, and the road into Draper was impassable. We were locked in for three weeks." She frowned, recollecting the experience. "The livestock were stranded without food or water, and we couldn't get to them. All the streams were frozen and the feed gone."

"I remember trekking out to the stream beside the house and breaking up the ice with a hammer for your mama so she could have water to cook with."

Rebecca shuddered. "We lost over a hundred head of cattle that year, didn't we?"

"That's right. Dozens of 'em died from dehydration and lung infections, and we lost half that many again that got caught in the drifts."

"Let's hope the next couple of months don't produce that kind of weather."

Patrick nodded.

As the wagon wheels crunched over the snow, Rebecca's thoughts turned to her work at the mercantile. She appreciated Mr. Rideout's kindness in allowing her a few days at home for the holidays but knew that a stack of work would be waiting for her at the store when she returned. She wondered if Lettie had had a nice Christmas with her family. Lettie was the oldest of nine children, and her family lived in Draper, but Lettie had moved into a place of her own as soon as she turned 18 to give her siblings more space in the crowded household. Thinking about Lettie triggered an idea. "Patrick, do you remember the girl I introduced to you at the store when you came in before Christmas? The one with the curly, brown hair?"

Patrick glanced over at her. "I don't think so."

"Sure you do. She has pretty, blue eyes and a friendly manner. Her name is Lettie Miller."

"Yes, now I remember; but I don't recall what she looked like," Patrick confessed. "Why?"

"Well, Lettie asked about you after you left the store. She'd like to get better acquainted."

"She would?" Patrick shrugged his shoulders.

"Yes, she would. When we get into town, will you come inside the mercantile for a minute and talk with her?"

"I don't know. I'll need to be getting back to the ranch; got a lot of chores there waiting for me."

"Five minutes, Patrick. Just take five minutes. It would mean a lot to Lettie." Rebecca put a hand on his shoulder. "And I promised her that I'd persuade you to stop in and say hello."

Patrick stared straight ahead, apparently not impressed by what Rebecca was telling him. "We'll see."

They continued talking together until they reached Draper. Patrick directed the team of horses to the house where Lettie and Rebecca shared a room, tied the reins to the hitching post, and carried Rebecca's traveling case inside for her. It had started to snow; big, thick flakes that clung to the ground and covered their wagon tracks without leaving a trace of their passing. He waited while she changed into a fresh dress, then drove her to the Rideout store.

He climbed down from the wagon and extended a hand to help her down, too; then reluctantly followed her into the mercantile. Rebecca said hello to the middle-aged clerk tending the counter. He was the same fellow who worked behind the counter when Mr. Rideout was busy with other matters or out of the store, and the one who had rung up

Rebecca's purchases when she'd come into the mercantile to shop shortly after her father's death. Since starting work at the store, she'd developed a friendly relationship with him; but she hadn't been able to foster much of a friendship with Mrs. Snowden, the prickly store manager in charge of keeping the shelves stocked with goods.

It took only a moment for Rebecca to spot Lettie at the far end of the counter arranging items on the shelves. She motioned for Patrick to follow her. "The goods on that shelf are as straight as a ruler," she said while Lettie's back was still to her.

Lettie turned her head. "Rebby! Welcome back. I'm so glad to see you." When she came around the counter, she caught sight of Patrick. "Oh! Hello, Mr. McKellar." She flushed and her freckles stood out vividly. "How nice to see you again."

Patrick whisked off his hat. "Good afternoon, Miss Miller."

"Did the two of you have a nice Christmas at the ranch?" Lettie asked, glancing at Rebecca, then returning her gaze eagerly to Patrick.

"We had a very nice holiday, didn't we, Patrick?"

He nodded, fussing with his hat.

I'll bet you were glad to be home," Lettie said, directing her comment to Rebecca. She made a quick stab at her hair, rearranging a curl that had fallen out of place.

"It was wonderful being at home again. Patrick has done an extraordinary job of keeping things running smoothly at the ranch."

"That's quite a compliment, Mr. McKellar," Lettie said to him.

"My cousin tends to exaggerate the truth at times," Patrick replied, showing the first glimpse of a smile.

Lettie giggled at his remark. "I've known Rebecca to be quite forthright when it comes to affairs at the Double K. She must trust your judgment."

"There's no question about that," Rebecca said. She glanced toward the open door of her office. "If you two will excuse me for a moment, I just want to duck inside and take a look at what's waiting for me on my desk." From the corner of her eye, she saw Patrick's apprehensive look. "I'll be right back. Wait for me, Patrick, and I'll walk with you to the door."

"All right," he mumbled.

As she stepped into her office, she heard Lettie's bright voice picking up the threads of the conversation. On the desk, Mr. Rideout had left some papers scribbled over the front with numbers. She glanced at the figures, quickly determining their relevance. She lifted another page from a pile of loose papers and looked at it. It would take her several hours to catch up on the work that had collected in her absence.

When she came back into the main part of the store a few minutes later, Patrick was responding to something Lettie had said. He was smiling and tapping his hat against his knee. He turned to Rebecca. "Did you find everything in order?" he asked.

Rebecca nodded. "I have a mountain of work on my desk."

"Then that should keep you occupied so you won't be worrying about things at the ranch," Patrick replied.

"She'll worry no matter what you say, Mr. McKellar," Lettie put in, tilting her head to give Patrick a smile.

Rebecca laughed. "Has it been busy here at the store while I was away?" she asked Lettie.

"I've been running around like a mad woman," Lettie responded with a dramatic sigh. "You'd think everyone in town had delayed their shopping until Christmas Eve."

Patrick chuckled at her remark. "I should get going," he said. "Nice to talk with you again, Miss Miller." He offered her a bow, then replaced his hat.

"And you, Mr. McKellar. I hope you'll stop by again soon."

He smiled, then turned to Rebecca. "I'll keep in touch."

"Thank you again for everything, Patrick." She accompanied him to the door of the mercantile. "Stay warm. It's bitter cold outside."

"I will."

Rebecca watched until he'd stepped up into the buckboard and driven away. Then she returned to where Lettie stood waiting for her.

Lettie was prancing on her toes trying to contain her excitement. "I could hardly believe it when I turned around and saw your cousin standing there!" she burst out.

"I told you he'd be back to talk with you."

"Did it take much convincing?" Lettie asked, her brow ruffling.

"A little, but that's only because he's so shy."

"Rebby, I'm more attracted than ever to him. I hope he'll return soon." She clasped her hands together, as if begging for such a favor.

"Now, Lettie, I thought you told me sometime back that you were looking for a man who was handsome, charming, and wealthy. Patrick doesn't fit comfortably into those categories," Rebecca teased.

"That was just foolish prattle," Lettie sniffed. "Mr. McKellar has all the qualities any girl would admire."

"Especially if that girl is you," Rebecca replied with a grin.

"Don't tease me, Rebby. I'm serious. I just have to see Mr. McKellar again, or I'll shrink like a fading violet."

"I wouldn't want that to happen," Rebecca said, "especially before I get a chance to tell you about Judson's visit to the ranch on Christmas."

"Oh, tell me!"

"I will, but not now because we both have work to do; but tonight when we're home."

"I'll be holding my breath until then," Lettie said. "And afterward when you're through, you must tell me everything you can about your cousin."

It took most of the week for Rebecca to catch up on her work at the store after being away during the Christmas holiday. On the next Saturday, the 4th of January in the new year, 1896, Rebecca arrived at the mercantile early and set to work in her office. Lettie's shift didn't begin until the afternoon, and so she was still at home.

Rebecca had been at her desk only a couple of hours when she heard a sudden, sharp sound that made her jerk. The noise was like a loud gunshot, and following the shot she heard someone shouting. Her back stiffened as another shot rang out. Leaping to her feet, she pushed aside the curtain on the window and stared out, but she could see nothing unusual taking place on the street. Then she heard a volley of shots coming from further up the road.

Just as she started toward the door of her office to see what was happening outside, she heard the store telephone ring. One of the clerks answered it. Rebecca was almost to the front entrance when the clerk hung up the receiver and dashed into the aisle. "President Cleveland has signed the Proclamation! Utah is a state!" For an instant, there was only stunned silence among the handful of customers and employees at the mercantile. Then the clerk cried out, "Three cheers for the State of Utah! Hurrah! Hurrah! Hurrah!"

The others joined in the refrain in a loud chorus, and then pandemonium broke out in the store. Each person congratulated the other, slapping one another on the back and all talking at once. The crescendoing wall of noise made Rebecca's head spin. Someone grabbed her hand and pumped it up and down in jubilation, then hurried on to the next person. Several people from the street burst into the mercantile exclaiming, "Have you heard the news?" The telephone began another strident ringing, and everything seemed to be in commotion.

As the significance of the declaration dawned fully upon her, Rebecca became caught up in the excitement. People were dashing in and out of the store, and she could hear more gunshots being fired in the streets. She hurried outside and stood on the walk in front of the mercantile watching the street filling with people. Shopkeepers stood at their doors waving American flags, and whistles and horns sounded all around her. She laughed aloud, thrilled by the cacophony of noise and eager to join the crowds in their impromptu celebrations. Someone rushed past her, nearly knocking her over. He offered an apologetic grin, then raced on. She could hear people whooping and cheering and hailing one another with a variation of the recent New Year's greeting by crying out, "Happy New State to you!" The sounds and colors and movements swirled around her as if she were on a carousel.

It was some moments before she remembered that her place was in the store attending to her work. She reluctantly left the pageantry of the street and returned inside. One of the clerks had located some red, white, and blue bunting and was hanging it along the store counter. Another was pulling flags of all sizes from storage boxes to display in the windows. The mercantile was being transformed into a colorful scene of patriotic spirit. It was like a celebration of the Fourth of July, only much more extravagant.

When Lettie arrived at the store in the early afternoon, she told Rebecca that the windows of every shop and place of business she passed on the way into work was decorated with flags, bunting, and national emblems. Lettie was too excited to concentrate on her job as was nearly everyone else in the store. The telephone continued to ring all afternoon as the news spread, and several people came in asking to use it to call their families or friends to report and discuss the grand news. Shortly before Rebecca was ready to leave the mercantile for the day, she received a telephone call herself. It was Judson on the line, calling from Salt Lake City, and telling her that the following Monday was to be a holiday in celebration of statehood; he asked if she could come to the city to share in the festivities with him. She eagerly told him she would.

When she left the store, she took a leisurely walk home, admiring the decorations that had sprung up on the windows and doors of houses and shops along her way, making the roads look like a parade route. A light snow was falling, depositing a thin layer of white on the roads and buildings. The flakes sparkled in the light of the gas street lamps giving the town a magical appearance. As she threaded her way through the crowds still celebrating in the streets, Rebecca drew her coat tighter around her, smiling.

When Rebecca arrived in Salt Lake City the following Monday, she found the streets crowded with people, and public spirit at a fever pitch. Even the train she had ridden into Salt Lake had been decorated with flags and bunting and had been thronged with passengers. Judson met her at the station, and they started for the Tabernacle where the inaugural celebration was to be held. Rebecca was amazed by the size of the crowd converging on Temple Square. Jostled on all sides, she had to keep a tight hold on Judson's arm in order to not get separated from him by the throng.

Once inside the spacious, dome-roofed building, she and Judson were seated with the thousands of others gathered in the auditorium. The scope and size of the decorations took her breath away. The ceiling was covered by a huge flag, so big that she had to crane her neck to see each corner of it. In the field of stars, the 45th, representing Utah, blazed brightly with electric light. Her gaze took in the red, white, and blue streamers running from the flag in every direction and the fringe of bunting and flags adorning the face of the gallery. At the head of the vast room, the pulpit and stand were draped in the national colors; and above them, mounted over the organ pipes, the word "Utah" was illuminated.

Rebecca stared in awe at the members of the First Presidency of the Church seated on the stand, along with state and territorial officials, dignitaries, and other prominent citizens. She listened to the prayer delivered by President George Q. Cannon, First Counselor in the First Presidency, and then afterward to a choir of a thousand voices singing the "Star Spangled Banner." She gripped Judson's hand, a thrill of excitement rippling through her, as the Proclamation admitting Utah to statehood was read.

The newly elected governor of the state, Heber M. Wells, was then installed into office, followed by the other state officials. At the conclusion of the swearing in ceremonies, a cannon salute thundered from Capitol Hill; Rebecca could feel the reverberations from the booming cannon in her chest. This was followed by a song entitled "Utah, We Love Thee," composed by Tabernacle Choir director Evan Stephens for the occasion and performed by the chorus. The melody and words were stirring and raised chills along Rebecca's arms.

Rebecca settled deeper into her seat as Governor Wells arose to deliver the inaugural address to the audience. He reviewed the long struggle for statehood and presented a glowing report of Utah's wealth and abundance of natural resources. "Our state," he declared, "has the greatest diversity of industry and offers the greatest variety of occupation of any state in the Union. The fame of Utah has gone forth to the world, not alone as a mining state, nor as an agricultural state, nor as a grazing state, nor as a manufacturing state, but she is famous in each and all of these various pursuits and is known not more widely for her gold and silver than for her potatoes and woolen goods." Rebecca smiled with pride as the governor spoke.

When the inauguration ceremonies ended and they had filed out of the Tabernacle, Judson took her for a buggy ride to see some of the decorations in town. The national colors were displayed on nearly every street corner Judson and Rebecca passed. East Temple Street was bordered by flags, and the Stars and Stripes waved from rooftops, windows, and doorways of buildings up and down the street. Judson reined his horse past the big store of F. Auerbach & Brothers, which was lavishly festooned in a patriotic theme. They paused in front of the Z.C.M.I. building so that Rebecca could get a look at the magnificent silver star mounted on the roof emblazoned with the number "45" in its center to represent the new state. Rebecca eagerly eyed the storefront which was draped with an immense, fan-shaped array of bunting, and stars and bunting embellished the multiple handsome windows. Judson showed her several more impressive sites, including the recently completed City and County Building where the new state officials were to convene that afternoon for their first legislative session. Rebecca's mind was swirling with all the sights and sounds surrounding her and the heady emotion of the occasion.

After their tour, Judson escorted her to a restaurant downtown where they ate amid a lively crowd, then he drove her to the boarding house where Rachel lived. They made plans to meet again in the evening to attend a patriotic concert to be held in the Assembly Hall on Temple Square. He kissed her when they parted, and Rebecca lingered on the doorstep to watch him until the buggy pulled away, then she entered the rooming house.

She had never been to Rachel's apartment before. Rebecca had telephoned her sister from Draper to tell Rachel she was coming to town for the celebrations and hoped she might spend the night at her place. Rachel had sounded pleased at the prospect of seeing her. She had given Rebecca directions to her room on the second floor and left the door unlocked in case she wasn't there when Rebecca arrived. Rebecca climbed the stairs, found the correct room, and knocked on the door.

"Was Rachel at home when you got there this afternoon?" Judson asked as he and Rebecca strolled the grounds of Temple Square.

"Not at first. She arrived about twenty minutes later." Rebecca pulled her winter coat tighter around her shoulders. The night air was chilly but clear, and stars speckled the sky. She and Judson had decided to take a walk across the Temple grounds after the concert to admire the beautiful buildings constructed there.

The Assembly Hall, where they had enjoyed the patriotic program, was a strikingly handsome structure made of gray stone with white painted trim and capped with 24 spires and a center tower. Rebecca thought the building's Victorian Gothic style made it one of the most picturesque edifices she'd ever seen. The elliptical domed Tabernacle, with its numerous sandstone piers and double-door entrances, was both innovative and impressive. Judson had mentioned that the building could seat 8,000 people, and that its acoustics were remarkable.

But the crowning jewel, of course, was the temple. Its gray granite walls stood as a monument to the faith and sacrifice of the Latter-day Saints—a hallowed place where the Lord could reveal His will to the prophet and where sacred ordinances and covenants were to be performed.

The gold-leafed figure of the angel Moroni affixed to the highest stone of the temple, with his trumpet raised to his lips as if to signal the people of the world, symbolized the restoration of the gospel of Jesus Christ. Tonight, the temple spires were illuminated by incandescent lights to celebrate Utah's admission into the Union, and the brilliant spectacle drew Rebecca's eyes and her thoughts heavenward. She remembered a particular passage in the Old Testament, a prophecy by Isaiah: *And it shall come to pass in the last days, that the mountain of the Lord's house shall be established in the top of the mountains, and shall be exalted above the hills; and all nations shall flow unto it.* A tingle passed through her as she gazed upon the literal fulfillment of that prophecy.

Her musings were cut short by the chatter of some passersby. A few people still milled through the Square and the streets outside of the temple grounds.

"Did you have a good visit with Rachel?" Judson asked, referring to his earlier remark.

"Yes. It was nice to see her again." Rebecca bit her lip and glanced away, deciding not to tell Judson about the argument in which she and Rachel had become entangled. They had quarreled over Rebecca's involvement with Judson, and both of them were angry and hurt by the exchange. Rachel had refused to speak to her for the rest of the evening.

"I'm glad you had a chance to visit," Judson remarked. "Did you enjoy the concert this evening?"

Rebecca was happy to leave the former topic behind. "Oh, yes. I love listening to the military bands. The music is so stirring and makes one feel proud to be an American."

Judson laughed. "That's the purpose of it."

"I couldn't keep my toe from tapping in time to the music," Rebecca confessed, smiling.

"I'm sure there was a lot of toe tapping tonight among the dignitaries and their wives at the Grand Inaugural Ball."

"I can just picture the ladies in their fine dresses and the gentlemen in their black suits dancing a polka or a minuet," Rebecca replied, imagining the colorful sight.

"Or waltzing to the strains of a Strauss melody."

"'The Blue Danube.' That's my favorite Strauss waltz," she said, nodding her head.

"Is it?" Judson responded. He began whistling the melody to the popular waltz tune, and when he smiled at her, a shaft of moonlight exposed the dimple in his cheek.

Rebecca felt a tingle race down her spine as she looked at him. It was difficult to draw her eyes away even when he put an arm around her waist to guide her toward the horse and buggy secured at the hitching post outside the walls of the Square.

"I'll make you a promise," Judson said as they walked, his eyes twinkling in the glow of the lamplight. "You and I will one day dance to the music of an orchestra playing 'The Blue Danube.' How would you like that?"

She laughed. "I'll hold you to that promise."

They passed through the gates of the Square and started toward Main Street where the buggy was hitched. It was growing late, and the streets were becoming deserted. Even so, Rebecca hated to see the evening come to a close. Crossing the road at the corner of Main and South Temple, they came abreast of a photography studio on Main Street where a handsome patriotic display was mounted on the door. The sign above the door read *Charles R. Savage, Art Bazar.* In the big twin windows facing the street were a number of photographs on display showing various scenes of the city. Judson paused in front of one of the windows and directed her attention to a large photograph of the Salt Lake Temple and another of Main Street showing the shops and places of business. In the other window, he pointed out a series of photographs taken by Savage at the World's Fair in 1892.

"I had an opportunity to visit the World Columbian Exposition in '92," Judson commented, gazing at the photos in the window.

"You were in Chicago?"

"Yes, in connection with my business," he replied. "It happened to be at the time of the Exposition."

"What impressed you the most?"

"Probably the buildings housing the exhibits, many of them constructed of white stone. They surrounded a man-made lake and large fountain. You see them here in Savage's photograph," he said, pointing to one of the pictures in the window. "The newspapers called it the White City."

Rebecca studied the photographs in the muted light of the street lamp on the corner.

"There were replicas of Christopher Columbus's three ships and a giant telescope with which to view the stars, and an automatic moving sidewalk to transport people," he added.

"A moving sidewalk? I can't even imagine that," Rebecca said. She thought about the remarkable new inventions that had come into existence over the past few years—electric lighting, the telephone, the phonograph, moving pictures. She shook her head in amazement.

"Before I left, I visited the Utah Building. It featured a scaled-down model of the Eagle Gate at the entrance to the building and a statue of Brigham Young. Mr. Savage had an exhibit of his photographs on display inside, for which he won a medal at the Fair. I heard the Tabernacle Choir sing there as well, and—"

Before he could finish his sentence, a group of revelers passing by on the sidewalk crowded Rebecca and Judson nearly off the walk and into the street. "Sorry," one of the men in the crowd muttered. The group was talking and laughing loudly, and Rebecca caught a whiff of alcohol clinging to them as they walked past. The statehood celebrations were cause not only for festivities, but a license for drinking too much, also. Just in the time she and Judson had been outside walking, they had passed several young men who were obviously intoxicated.

After the group moved on, Judson and Rebecca continued along the road until they reached the buggy.

Judson helped her inside and then seated himself next to her. Giving the reins a shake, he urged the horse forward toward Rachel's boarding house where Rebecca would be spending the night with her sister.

The house where Rachel lived was situated along a poorly lit street. It sat in the center of the block where the fingers of light couldn't quite reach. Few people were on the street by this time, and the road was deserted when Judson pulled up to the house with the buggy. They sat in the carriage for a few minutes talking and holding hands, both of them reluctant to end the evening. Finally, Judson stepped out and extended his hand to Rebecca to help her down from the buggy. Just as she was about to take his hand, a man emerged from the shadows weaving drunkenly along the sidewalk. As he was approaching, he stumbled into Judson. "Watch your step, mister," Judson said, reaching out to steady the intoxicated man.

"Get out of my way," the man growled, "unless you want trouble."

Rebecca stiffened when she heard the man's harsh, snarling voice. Even though his hat was pulled down over his forehead, hiding his face, she recognized him. In the dim light, she could see the hawk feather in the brim of his hat. She ducked back inside the covered buggy, not wanting Jake Baxter to see her so she wouldn't have to speak to him.

But to her surprise, Judson seemed to recognize Baxter, too. "I'd like nothing better than to even the score," he snapped, taking a step toward the stocky man.

Baxter pushed back his hat, squinting in the poor light to get a better view of Judson. At first his expression was puzzled, then his face twisted into an ugly grimace of recognition. "Nice to see you again," he sneered.

"I can't say the same for you. I dislike anyone who's a thief and a bully."

Rebecca was bewildered by the exchange going on between the two men; she didn't think Judson had ever met Baxter at the ranch. She leaned forward to peer out from the buggy so she could watch what was taking place between her former ranch hand and Judson. Her heart was beating hard, knowing Baxter's explosive temper.

"You can't prove nothin'," Baxter scoffed. "I would have won that hand if you hadn't been playing cards under the table." He snorted scornfully.

"I wasn't cheating, and you know it. But that's not what rankles me. I haven't forgotten that you threatened my friend with a knife."

Rebecca saw Baxter's eyes narrow, and she shivered. She wanted to warn Judson to stay away from the volatile cowhand, but she remained huddled in the carriage hoping Judson would end the confrontation.

"I remember you now," Baxter rasped, his words slurred in a drunken blur. "It was you that night with the redskin. You stopped me then from giving that Indian what he deserved." He moved forward a step and glared at Judson. "But I made up for it."

Judson blanched. "What did you say?" he asked in a strangled voice.

Rebecca gasped when she heard Baxter's boasting words and saw Judson's reaction to them. She gathered her skirts and prepared to climb down from the buggy, frightened by what she knew might happen next.

"I showed that swaggering redskin," Baxter bragged, planting his legs firmly apart as if daring Judson to contradict him. "When I gutted him, he squealed like a piglet. I can still smell the stink of Indian blood on my knife."

Judson cried out in a convulsion of anguish and rage. He hurled himself against Baxter, knocking him to the ground. Then in a flash he was on top of him, smashing Baxter's face with his fists.

Horrified, Rebecca leaped down from the buggy, her heart banging wildly. "Judson!" she shouted. "Stop it! You'll kill him!"

Judson's face was white with fury. He kept hammering at Baxter, railing and cursing with each blow. Baxter was squirming, trying to escape the punches and wiggle out of Judson's grasp, but Judson held him pinned to the ground.

Then, somehow, Baxter managed to pull his knife from his pocket and thrust the blade at Judson's chest.

Rebecca screamed when she saw the knife flash into sight. She rushed toward the men, desperate to stop them from fighting.

Swerving out of reach of the blade, Judson grabbed Baxter's wrist and twisted, wrenching the knife away from him. Then he pressed the point of the blade to Baxter's throat. The cowhand's eyes bulged with fear.

"Judson, no!" Rebecca crouched next to him on the roadside. "That's enough! Killing him won't bring Daniel back!" A sob caught in her throat, nearly choking her.

Judson lifted his head to glance at her, loosening for an instant the pressure on the knife. But when Baxter squirmed to free himself, Judson refocused his gaze. He forced the blade against Baxter's throat until it drew blood.

Rebecca leaned close to Judson's ear, struggling to control her voice. Her pulse was racing, and she felt sick to her stomach. "Vengeance isn't the answer," she whispered frantically. "It will only make things worse—make Daniel's loss harder to bear than before." She put a hand on his shoulder. "Listen to me, Judson. Please let him go."

Judson stared at her for an instant, his eyes wild, and Rebecca was afraid he was so consumed with revenge that he'd lost his mind. His hand gripped the knife tighter. Then dropping his head, he swore under his breath and hurled the knife as far from him as he could.

Standing up abruptly, he jerked Baxter to his feet. "Start moving," he commanded. He shoved Baxter toward the buggy, breathing hard and still shaking with rage. He pushed Baxter into the carriage. "You move a muscle, and I'll kill you," he warned. He climbed in beside him and grabbed the reins. "Go inside," he said gruffly to Rebecca. His chest was heaving, and his voice shook.

With her legs quivering beneath her, Rebecca approached the buggy. "What are you going to do, Judson?" Her eyes flicked to Baxter who sat cowering on the seat, his face ashen. His lip was cut and bleeding, and purple bruises were already puffing up under his eyes.

"See that he pays for what he did to Daniel," Judson snapped. He whipped the reins against the horse's broad back, and the buggy lurched forward.

The next morning Rebecca arose at sunup and quietly dressed so she wouldn't wake her sister. She hadn't slept at all the night before, worrying that Judson had changed his mind about sparing Jake Baxter's life. Her mind and heart were still reeling from witnessing the harrowing scene the previous evening, and even her prayers had not brought her the peace she desperately sought.

She put on her coat and slipped out the door, shutting it softly behind her so she wouldn't disturb Rachel. She crept down the staircase, crossed the parlor, and let herself outside. Each breath formed a plume of vapor in the cold morning air as she hurried toward the one place she hoped might offer her comfort and solace. Few people were on the street so early in the morning, and all of the shop windows were still shuttered. She walked quickly, hugging her coat to her body to keep out the cold. Only once did she lift her eyes to look at the snow-covered mountains hemming in the valley. A cold, brisk wind blew across her face. She lowered her head and pulled the collar of her coat up around her neck.

It took several minutes to reach the location Rebecca had in mind to visit. When it came into sight, she kept her eyes focused on the soaring, silver spires. As she walked the remaining distance to the temple, she offered a silent prayer in her heart. She slipped through the open gate leading onto the grounds at Temple Square and then paused abruptly, staring. A gigantic flag draped one whole side of the temple. It floated between the stately east and west towers, the stars and stripes rippling in the crisp, morning breeze. Rebecca's heart swelled as she gazed at the handsome granite temple and the flag gracing it. She stood without moving, barely drawing a breath, taking in the spectacular scene. Finally, she went to one of the benches situated on the temple grounds and sat down.

As she stared at the temple and the flag draping it, she realized that it must be the same flag that had hung in the Tabernacle yesterday during the inaugural celebration. Secured at each of the four corners, it fluttered in the brisk breeze. Her gaze lifted to the temple spires sparkling in the sunlight, and her thoughts traveled back to the day she had attended the temple's dedication with her father and sister. That had been nearly three years ago, in April of 1893. The edifice, with its striking architecture, had taken forty years to complete, but it was the spirit that had filled the building on that sacred occasion that Rebecca remembered most. She recalled President Wilford Woodruff's words at the dedicatory ceremonies when he had promised that from this time forth the power of the Adversary over the Saints would be diminished, and that the gospel message would go forth with greater strength and power than ever before.

The memory of those words sank deeply into her heart as she sat gazing at the temple adorned with the majestic American flag. She knew that those promises extended to her and to Judson. She reflected on Judson's agony over his friend's death, and his fury at the discovery of Daniel's murderer. She closed her eyes in prayer, begging God to comfort Judson and to heal his heart.

CHAPTER TWENTY-FOUR

Rebecca gripped Judson's hand as the two of them started across the bare, frozen ground of the Draper cemetery.

"The grave is over there near the west boundary," Judson told her, gesturing toward the far edge of the grounds. "He's buried next to his father."

Rebecca nodded. Her legs felt shaky as she and Judson picked their way through clumps of melting snow. The sky was as gray and hard as iron, and the air was still; not a whisper of wind disturbed the barren branches of the trees dotting the cemetery. She clutched the bouquet of evergreen boughs she was carrying to lay on the grave. Their clean, fresh scent comforted her and would provide a touch of green to enliven the stark landscape.

In a few more strides, they reached the spot. Judson stopped beside a pair of markers set into the ground. Rebecca stood beside him, staring at the graves. At the head of one stood a marker carved of new wood with the name *Daniel Briggs* incised into it and the inscription *Died 30 November 1895*. Above the name and date was carved in bold letters a single Indian word, and at the base of the marker the image of a wolf was cut into the wood. Rebecca blinked back tears as she handed the bouquet to Judson.

He bent down and cleared away a patch of snow from the grave and brushed off a fleck of dry brush clinging to the carved wooden marker, then laid the evergreens on the plot. He remained on one knee for a moment, staring at the grave. Finally, he let out a sigh and rose to his feet. "I hope it was the right thing to do to bury Daniel beside his father," he said quietly.

Rebecca's eyes moved to the adjacent grave where a rough, unpolished stone marked the ground, its face blank giving no indication of the name of the person who was buried there. Atop the stone lay a handsome Indian necklace with brightly-colored beads accenting a carved, wooden ornament. The ornament was in the shape of a wolf.

Judson saw her looking at the necklace. "It belonged to Daniel," he said, nodding toward the unusual piece. "He carved the wolf and wore the necklace over his shirt. He intended to give it to his father, when he found him, as a token from his son." Judson drew a long breath. "I was never sure whether Daniel wanted his father to have the necklace as a remembrance of the son he'd fathered or as a reminder of the child he'd abandoned. I don't think Daniel himself fully knew."

"Did Daniel place the necklace here?" Rebecca asked. The story Judson had just related tore at her heart.

"Yes. When we learned his father had died, we came here together and Daniel put the necklace on the grave."

Rebecca eyed Solomon Curtis's grave a moment longer, then her gaze shifted to the wooden monument memorializing Daniel's gravesite. "Did you carve this marker?" she asked, glancing up at Judson.

He gave a brief nod.

"What is the meaning of this word across the top?"

He stared silently at the marker for a moment before answering. "That's Daniel's Ute name. I never could pronounce it properly," he added, smiling. "It means Gray Wolf."

"Gray Wolf," Rebecca repeated softly, thinking on the meaning of the name. "That's why he carved the wolf for his necklace."

"Yes."

"And why you made a carving of a wolf on the marker."

"That's right."

Rebecca studied the image carved into the wood. It depicted a wolf loping through the short grass, its body lean and powerful. "It's beautiful," she said, lifting her eyes to Judson.

"Well, I hope Daniel likes it," he replied with a somber smile.

Rebecca pulled her coat tighter around her and glanced up at the bleak sky. The sun was struggling to break through the clouds. In the distance, she saw a small patch of blue like a cool pool of water. "Do you think Miss Addams has visited the grave?" she asked.

Judson shrugged his shoulders. "I don't know. I received a note from her a few weeks ago, thanking me for giving her Daniel's Book of Mormon. She said she'd begun reading it."

"That's good," Rebecca said, nodding her head.

Both of them stood silently without speaking, then Judson cleared his throat. "I'm thinking of making an appointment with President Woodruff to talk with him about the possibility of doing the temple work for Daniel. I'd like to be the proxy for the baptism, if that's allowable."

"How wonderful," she returned. "You could do something important for Daniel that he wasn't able to accomplish for himself."

"Yes, I hope so." He gazed out over the grounds of the cemetery, and his thoughts seemed to be far away. "But I'll have to get my own life in order first."

"I know you can do that," she encouraged.

"Even so," he went on, "it may not be possible. I've been told that at a recent general conference of the Church, President Woodruff announced a new emphasis on family relationships. He directed family members to trace their genealogies as far back as they can and be sealed to their mothers and fathers. It might not be feasible for me to do Daniel's work."

"Perhaps your visit with the Prophet will clarify the situation."

"We'll see," he said. "Are you ready to show me where your parents are buried?"

Rebecca knew he was struggling with his own testimony and was troubled with doubts concerning his personal worthiness, and she sensed that he didn't want to discuss the matter further. She took his hand and led the way to her parents' graves that were situated on the opposite side of the cemetery, and they lingered there for a time.

"We'll come back here in the spring," Judson suggested, "and bring flowers for the graves."

"Do you think the caretaker would allow us to plant a few wildflowers at the graves?" Rebecca asked, musing.

"We'll ask him," Judson said, leaning down to kiss her cheek.

Before Judson boarded the afternoon train back to Salt Lake City, he and Rebecca stopped for lunch at a small café in town. After he'd placed their order, he reached across the table for her hand. "Thank you for coming with me to the cemetery," he said, stroking his thumb across her hand. "I wish you could have met Daniel."

"So do I."

"He was a remarkable young man." Judson's eyes reflected the deep sorrow he felt over Daniel's passing.

"I'm glad the person responsible for his death is locked away where he can't harm anyone else." Rebecca frowned, thinking about Jake Baxter and her own unpleasant experiences with him. "Did you know beforehand that Jake was employed at the Double K?"

Judson shook his head. "Not until you told me. I'd never met him there."

"It's good you didn't; I wish I'd never met him." A shudder shook her body. "I'm sure it was Jake who stole my father's money and then set fire to the barn in revenge after I discharged him." Thinking about these incidents now, months later, still made her shake with anger.

"You can press charges against him for that." Judson's voice was bitter and harsh.

"Yes, both Micah and Patrick think I should." She glanced down at Judson's hands resting on the table. Those hands made her feel safe, much like her father's hands had always done. "It was Jake, too, who ruined a necklace that belonged to my mother."

Judson looked at her questioningly.

Rebecca told him about the cameo necklace and how she'd worn it to the dance in Draper, and how Jake had accosted her afterward. It was a painful memory for her to recall.

"Perhaps I can do something to repair the cameo," Judson said after they'd discussed the incident. "If you want to give me the necklace, I'll take a look at how badly it's damaged. I have some tools at the shop I might be able to use to buff out the scratches."

"I'd be so grateful if you could. My mother treasured that necklace."

In response, Judson raised her hand to his lips and kissed it.

His touch made her quiver; she was falling more deeply in love with him each time they were together. "Patrick is coming into the store later this afternoon," she said, striving to catch her breath.

"Is he?" he replied. "You must be looking forward to that."

"Yes, I am. I'm anxious to hear how things are going at the ranch and to visit with him for a little while. Whenever he comes to see me, it's as if he brings a bit of the Double K with him."

Judson chuckled. "You're never happier than when on the ranch, are you?"

"I'm happy now. Here with you." She flushed at her own words.

Judson leaned forward in his seat. "And I'm happy being with you, much more so than you probably realize."

Just then, the hostess appeared with their food. She set down two bowls of steaming soup and a loaf of tangy-smelling sourdough bread. "Enjoy your lunch," she said before stepping away from their table.

They ate their soup and bread while continuing to visit. All too soon, Judson reached into his vest pocket for his watch. His face clouded as he glanced at it. "If I don't hurry, I'm going to miss the train back to Salt Lake," he said regrettably.

Rebecca hid her disappointment behind a smile. "I'll walk with you as far as the store."

Soon after Rebecca returned to her desk at the mercantile, Patrick arrived. She ushered him into her office and the two of them sat together discussing affairs at the ranch. Patrick brought good news—the cattle were tolerating the cold weather well, and there was enough money in reserve to buy winter feed for them. He and Rebecca discussed the possibility of her returning to the ranch to stay before the spring roundup began. When he got up from his chair to leave, Rebecca was in high spirits. Just the thought of moving back to the Double K put a bloom on her cheeks.

"Thank you for coming, Patrick," she said. "I always look forward to your report."

"And I thought it was me you looked forward to seeing," he joked as he clamped his hat on his head.

"You know that's true, too," she laughed. She walked with him to the door of the office.

"Is Miss Miller here at the store this afternoon?" Patrick asked, trying to sound nonchalant.

Rebecca knew him too well to be fooled by his tone, and she couldn't resist teasing him. "Why, Patrick McKellar, I'm surprised at you. I didn't think you cared for Miss Miller's company."

"I was only going to say hello if she were here," he said quickly. His ears turned red with the words.

Rebecca slipped her arm through his. "Well, in that case, you're in luck. Lettie is here today." She glanced down one aisle and spotted Lettie sorting goods on the shelf. "There she is," Rebecca said, gesturing toward her friend.

"Why don't you come with me to say hello to her?" Patrick suggested. He whisked off his hat and began fidgeting with it.

Rebecca patted his arm. "I think you can manage without me." She gave him a grin and a peck on the cheek and then returned to her office, chuckling to herself.

January drifted into February, and with the new month came more winter snowstorms. Rebecca didn't mind the snow, however; it lay clean and sparkling outside her office window like a downy coverlet. She didn't even mind walking to work and back in the cold weather. She knew spring wasn't far away now, and with it the opportunity to return home to the ranch.

She was contented for another reason, too—Judson had been calling on her regularly. Over the last month and a half he'd come to Draper to see her nearly every weekend. His spirits seemed to be lifting, although he often spoke about Daniel. But he was still troubled; Rebecca could read that in his eyes with every visit. He couldn't seem to reconcile himself to Daniel's murder, and his hatred for Jake Baxter was eating at him. The last time she and Judson had been together, she had raised the subject of forgiveness. She, also, carried bitter feelings for Jake because of what he'd done, she'd explained to Judson, but neither of them would be able to go forward with a light heart and a clear conscience until they forgave him. Judson had responded to her suggestion with a glib remark, but before the conversation ended, he had told her that he would never forgive Baxter for Daniel's murder.

That thought lay heavy on Rebecca's mind as she packed a few things for a brief trip to the ranch. Mr. Rideout was out of town on business for several days and had told Rebecca she could take the weekend off if she liked. He'd said he was pleased with her work in keeping the financial records and had promised her a raise in salary. Rebecca was happy with her job at the mercantile, but she yearned to be home at the ranch.

Patrick came for her with the buckboard, and they had a good visit while he drove her out to the Double K. When she spotted the ranch house, nestled beneath snow-flocked trees and fronted by a winding, ice-crusted stream, she breathed a sigh of contentment. Patrick carried her bag inside the house, and she unpacked and then prepared lunch for the two of them. In the afternoon, she rode her father's horse into the pastures to check on the cattle. As Patrick had told her earlier, they seemed to be in good condition. Snow lay heaped on the ground, but the cowhands had done their jobs of making sure there was feed and water available for the animals. Afterward, she made supper and invited both Patrick and Micah to join her. Their conversation at the table revolved around the cattle and ranch matters.

It felt good to be part of the discussion and decision-making again.

After the two men had finished their supper and returned to the bunkhouse for the night, Rebecca washed up the dishes and then went to her room. She had been thinking lately about the pencil sketch Patrick's mother had given her and wanted to look at it again. She went to her bureau and pulled out the bottom drawer, slid aside a small pile of clothing folded there, and withdrew the framed pencil portrait Patrick had brought when he arrived at the ranch four months ago. She carried it with her to the bed and sat down. Removing the soft cloth she'd kept around it to protect it, she turned the drawing toward the light streaming from the coal oil lamp on her nightstand. She studied the portrait, her eyes sweeping along the lines that formed the face and hair. The features were skillfully drawn, reflecting an attractive woman with almond-shaped eyes, a petite nose, and slender lips. The woman's hair was depicted long and loose, flowing to her shoulders. She suddenly remembered her father telling her that Lydia Kade's hair had been as red as the setting sun; she smiled, pleased to have recalled this detail.

Gripping the portrait in her hand, she stood and walked to the oval mirror mounted on the wall of her room. She held the picture next to her face and examined the features, comparing each one to her own in an attempt to find a resemblance. There was nothing much about the two of them that matched, she concluded, turning the picture to better catch the light of the lamp. Perhaps some slight resemblance in the shape of the nose, she mused. Again, she wondered who had made the drawing and what the relationship had been between them. She decided to write her Aunt Birgithe and ask her; Birgithe always seemed to have the answers when it came to the family history.

Rebecca gazed at the drawing again, then walked with it into the small parlor. It was a precious heirloom that deserved to be displayed where she and other family members could enjoy it. She found a nail in the kitchen drawer and a hammer, selected an appropriate spot on the parlor wall, and pounded the nail into it. Then she hung the framed portrait on the wall and stood back to judge her handiwork. It was perfect. The place where she'd mounted it caught the light from the parlor lamp and reflected it in the lines of the drawing. Lydia's eyes seemed to sparkle with life, and her smile appeared to broaden. Rebecca smiled back at her, feeling a surge of emotion. As she stood staring at the portrait, her mind wandered back to what Judson had told her about President Woodruff's instructions to identify deceased ancestors and perform the sealing ordinances for them, thus creating an unbroken chain through the generations. She thought about the Kade family names and dates recorded in her parents' copy of the Book of Mormon; she knew Lydia and her husband had been baptized into the Church and had their marriage sealed in the Nauvoo temple before coming west, but she wondered about the status of earlier generations, if anyone had performed baptisms on their behalf. As long as she was writing Birgithe about the portrait, she decided to ask her about Lydia's forebears as well as earlier ancestors on the Kade side of the family. That thought made her smile with satisfaction.

The next afternoon, Judson came to the ranch as he and Rebecca had planned. He gave her a kiss in greeting right in front of Patrick who happened to be working in the front yard when Judson rode up on his horse.

Rebecca blushed when Patrick teased her about the kiss. After talking with Patrick for a few minutes, she and Judson went into the house. Rebecca took his coat for him. "How was your ride here?" she asked.

"Fine. The weather stayed dry the whole way." His mouth curved into a smile.

"I'm glad to hear that," Rebecca replied. She noticed that he'd been wearing the same contented smile ever since he'd reined his horse into the yard. He had a twinkle in his eye, too, and a spring in his step.

"Yes, indeed, fine weather for an exceptional day," he said.

She raised one brow in a puzzled look.

"It's February 29. Leap day," he said, as if that explained everything.

She knew he was joking with her about the reason for his cheerful mood. "Is that why you're so happy?" she asked, as they sat down on the parlor couch.

"It could be because of the new shirt I'm wearing," he teased. "I bought it only yesterday."

Rebecca eyed the white, starched shirt he had on. "It looks very handsome on you, but I don't think that's the reason for your smile."

Judson leaned forward in his seat and his eyes grew serious. "I had a visit with President Woodruff yesterday. I finally worked up the nerve to make an appointment with him." He pressed his hands together. "I told him about Daniel and his desire to be baptized into the Church and about his murder."

"What was his response?" Rebecca asked breathlessly. The very thought of having an audience with the Prophet and President of the Church filled her with awe.

"He sat patiently and listened to everything I had to say. Then he leaned back in his chair and folded his hands, silently gazing at me. I can tell you that I was trembling in my boots. I felt sure he could see straight into my soul and detect every unrighteous deed I'd ever done."

"That must have been sobering," Rebecca said with a nervous laugh.

"More than you can imagine." Judson smiled and eased back into the couch. "But he couldn't have been kinder or more understanding. In spite of his 89 years, that man is as sharp-minded and clear-sighted as anyone I've ever met."

"What did he say about your doing the baptism for Daniel?"

"When I told him I'd like to be the proxy for Daniel, he asked me to tell him a little bit about myself. I began pouring out the whole story of my conversion to the Church and my commitment to keeping the commandments, and then how I later drifted away from the principles I had known to be true."

Rebecca bit her lip. "Oh, my. How did he reply to that?"

Judson looked past her, as if gazing on the words the Prophet had spoken to him. "He responded with only a single question. 'Do you have a testimony of the Savior?'" Judson sat forward on the edge of his seat, his eyes intense. "I had to think about the answer."

"And?" Rebecca asked, holding her breath.

"And I realized that I do. It came as a shock to me, that's for certain." He chuckled softly.

"Then what did President Woodruff say?"

"He told me to do some fasting and praying, read the scriptures and pay careful attention to following the commandments, and then come and see him again in a month and he would write me a recommend to give to my bishop so I can do the baptism for Daniel."

"Judson, that's thrilling." Rebecca leaned forward to give him a hug. "I'm so happy for you and for Daniel."

Judson's voice took on a solemn note when he spoke again. "Daniel had wanted to meet with President Woodruff. He had the mistaken notion that only the President of the Church could baptize him," he added. "But he wasn't willing to meet with the Prophet until he had purged himself of the hatred he carried in his heart for what his father had done in abandoning him and his mother. That was the only thing holding him back. He was struggling to forgive his father."

Rebecca nodded as she listened intently to what Judson was telling her.

Judson took her hand in his. "I don't want that to be the thing holding me back from doing Daniel's work . . . my hatred for his killer. Even though I hadn't mentioned my feelings on that point to President Woodruff, I'm sure he sensed that my heart was not right with regard to it. I suspect that is the very thing he wants me to pray and fast about—cleansing my heart of hate and finding the strength to be able to forgive."

Rebecca could scarcely speak. She squeezed Judson's hand, communicating her empathy.

"So that is the reason for the gleam in my eye," he said after a moment's pause. "I could hardly wait to tell you."

"It's the best news you could have brought me," she replied. She was glad for Judson, and the joy she saw in his eyes offered her hope for her own redemption. Perhaps she could find a way to forgive herself for her part in her mother's death and lay aside the guilt and remorse she'd been carrying.

"I was reading in the New Testament the other day and came across a scripture in Matthew. It made a big impact on me when I read it, and I haven't forgotten it since. The words keep circling in my head." He glanced past her. "Have you a Bible here? I'd like to show you the verses."

She stood up and went to her father's desk to get the book of scripture. When she returned to the couch, she handed the Bible to Judson.

He smiled and began thumbing through the pages. "Here it is," he said, pointing to the passage of scripture. He turned the book toward her. "Will you read it for us?"

She swallowed and lifted her eyes to his face. A sudden swell of emotion made her doubt if she could read without her voice trembling. Judson nudged the book closer. She took it from his hand, and then he pointed to the scripture in Matthew, chapter 11, verses 28–30. She cleared her throat and blinked to bring the words into focus, then she began in a low voice. *"Come unto me, all ye that labour and are heavy laden, and I will give you rest. Take my yoke upon you, and learn of me; for I am meek and lowly in heart;"* she paused, swallowing back a sob that came unexpectedly to her throat, *"and ye shall find rest unto your souls. For my yoke is easy, and my burden is light."*

She looked up at Judson, tears starting in her eyes.

"Come unto me, all ye that labour and are heavy laden, and I will give you rest," he repeated quietly.

He said the words so softly and reverently that Rebecca heard them only as a whisper. She closed her eyes, concentrating, unsure if it was Judson's voice she'd heard in her ears and in her heart, or if it was the whispering of the Spirit.

Judson and Rebecca spent the rest of the afternoon together. She brought out the cameo necklace that had belonged to her mother and showed it to him, and after looking it over carefully, he thought he might be able to smooth out the scratches and scrapes. Later, they went for a ride into the hills, and by the time they returned, a light snow was falling. Rebecca started a fire in the hearth, and she and Judson sat beside its cozy flames to eat their supper.

After they'd finished, Rebecca carried their empty plates into the kitchen. When she returned to the parlor, Judson was standing at the window. She joined him there and pushed aside the eyelet curtains so she could see outside. "More snow," she declared, gazing up at the sky to watch the big, soft flakes falling in the light of the porch lamp.

"Yes," he said. "Look there, along the fence." He pointed to a section of split-rail fencing just beyond the yard. "The snow piled up along the fence line looks like a company of angels spreading their shining, white wings."

"Angels don't have wings," she reminded him with a grin.

"But it was a pretty metaphor."

She laughed. "Yes, very pretty."

He turned away from the window and took both her hands into his. "I see a real angel standing right here before me," he said. "One who is not only beautiful, but courageous, too."

Rebecca's heart fluttered as she looked into his eyes. Across the room, the fire crackled in the hearth, and its flickering light cast a reddish glow onto Judson's face, transforming his brown eyes to a gleaming gold.

He remained silent for a moment, gazing at her, before he spoke again. "There's one thing I haven't told you yet about my conversation with President Woodruff."

"What's that?" she asked.

"I told him about you—how kind and strong and smart you are. We discussed you for quite some time," he replied.

Rebecca blushed, not only at his flattering words, but at the thought of having her name resting on the lips of a prophet of God. She pictured President Woodruff's kindly face—his blue, penetrating eyes, his snowy hair, and his gentle smile. He had been the Prophet of the Church for the last half a dozen years, ever since she was thirteen, and she had grown to love and admire him. She respected his dedicated leadership and relied on his example of unwavering faith.

"He told me I shouldn't let a girl like you slip away. I replied that I had no intention of letting that happen."

Rebecca sucked in her breath, and her whole body began to tingle as she guessed what he was about to say next.

Still holding her hands in his, Judson slipped down onto one knee. "I love you with all my heart, Rebecca. I can't imagine my life without you beside me." He took a gulping breath. "Will you marry me?"

"Oh, yes!" Rebecca exclaimed. Tears surged to her eyes in an overwhelming swell of emotion. "I would be proud to be your wife."

With a gentle touch, Judson wiped away the tears slipping down her cheeks. "I was afraid you might say no," he whispered. "And I don't think I could have borne that."

His tender words went straight to her heart. "Oh, Judson, how could I have refused you? I started falling in love with you the first moment I saw you step out of that buggy with Rachel on your arm."

As they sat down on the couch beside the fire, a shadow passed across Judson's eyes. "Rachel won't be happy when she hears this news. I ran into her on the street a few weeks ago, and she turned her face away and wouldn't speak to me."

Rebecca sighed, feeling the same frustration as Judson. "She's been avoiding me as well. She's slow to answer my telephone calls and letters, and when we do get a chance to speak, she finds an excuse for not being able to meet for a visit." She glanced down at her hands. "We had an argument when I was staying with her during the statehood celebrations, and her feelings haven't softened toward me since."

"I'm sorry," Judson said, his voice pained. "I apologize for causing trouble between the two of you. Believe me, it was not my intent."

"The difficulties between my sister and me started long before either of us met you," she confessed, thinking back on their troubled relationship during the past few years. "If we can't persuade Rachel to change her feelings toward us, then we'll have to accept them as they are. But I won't allow her to spoil our happiness, no matter her objections."

Judson took her into his arms and kissed her, and Rebecca could feel his heart beating where her hand rested against his chest. Holding her close, they sat beside the fire and made plans for their wedding day.

"After we're married, I'd like to celebrate our wedding here at the ranch, if you are agreeable," Rebecca suggested, tilting her face toward his. "It would mean so much to me."

"Of course." Judson kissed her forehead. "A wedding party at the Double K is exactly the thing we need—with our families and friends to enjoy it with us."

Rebecca snuggled beside him and rested her head on his shoulder.

Judson fell silent for a moment, and when he spoke again, his voice was husky. "We haven't talked yet about where the ceremony will take place." He looked into her eyes, and his expression was earnest. "I want to take you to the temple and have our marriage sealed so that it will last forever."

Rebecca's breath quickened. "That is what I want, too."

"I hoped that would be your response." Judson pressed her fingers to his lips and kissed them.

"I remember my parents counseling me to marry in the temple. They stressed the importance of a temple marriage to a worthy man who honors his covenants." Her voice trembled as she contemplated the path that lay open, bright and beautiful, before her.

Judson leaned forward. "I promise you, I will strive to be that man."

CHAPTER TWENTY-FIVE

When Rebecca heard the sound of wagon wheels approaching the house, she set aside the letter she'd been reading from her Aunt Birgithe and went to the window. Pushing aside the curtain, she looked out. A buckboard pulled by a pair of matching chestnut horses rolled into the yard. "Whoa," Rebecca heard a man's voice say. Her heart beat faster as she started for the door.

When she stepped onto the porch, Rachel was just alighting from the wagon, helped by a young man dressed in a dapper suit and hat. Spying Rebecca on the doorstep, Rachel arranged her face into a brittle smile. "Hello, Rebecca," she said without emotion.

Rebecca hurried down the porch step and across the yard to where the man was hitching the horses to the post. "I'm so glad you've come, Rachel. I wasn't sure you would,"

Rebecca said, giving her sister a hug before Rachel could rebuff her.

The man finished tying the reins around the post and stepped to Rachel's side. Rachel straightened her broad, frilly hat and turned to him. "This is Charles Sims. Charles, my sister."

The young man held out a gloved hand to Rebecca. "How do you do, Miss Kade," he said. His voice was nasal and his handshake limp and prissy, but he had a handsome face with thick, dark hair and blue eyes framed by long lashes.

"Very well, Mr. Sims. Welcome to the Double K." Rebecca smiled to herself. Rachel had made no mention of bringing a gentleman friend with her to attend the wedding celebration. Much like the occasion when Judson had accompanied her to the ranch, Rachel preferred to keep her relationships private until the moment she deemed appropriate to unveil her prize. "Please come inside," she said to Rachel and her friend. "Judson will be pleased to see you, Rachel, and to meet Mr. Sims. He's gone with Micah for a few hours to attend to some ranch business, but then he'll be back."

Rachel's reply was an unblinking stare as she marched rigidly to the house. Poor Mr. Sims had to take little running steps to keep up with her.

Rebecca sighed, then followed them inside. She had written Rachel several weeks earlier asking her to help with the celebration party. The letter she'd received in reply had been noncommittal, and so Rachel's arrival at the Double K was somewhat of a surprise.

Rachel took off her cloak and hat and laid them across a parlor chair. Then she seated herself on the couch. Her beau stood beside her, obviously unsure whether to sit or remain standing without some word from her. "Would you mind getting the bags, Charles?" Rachel asked him.

He turned and hurriedly left the room. Rebecca thought he seemed eager for the opportunity to absent himself from the two of them.

Rebecca sat down on the chair opposite Rachel and folded her hands in her lap. "Mr. Sims seems to be very nice," she remarked, unable to think of anything else to say. Sitting stoically across from her, Rachel seemed like a stranger.

"Thank you. He's a gentleman in every sense of the word."

Rebecca knew her sister's comment was barbed with a double meaning, but she refused to take offense at it.

Rachel glanced at her. "I suppose now that you and Judson are to be married, the two of you will be taking over the ranch house."

"No, not at all," Rebecca replied, leaning forward in her chair. "It's as much your home as it is mine."

"Is it?" Rachel snapped.

Rebecca drew in a deep breath, striving to keep her response positive. "I wrote you about my idea to ask Patrick to stay on at the Double K and run it, with Micah continuing as the ranch foreman. Did you get my letter?"

Rachel gave a short nod.

"Since I didn't hear from you, I assumed you had no objection to that plan."

Rachel's gaze was harsh, but she didn't disagree or offer comment.

"Judson has a small interest in a silver mine in Park City that is producing a little cash. He told me I could use that money to pay Patrick a monthly wage until the ranch is turning a profit. The economy seems to finally be improving, and Micah and Patrick think that the ranch may see its way out of debt in the coming months."

"And I suppose Judson is in favor of this whole idea," Rachel sniffed.

"He is." Rebecca clasped her hands together more tightly. "I was hoping you and I could have a private chat regarding Judson before he gets back."

"Whatever for?" Rachel asked coldly. "Now that you are to be wed to him, you and I have little to say to one another."

Rebecca was quickly losing her patience. "Please stop being so dramatic, Rachel," she fumed. "I didn't take Judson away from you."

Rachel turned angry eyes onto her. "Even if I did grow tired of him, you should have had the good sense to shun his advances."

"Why?" Rebecca asked simply. "Because his affection for me hurt your pride?"

A spot of color sprang to Rachel's cheeks, and she set her jaw.

"If that's the case, then what a foolish reason it is." Rebecca's flare of temper faded. She reached across and covered Rachel's hand with hers. "I love Judson with all my heart. I hoped you'd be happy for me—for both Judson and me."

Before Rachel could reply, the front door slammed shut and Mr. Sims staggered into the parlor under the weight of a suitcase in each hand and several packages tucked under his arms. He set them all on the floor with a plop. "Here they are, Rachel," he said. His voice sounded almost whining.

Rebecca turned her gaze to him. Although his features were attractive and his dark hair thick and wavy, his looks were marred by the petulant expression on his face.

"Thank you, Charles," Rachel said, unsmiling. "Would you hand me that large box, please?"

He sorted through the half dozen boxes he had carried inside until locating the biggest one, and then passed it to Rachel.

"In spite of what you may think of me, Rebecca, I am not so callous as to ignore your engagement and marriage. I have brought you a wedding gift." She handed the box to Rebecca.

Although her tone was as prickly as a burr, Rebecca sensed that her sister's motive was genuine. "Thank you so much, Rachel. Shall I wait until Judson comes to open it?"

"No, no," Rachel said with a wave of her hand. "This present is for you. Go ahead and open it now."

Rebecca set the box on her lap. It was lightweight and wrapped with a pretty pink bow. She untied the bow and removed the lid of the box. Pushing aside the paper, she looked inside. "Oh, my!" she exclaimed, dipping her hand into the box and pulling out a big, wide-brimmed straw hat. The straw was dyed a bright blue, and blue and pink ribbons crafted into clusters of flowers decorated the brim. Rebecca chuckled at the sight of the gaudy hat, both delighted and shocked by its ostentation. "Did you make this yourself, Rachel?"

"Yes, and only the very best materials went into it. Those ribbons are pure silk, Rebecca, and it's styled in the latest fashion."

Rebecca grinned at her sister. "Thank you, I love it." She threw her arms around Rachel's shoulders, and Rachel begrudgingly returned the hug.

"It's very pretty," she heard Mr. Sims say from his position near the pile of parcels and suitcases. "Your sister has exquisite taste."

Rebecca glanced over at him and smiled. If he weren't so fawning and obedient, she suspected she'd like him better.

The gift-giving seemed to thaw the icy wall Rachel had erected between them. As the afternoon wore on, she grew less antagonistic as Rebecca drew her into the preparations for the wedding celebration that was to take place in three days, and by the time Judson returned to the house, Rachel was nearly her old self. But her expression hardened when she saw him.

He entered the parlor, came to Rebecca's side, and slipped an arm around her waist. Then turning to Rachel, he said in a friendly tone, "It's nice to see you, Rachel. I hope your ride here was pleasant."

Rebecca held her breath to see how Rachel would react.

She nodded briefly in response to his greeting. "May I introduce you to Mr. Sims, a close friend of mine," she said, barely glancing at Judson.

"How do you do, Mr. Sims," Judson said, reaching over to shake the man's hand.

"Well enough," Sims answered stiffly. "And you?" It was obvious that Rachel had filled him in beforehand on the situation concerning Judson.

After the introductions were completed, Rebecca turned to Judson. "Look what Rachel has brought me. Isn't it attractive?" She placed the blue hat on her head. Her blonde hair peeped out beneath it in startling contrast, and the silk flowers along the brim nearly hid her eyes.

Rachel immediately stepped to her side. "You don't know a thing about fashion, Rebby," she scolded. "The hat is to be worn at an angle, like this." She adjusted the hat on her sister's head. "There. Now it looks as it should."

"Thank you," Rebecca said, stifling a grin. She turned toward Judson and tilted her head. "How do you like it?"

As he stared at her, the corners of his mouth twitched with a smile, and his brown eyes twinkled, but he responded in a solemn tone. "It's lovely. You look magnificent in it."

"There, you see," Rachel said smartly. "At least Judson has some sense of style."

Judson chuckled, and Rebecca started giggling, too. Even Mr. Sims gave a weak laugh, although he looked uncertain about whether he should or not. Before Rachel could puff up with indignation, Rebecca enveloped her in a hug. "I love you, Rachel," she said.

The four of them sat outside on the grass to eat lunch. The weather was a little cool, but Rebecca wanted to enjoy the spring air and the beauty of the greening hillsides. Snow still lined the deep gorges and canyons of the mountains, etching a zigzagging pattern of white along the granite face. Above the jagged peaks, the sky was a seamless blue. The fruit trees in the yard were in full bloom. As Rebecca gazed across the lawn, she noticed how the pink blossoms on the plum and peach trees stood out in a vivid splash of color against the backdrop of the snow-capped mountains. It was going to be difficult to leave the ranch during the splendor of spring time, she mused, when the colors were vibrant and the grass new and the calves roamed in the pastures beside their mothers. If she didn't love Judson with her whole heart, she couldn't have borne being away from the ranch at this time of year.

Patrick had accepted Rebecca's offer to run the ranch in her stead, and she felt at peace about the decision. Patrick was thoroughly acquainted with the operation of the Double K from the last six months he'd spent on the ranch while she'd worked in Draper, as well as from the years he had lived there with his family. She was confident that he would be a capable, honest, hard working manager, and that the affairs at the Double K would be resting in excellent hands.

When she'd told Micah of the proposal, he had raised no objections and was agreeable with the arrangement to take instructions from Patrick and to report directly to him instead of to Rebecca. Rebecca was grateful to him for all he had done in the past to keep the ranch operating smoothly and efficiently. To show her appreciation, she'd given Micah her father's chestnut gelding to use on the ranch. She knew he'd always admired the animal, and he'd seemed pleased with her gesture. She'd assigned him the job of hiring a new wrangler to replace Jake Baxter, which he'd already done, and everything seemed to be in order in preparation for her to leave the ranch after her marriage to Judson.

She and Judson had discussed where they would make their home once they were wed. Judson had his shop in the city, of course, and needed to be there to conduct his business; during the intervening months between their engagement and their upcoming marriage, he had built a small, adobe house behind the workshop for them to occupy. It was a cozy cottage with electric lights, indoor plumbing, and a telephone. She was thrilled to become the mistress of such a modern home and excited for the opportunity of living in the city with all its conveniences, but still a shadow crossed her heart whenever she thought about leaving the Double K. Judson had assured her that they'd come to the ranch often, and she clung to that promise.

"And just how did you pop the question to Miss Kade, if I may be so bold as to ask?" Mr. Sims was saying to Judson.

Judson chuckled and took Rebecca's hand. She gazed into his face, her uncertainties forgotten in the warmth of his smile. "It was leap day," Judson began with a mischievous gleam in his eye. "I came to the ranch to visit Rebecca and had high hopes that she would take advantage of the custom associated with the day."

He grinned at Rebecca, and the familiar dimple in his cheek sprang into view.

"As you know, it is a common tradition on February 29 for the woman to propose marriage to the man if she so chooses," Judson said.

Rebecca rolled her eyes.

"Even though I hinted most pointedly and gave her every opportunity, she didn't raise the subject. So I had to do the proposing myself."

Mr. Sims chuckled, and even Rachel came close to a smile. Judson leaned over and kissed Rebecca's cheek.

"That was an interesting story," Rebecca said, a smile tugging at her mouth, "in spite of the fact that you embellished it quite a bit."

"I thought it made the telling more eventful," Judson responded with a wink.

"The occasion was quite eventful enough." She laughed and gave Judson an affectionate look.

Rachel brushed a blade of grass off her skirt. "Well, before the grand day of your marriage arrives, I have something for you, Rebecca," she said. "I was going to wait until later to give it to you, but now seems an appropriate time."

Rebecca's brows rose in question. "What is it?"

Reaching into her skirt pocket, Rachel pulled out a small box that fit easily into the palm of her hand. "I thought you might be planning to wear Mother's cameo necklace on your wedding day. So I brought these to go with it." She opened the lid to the box and took out a pair of earrings and handed them to Rebecca.

Rebecca's heart skipped a beat as she stared at the coral earrings nestled in her hand. The earrings matched the cameo necklace Rebecca had inherited; their lustrous surfaces, each carved with the profile of a woman's face, shimmered in the sunlight.

Rebecca leaned forward and hugged her sister. Then she held the oval-shaped earrings up for Judson to see. "These go with the cameo pendant you polished for me, Judson. They belonged to Mother. Papa gave her the matching set of jewelry as a gift for their tenth wedding anniversary."

Judson studied the pair of earrings. "Then it's fitting that you should wear them on your own wedding day," he said.

Rebecca nodded as she cradled the earrings in the palm of her hand. Since her parents' deaths, she had thought often about the coral necklace and pair of earrings and all that they represented. When the necklace was damaged on the night of the dance in Draper, she had been devastated. After Judson had repaired the nicks and scratches and polished the surface, the cameo pendant looked new; it had seemed to mark the beginning of the process of forgiving herself and cleansing her heart from the guilt and remorse she'd been carrying in connection with her mother's passing. She recalled the brief image, whether real or imagined, she'd glimpsed of her parents standing in the meadow on the far side of the gully. As she thought back to that experience of riding with Judson into the ravine where her mother had died, she recognized the healing that had come from it. A feeling of peace, of wholeness, entered into her heart as she gazed at the set of earrings. She turned back to Rachel. "Thank you so much for bringing these to me."

The four of them sat together talking while they finished their lunch, and when they were through and had packed up their picnic dishes, they prepared to go inside. With the earrings tucked safely in her pocket, Rebecca was standing near Judson when she saw him approach Rachel. "That was thoughtful of you to bring the earrings for Rebecca. I know how much they mean to her," Rebecca heard him say.

"Thank you," Rachel replied without smiling. She started toward the house.

"Rachel?" Judson repeated.

She turned around, her face stony.

"I hope we can be friends," he said with sincerity.

Rebecca watched her sister stare at him without any change in expression, then just as Rachel was about to turn away, Rebecca saw her grant Judson the slightest glimmer of a smile.

The sounds of laughter and joyous celebration filled the ranch house and spilled outside onto the lawn. Sunlight flowed through the windows and reflected off the streamers, bows, and paper bells adorning the parlor. The boxes Charles Sims had carried inside when he and Rachel arrived at the ranch had been stuffed with wedding decorations, and Rachel had placed them throughout the house and yard for the occasion of the wedding celebration. On the parlor table was a vase filled with yellow, decorative sunflowers that Judson had purchased in Salt Lake City as a gift for his new bride.

Rebecca, her hand clasped tightly in Judson's, took a moment to savor the scene. She glanced around at the guests crowded into the adobe house. Nearly everyone she loved was present. Her Aunt Birgithe and Uncle Samuel along with their spouses and children were milling about the room visiting with the other guests; Jessica and Rory McKellar and their five sons sat outside on the grass eating wedding cake; a few relatives on her mother's side of the family were in attendance, as well as many of Judson's friends and relations. Even Mr. Sims seemed to be enjoying himself standing at Rachel's side as she chatted with the guests. Each one had offered heartfelt congratulations to the newly married couple. The happiness Rebecca felt, not only for this occasion to have her loved ones near, but for her marriage yesterday in the temple of the Lord, was almost more than she could take in. As she turned her eyes to her new husband, Rebecca marveled at the depth of love she felt for him. She had not thought it possible to love someone as completely and as ardently as she did Judson.

As if sensing her thoughts, Judson drew her close to him. He bent his head so he could whisper softly in her ear. "Are you happy, Mrs. Carter?" he asked.

"Unbelievably so," she whispered back, giving him a kiss.

He squeezed her hand, communicating his love for her.

Rebecca looked out again at the crowded room. The only thing that could have added to her joy would have been to have her father and mother present with her. Her hand caressed the cameo pendant at her throat. She felt its smooth, polished warmth against her fingertips. She smiled, remembering Rachel's comments as she'd helped Rebecca fasten the necklace and slip on the earrings—"You look every bit as beautiful as Mother ever did," she'd said; "Mama and Papa would be so proud of you today." Those words had touched her deeply.

Her thoughts returned to the present as a couple approached with whom she was not acquainted. The woman carried a young baby in her arms.

"Finally, I get a chance to congratulate you. Catherine and I have been squeezing our way through the crowd to greet you and your pretty wife."

Rebecca smiled at the pair who had just stepped up to them and watched as Judson shook the man's hand and kissed the woman's cheek.

"Rebecca, these are friends of mine, Lorin and Catherine Stott," he said, "and their new baby boy."

"How do you do?" Rebecca replied. She glanced down at the baby, swaddled in a soft blanket, and thought how adorable he was.

"You outdid yourself, Judson," Lorin said, clapping a hand on Judson's shoulder. "What a beautiful bride you have."

"You're right on both counts," Judson returned.

"Congratulations, Mrs. Carter," Catherine offered, taking Rebecca's hand into hers. "We wish you and Judson much happiness."

"Thank you." Rebecca immediately liked the tall, friendly woman whose smile radiated warmth and genuineness.

"I haven't seen you in the Blue Fly for quite a while now. Are you taking your refreshment elsewhere these days?" Lorin said to Judson with a grin.

"I've mended my ways somewhat," Judson replied, smiling. "But I've missed your company. In a week or so, why don't you and Catherine join us for supper? Rebecca and I would like that."

"Yes, please do. I'd look forward to getting to know you better," Rebecca said sincerely.

After a few more words of conversation, the couple moved away to allow the opportunity for others to greet the bride and groom.

"I like meeting your friends," Rebecca remarked as she watched the Stotts blend into the crowd.

"I'm glad," Judson said, bestowing a kiss on her cheek. When he raised his head, his gaze was drawn to a young woman who was threading her way toward them. "Rebecca, there's someone I want you to meet," he said, nodding toward the woman.

Rebecca took his arm as Judson led her to the woman's side.

"Miss Addams, I'm delighted you could come. Let me introduce you to my wife." He turned to Rebecca. "This is Miss Louisa Addams, a special friend of mine."

"Miss Addams, how nice to meet you at last," Rebecca said with genuine feeling.

"Thank you, Mrs. Carter; and congratulations on your marriage."

The young woman's voice was soft and sweet, and her features were pretty. She reminded Rebecca of a delicate porcelain doll.

"How are you getting along?" Judson asked her. There was no mistaking the meaning behind his question.

"I'm doing much better." Even though her words were cheerful, the smile that accompanied them was forced.

Judson took her hand into his. "I hope all will go well with you and you find happiness," he said sincerely.

"Thank you. And thank you for everything you did for Daniel and me. I can never repay your kindness."

"I only wish things had turned out differently."

Rebecca heard the ache in Judson's voice and knew that her husband still mourned the loss of his young friend.

Louisa turned to Rebecca. "Your husband was a great friend to Daniel and me. Daniel frequently spoke of him and always in glowing terms."

Rebecca felt a lump starting in her throat. "I am so sorry for your loss, Miss Addams. I wish I could have met Mr. Briggs."

"Oh, you would have liked him so much," Louisa replied, her eyes brightening.

"I'm sure I would have." Rebecca's heart was drawn to this young woman who had suffered such a horrific tragedy, and in spite of it comported herself with grace and poise.

"I hope you'll stay throughout the afternoon and enjoy yourself," Judson said to her. "Have you an escort?"

"My uncle and aunt were kind enough to accompany me." Louisa's eyes flickered toward the door of the parlor in search of them.

Rebecca wondered if the young woman's parents had refused to bring her, and so she had been forced to rely on the kindness of relatives. That thought tugged at Rebecca's heartstrings, and she deeply appreciated the effort Louisa had made to come all the way to Draper to attend the wedding celebration.

As Louisa concluded her conversation with them, Lettie Miller and Patrick approached, her arm tucked in his. Rebecca noted the sparkle in Lettie's eyes and the spot of color on Patrick's cheek. She smiled, pleased and somewhat surprised to see them together. They visited with Judson and her, offering their congratulations, and then the conversation turned to the ranch and Patrick's new responsibilities as manager of the Double K. Rebecca had invited him to stay in the ranch house and take over her parents' bedroom after she and Judson left for their new home in Salt Lake City. She was glad knowing someone she could trust would be living in the house.

As Lettie and Patrick chatted with them, the rest of Patrick's brothers congregated around the newly wed couple, teasing Rebecca and congratulating Judson. The eldest, Wyatt, informed Rebecca that he was engaged to be married to a young woman he'd met in Arizona; and the youngest, twelve-year-old Gideon, couldn't wait to tell her about a stray calf he had rescued from a canyon ledge on their ranch. She scarcely had time to talk with them before other relatives and friends pressed upon her, taking her attention.

In between visiting with their guests, Rebecca's eyes kept wandering to Louisa Addams. The young woman had touched a chord in her heart, and Rebecca wished she could do something nice for her. She spotted her once seated in a chair by herself, watching the others in the room; and another time standing beside the door in conversation with an older man and woman, whom Rebecca presumed were her uncle and aunt. She noticed the attractive, blue silk dress Louisa wore accentuated with lace and ribbons, the white gloves that came to just above her elbows, and the stylish slippers on her feet, and an idea took root in Rebecca's mind. "Excuse me for a moment, will you, Judson?" she said, patting his arm. Then she slipped through the throng of people until she found Rachel.

Her sister was just concluding a conversation with one of the guests, and Mr. Sims was hovering at her elbow.

Rebecca stepped to their side. "Would you mind if I talked privately with Rachel for just a minute?" she said to her sister's beau.

"Certainly, you may," Mr. Sims replied. Bowing to the two of them, he excused himself and disappeared into the crowd.

Rebecca took her sister aside and briefly told her about Louisa Addams. She asked her to make Louisa's acquaintance and to spend some time keeping her company. "She doesn't know anyone here, really, except for Judson," Rebecca concluded.

"Yes, of course. Point her out to me," Rachel responded.

Rebecca nodded toward Louisa, who was still hovering near the door and looked as if she was feeling uncomfortable and out of place. "I think you'll like her, and she needs a friend right now," Rebecca said.

"I'll take good care of her," Rachel assured her sister. She left Rebecca's side and made her way through the crowded room to where Louisa stood. Rebecca watched her walk over to Louisa and begin talking with her. Rachel had the ability to strike up a friendly conversation and put people at ease, even those she'd only just met; Rebecca hoped her sister would put that talent to use now.

As she started back toward Judson, the stringed band he had hired to play throughout the afternoon fell silent, and the band leader tapped his baton on his music stand to garner the attention of the guests. Judson was standing beside him, wearing a grin on his face.

"Ladies and gentlemen, the dancing is about to commence," the band leader announced in a loud voice. "A special piece has been requested by the groom. If he will take his bride's hand, their first dance as husband wife will begin."

The guests surrounding Rebecca stepped back against the walls as Judson crossed the room toward her. Dressed in his black tailcoat and pants, and crisp white shirt with a white folded and knotted tie, he looked like a handsome prince coming to whisk her away on his white steed. As he approached, she, too, felt like a princess in the middle of a fairy tale; one whose ending of happily ever after was coming true. Judson met her in the center of the room, bowed slightly, and took her hand. "May I have this dance?" he crooned.

"I'd be delighted," she replied with a curtsy. She placed her hand in his as the first strains of a waltz flowed sweetly from the violins, cello, and viola.

Judson took her in his arms and leaned close to whisper in her ear. "With just a little stretch of the imagination, my love, you can hear a whole orchestra playing."

The violins finished the few bars of introduction, and then broke into the enchanting strains of a familiar waltz.

"Oh, Judson," Rebecca said, her heart swelling at the thought of his romantic gesture. "It's 'The Blue Danube.'"

With his arm around her waist and his hand clasping hers, Judson began to move with a fluid grace in time to the music. "Exactly as I promised you," he said, holding her close.

After seeing the last guest out, Rebecca and Judson stood arm in arm beside the door reflecting on the afternoon's success. "What an amazing day," Rebecca declared.

"I hope it was everything you wanted it to be," he replied, leaning down to kiss her.

"It couldn't have been more perfect. And may I add that you dance beautifully," she said, returning his kiss.

"If that is so, it was only because you were my inspiration."

They shared an embrace, then they began to clear away the streamers and other decorations from the parlor. "I think our guests had a nice time. Wasn't it lovely to see them join in the dancing?" Rebecca asked.

"It was, until Patrick suggested we change partners. I'm afraid Miss Miller scuffed the shine off my shoes."

Rebecca laughed. "Well, I enjoyed my turn with Patrick. Although I have to confess he is a much better cattle rancher than he is a dancer."

"Then your cousin and Miss Miller should make a fine pair."

Rebecca folded her handful of streamers into a tidy stack to save and use again when needed. "I hope they become a couple. Patrick seems to like her, and I know Lettie is smitten with him."

"These things seem to have a way of working out," Judson replied, handing her the decorations he'd picked up.

"And perhaps Rachel is fonder of Mr. Sims than she lets on. I'll save these decorations just in case."

"Ah, yes, the simpering Mr. Sims," Judson responded with a twinkle of good humor in his eyes.

"Perhaps you'll approve more of my cousin, Rourke. Did you see him dancing with Miss Addams? I asked Rachel to befriend her for the afternoon, and later I saw her introduce Louisa to my cousins when all five of the boys were standing together in a group."

Judson's expression sobered. "Which one is Rourke?"

"The middle one. He's eighteen and such a nice fellow. He's rather quiet and sensitive, but always fun to be around."

"I'd like to see Louisa have some happiness. She's suffered greatly over Daniel's death."

"When we get settled in Salt Lake City, perhaps I can pay her a visit. I was so impressed with her; I'd enjoy getting to know her better."

"I can't think of a better friend for her than you," Judson said, kissing the tip of Rebecca's nose.

Rebecca gathered up an empty plate and cup left by a guest on the parlor table and carried them into the kitchen. All the guests had departed the ranch except for Jessica and Rory and their sons. They were spending the night in the bunkhouse, which Micah had cleaned and prepared for overnight guests, and would stay a few days afterward before starting back for Arizona. She set the dishes in the sink and then went back to the parlor. Judson was standing in front of the pencil portrait hanging on the parlor wall; he turned when she entered the room.

"This is a nice drawing," he said, smiling at her. "Did you say it's a portrait of your grandmother?"

"My great-grandmother." Rebecca joined him in front of the picture and stood gazing at it alongside him. "Her name was Lydia Kade. I didn't know much about her apart from the few things Papa had told me. I wrote my Aunt Birgithe to ask her about the portrait, and she informed me that Lydia's husband, Christian Kade, had drawn it before the two of them were married."

"That sounds romantic," Judson said.

"Yes, I think so, too." Rebecca reached out a hand to stroke the glass frame. "She told me a little bit about Lydia's life; how she was married to her first husband, Abraham Dawson, when she became acquainted with the gospel through some Mormon missionaries preaching in Green County, Illinois, where she lived. Later, her husband was killed in a mining accident, and Lydia moved with her two children, Elizabeth and James, to Independence, Missouri. It was there she met Christian, and they married. The family lived in Nauvoo, Illinois, for a time and then came out west with the Saints."

"And James was your grandfather, right?"

"That's right. He was a doctor in Salt Lake City. He married a young woman named Inger Johanssen whom he'd known since childhood. My father was the oldest of their three children. Papa told me many stories about his parents; he adored them." She smiled, thinking about her father and the pride and love he had for his family which he'd instilled in his daughters. "Let me show you something."

Rebecca went to the mantle over the fireplace and picked up the Book of Mormon resting there, then walked to the couch with it. She and Judson sat down side by side on the couch, and Rebecca turned to the back few pages of the book. She pointed at the list of names and dates inscribed there. The fading light coming through the window behind them cast a glow on the pages.

Judson whistled softly. "Look at that—a family record."

Rebecca tapped her finger next to Lydia's name. "My great-grandmother had two brothers, Aunt Birgithe told me, whose names were John and Philip Ross. Those brothers have been on my mind ever since you performed the proxy baptism for Daniel. I've wondered if their baptisms and temple work have ever been done."

Judson's brows rose, and he nodded his head in thought. "If not, you could have it done for them."

"That's just what I was thinking, as well as other members of the family who have gone before. Aunt Birgithe said that Christian, too, had a brother. His name was Jarrett Kade."

Judson bent closer to study the list. "Will you be recording the names of our children in this book?" he asked, smiling at her.

"Wait right here." She handed the open book to Judson while she stood up to fetch a pen and a pot of ink. Returning with them, she gave Judson the ink bottle to hold and took the book into her lap. She smoothed the page, dipped the tip of the pen into the ink, and then began to write. She formed each letter and numeral with care, her heart seeming to beat in rhythm with each pen stroke. When she had finished, she set down the pen and looked into Judson's face. He was staring at the record she'd just written.

"Rebecca Ann Kade and Judson Carter married 25 April 1896 in the Salt Lake City Temple," he read aloud. He lifted his eyes to meet hers. "I'm proud to see my name standing next to these others and to become part of such a noble family."

Rebecca slipped her hand into his. "As our children are born, we'll record their names next to ours; and when they marry and have children of their own, we'll write down those names and dates, too." Rebecca's pulse quickened as she gazed again at the record written on the back pages of the book of scripture. "Each of us will be linked together in a continuing chain welded by love and sealed as a family throughout all eternity," she said softly.

Judson nodded and squeezed her hand.

Rebecca shifted her gaze to the portrait of Lydia Kade smiling at them from the framed picture. The portrait would be a priceless keepsake to be treasured through the years, Rebecca mused; a reminder of their heritage, both as a family and as members of the Church. Christian and Lydia's story of sacrifice and devotion to the gospel would be recounted down through the generations, and their example would build faith, testimony, and spiritual strength among their descendants.

Judson tucked a straying curl behind her ear. "Your hair looks almost red in the fiery light of the setting sun. I told you that once before; do you remember it?"

"Yes. It was here at the ranch, and we were sitting outside on the porch. You made stew while I was on the range tending to the sick cattle and brought me a bowl of it to eat when I returned." She smiled, recalling how his touch on her cheek had made her quiver and how attracted she was to him even then.

"That's right." He wound a curl around his finger. "I told you then how pretty your hair looked in the evening light."

She glanced at the portrait again. "My Great-Grandmother Kade had red hair. Maybe I've inherited a little something from her after all."

"I'm sure you have," Judson said, closing the book that was resting on Rebecca's lap and setting it aside. "And I know she must be proud of you."

Rebecca smiled at that thought. "I hope so."